When Informal Institutions Change

Huseyn Aliyev examines how, when, and under what conditions democratic institutional reforms affect informal institutions in hybrid regimes (that is, countries transitioning to democracy). He analyzes the impact of institutional changes on the use of informal practices and what happens when democratic reforms succeed. Does informality disappear, or do elites and populations continue relying on informal structures?

When Informal Institutions Change engages with a growing body of political science, economic, and sociological literature on informal practices and institutions. Aliyev proposes expanding the analysis of the impact of institutional reforms on informal institutions beyond disciplinary boundaries, combining theoretical insights from comparative politics with economic and social theories on informal relations. In addition, Aliyev offers insights relevant to democratization, institutionalism, and human geography. Detailed case studies of three transitional post-Soviet regimes—Georgia, Moldova, and Ukraine—illustrate the contentious relationship between democratic institutional reforms and informality in the broader post-Soviet context.

Aliyev shows that for institutional reform to strengthen, democratize, and formalize institutions, informal practices and institutions must be approached as instrumental. These findings have implications not only for hybrid regimes but also for other post-Soviet or post-communist countries.

Huseyn Aliyev is a postdoctoral researcher at the Center for Security Studies at Metropolitan University in Prague, lecturer at the University of Bremen, and a visiting academic at the School of Interdisciplinary Area Studies at the University of Oxford.

When Informal Institutions Change

INSTITUTIONAL REFORMS
AND INFORMAL PRACTICES
IN THE FORMER SOVIET UNION

Huseyn Aliyev

University of Michigan Press
Ann Arbor

Published in the United States of America by the
University of Michigan Press
Manufactured in the United States of America
♾ Printed on acid-free paper

2020   2019   2018   2017   4   3   2   1

A CIP catalog record for this book is available from the British Library.

Library of Congress Cataloging-in-Publication data has been applied for.

ISBN: 978-0-472-13047-4 (hardcover: alk. paper)
ISBN: 978-0-472-12310-0 (e-book)

To my parents
I dedicate this book

Contents

Preface

WHAT HAPPENS TO informal institutions and practices when political actors decide to implement democratic institutional reforms aimed at relieving formal institutions of informal constraints? Does informality disappear, or do the elites and affected populations continue to apply and abide by informal rules? What do we know about the relationship between institutional reforms and informal institutions? This book improves our understanding of how, when, and under what conditions democratic institutional reforms affect informal institutions and practices in countries transitioning to democracy (hybrid regimes). With an empirical focus on three transitional post-Soviet regimes—Georgia, Moldova, and Ukraine—this book explains the contentious relationship between democratic institutional reforms and informality in the broader post-Soviet context. These findings have implications not only for hybrid regimes but also for the majority of other post-Soviet and postcommunist countries. This book engages with a large and growing body of literature on informal institutions and practices and offers theoretical insights relevant to comparative politics, democratization and institutional development studies, political sociology, human geography, and political economy.

Acknowledgments

I FIRST STARTED thinking about the relationship between institutional change and informal institutions while on a research trip to Tbilisi, nearing the end of my doctoral studies at the University of Otago in New Zealand. The complex institutional transformation that had occurred in Georgia since 2004 was easy to note for an observer with experience in other post-Soviet states. The most striking observation was that Georgian institutions—modernized, reconstructed, and relieved of petty corruption—seemed to harmoniously coexist with the informal relations that continue to thrive in Georgian society. I conceived the idea for a book that would explore and explain how institutional reforms exist side by side with informal institutions. I developed the plan for this book and wrote its first pages of in the idyllic remoteness of Dunedin, on the South Island of New Zealand. Although portions of the draft manuscript were written in the Auckland City Library and the library of the University of Hamburg, the majority of the writing was completed during my stay as an Alexander von Humboldt visiting researcher at the Research Center for East European Studies (Forschungsstelle Osteuropa) of the University of Bremen (Germany).

I am grateful to the Alexander von Humboldt Foundation for its generous financial support, which enabled me to conduct extensive fieldwork in Ukraine and to collect empirical insights for Moldova as well as to conduct final stages of research for this book. The first leg of my fieldwork in Georgia (in 2013) was funded by the University of Otago Humanities Division and the Department of Politics research awards.

I specifically thank the numerous interviewees who sacrificed their time and braved the potential risks of providing me with invaluable insight into the functioning of informal institutions in their countries. In Georgia, I thank the staff of the Caucasus Research Resource Center (CRRC) for their friendly welcome and extensive interview materials. I have also benefited from discussions with the staff of Ilia State University of Tbilisi, ISET, and the attaché of the European Union to the Republic of Georgia. In Ukraine, I thank representatives of the Reanimation Package of Reforms, Gorshenin Institute, Transparency International–Ukraine, Ukraine Crisis Media Center, and the Ukrainian Center for Independent Political Research, as well as many other organizations, agencies, and individuals who chose to remain anonymous. In addition, I extend my gratitude to Katerina Bosko, Pavlo Illashenko, Olena Shubkina, Tetiana Stepurko, and Mychailo Wynnyckyj for providing me with indispensable networking in Ukraine.

Among those who have commented on this research, provided me with feedback, and in various other ways assisted in finalizing this manuscript, I acknowledge Heiko Pleines, Abel Polese, Jeremy Morris, and Megan Ouellette. I particularly express my special gratitude to Pleines for agreeing to host me at the Forschungsstelle Osteuropa and for providing me with all the resources and support that proved crucial for the completion of this monograph. I also thank Pleines for organizing a May 13, 2016, research colloquium dedicated to the discussion of my book. Special thanks go to four participants in the colloquium—Pleines, Tatia Chikhladze, Yana Zabanova, and Bosko—for their extensive comments and feedback on the chapters.

I thank four anonymous reviewers for the University of Michigan Press for their incisive comments and comprehensive feedback, which have allowed me to significantly improve this book. I express my appreciation to the former editor of Political and Social Sciences at the University of Michigan Press, Melody Herr, for her professionalism and invaluable advice throughout the publication process. To a large extent, Melody's enthusiasm for this project steered it through numerous editorial checks and approvals. Last but not least, I thank Melody's successor, Meredith Norwich, for advancing this project through its final stages.

Introduction

THE 2014 VICTORY of the Ukrainian "Euromaidan" movement, similar to Georgia's 2003 "Rose Revolution" and Ukraine's 2004 "Orange Revolution," marked another stage in institutional transformation of the post-Soviet region. Today, more than a decade after the success of first "color revolutions" in the former Soviet Union (fSU), democratic institution-building continues to face a number of challenges. The resilience of autocratic elites, difficulties of transitioning to market economy, and other notorious problems of postsocialism continue to haunt institutional transformation in the fSU. Less notable to an outsider's eye is the stealthy yet consequential, influence exerted on institutionalization by the "invisible hand" of informal institutions. Brought to life under Soviet totalitarianism, post-Soviet informality remains stubbornly resilient to political regime changes, massive economic transformations, globalization, and other metamorphoses of postcommunism. This book explores the effects of democratic institutional reforms on informal institutions and practices in post-Soviet spaces. It shows how, to what extent, in which ways, and under what conditions institutional changes—aimed at creating democratic, modern, and transparent institutions—affect the reliance on informality among postcommunist societies.

Twenty years after the collapse of the Soviet Union, informal institutions and practices are still widespread in most post-Soviet societies. The economic hardships, political instability, and social insecurity of the immediate postcommunist period have forced the population of the fSU to rely on informal institutions. As a consequence of the weakness and inefficiency of state institutions throughout the postcommunist period, informal institutions were often indispensable not only as private safety nets in day-to-day life but also as long-term coping mechanisms. Many scholars have argued that during the first postcommunist decade, support for informality increased throughout the post-Soviet region. The failure of most non-Baltic former Soviet states to democratize and to effectively reform their institutions has been further exacerbated by the entrenchment of authoritarianism. Only a handful of post-Soviet states have embarked on democratic institutional reforms, challenging the old forms of governance and widespread institutional stagnation.

More specifically, this book focuses on the few non-Baltic former Soviet states that seek to implement democratic institutional reforms to rebuild and transform ineffective old institutions riddled by systemic corruption and clientelism. Particularly notable are institutional reforms implemented between 2003 and 2015 by transitional (hybrid) political regimes in Georgia, Moldova, and Ukraine. Although fragile and often short-lived, these recent developments have heightened the need to reexamine the boundaries between formal and informal spheres.

Nevertheless, little is known about the extent, if any, to which institutional transformation and formalization pose a challenge to the importance of informality—interpersonal connections, informal networks, reciprocal exchanges of favors, and other practices widespread across the fSU. While the research has tended to focus on economic aspects of informality, this book examines the effects of institutional transformation on the informal sphere beyond the realm of research on informal economy. This book explores informal relations primarily in the political and social spheres, presenting a comprehensive account of the relationship between institutional changes aimed at constructing democratic state institutions and informality across the post-Soviet region. To explain this complex and multidimensional relationship, this volume offers a comprehensive analysis, offering fresh insight into the phenomenon of informality in postcommunist spaces.

RATIONALE BEHIND THE BOOK

More than forty years after Keith Hart coined the concept of the informal sector,[1] the literature on informality has reached a rough consensus that democratic state- and institution-building processes affect the informal sector.[2] Many scholars have noted that the weakness of formal institutions[3] and the deficit of good governance result both in the strengthening of informal institutions and in the spread of informal practices, not only in postcommunist countries but also in other developing regions of the world.[4] Scholars have also argued that institutional reforms, implemented during the process of democratization, undermine the support for informal practices and reduce the size and spread of the informal sector.[5] The literature on institution-building and informality has nevertheless been ambiguous about the effect of democratic institutional reforms on informality across the post-Soviet region. As Gretchen Helmke and Steven Levitsky admit, "Systematic research on the subject remains at an incipient stage."[6]

In general, research on informality as a phenomenon extending beyond the economic sphere in the fSU is less widespread than studies on informal entrepreneurship and other aspects of informal economy. While many scholars have focused on informal economy of post-Soviet states, there has been relatively little empirical research into informal practices that perform not only economic but also political and social functions.[7]

Notable exceptions are the studies by Ledeneva[8] on informal networks and practices and their relationship with institution-building in post-Soviet Russia. Works by Paul J. D'Anieri and Vladimir Gel'man have highlighted various aspects of informal relations in the politics of post-Soviet regimes, including those of transitional post-color-revolution states,[9] and a recent book by Henry E. Hale explores the relationship between democratization and informal politics in hybrid regimes of Georgia and Ukraine, among other former Soviet states.[10] The majority of recent literature on the topic, however, has prioritized informal political networks and the use of informality by postcommunist elites. Little effort has been made to examine the broader aspects of informality, such as informal behaviors of the general public or the role of informal practices among particular types of formal institutions. The significance of informal practices for the ruling elites and populations across the fSU has led many scholars to believe that informality, at both institutional and individual levels, must be taken into account when studying postcommunist transformations.[11] As Gel'man emphasizes, "The distinction between types of predominant institutions (formal or informal) marks a watershed between 'transitions to democracy' (where the 'rule of law' is assumed almost by default) and post-Soviet transitions to a somewhat different regime."[12]

With the bulk of research on post-Soviet informal practices focused on Russia, little is known about informality in other parts of the fSU. Even less is known about the relationship between institutional change and informality in those post-Soviet regimes that have attempted to implement democratic institutional reforms. According to the recent research on informal practices

in Russia[13] as well as in other undemocratic post-Soviet regimes,[14] informality
has not retreated. In addition to economic instability, which continues to
sustain the booming informal economies of post-Soviet countries, the lack of
political and social reforms and the failure of governments to reform, modernize, and decentralize formal institutions encourage the reliance on informal practices on a much broader scale than was the case during the Soviet
period.[15] The recent literature on democratization and institution-building
in hybrid or transitional post-Soviet regimes—Georgia, Ukraine, and
Moldova—suggests that informality presents a challenge to institution- and
state-building processes.[16] To date, however, no studies have specifically in-
vestigated the effects of democratic institutional transformation on informality in post-Soviet hybrid regimes beyond informal politics and informal
economy. This study contributes to a growing body of literature examining
the role of informality in postcommunist institutionalization processes, adding to studies by such scholars as Hale, Alena Ledeneva, and Richard Rose.

Following Helmke and Levitsky's suggestion that when studying informal institutions, it is "essential to maintain a broad and pluralistic research
agenda that encourages fertilization across disciplines, theoretical traditions, and methods,"[17] this book synthesizes various theoretical and empirical approaches. Bearing in mind the cross-disciplinary nature of the phenomenon of informality, this book draws its theoretical insights from a
broad range of disciplines, including political science, political economy,
anthropology, and sociology.

SUMMARY OF THE ARGUMENT

This book examines the relationship between democratic institutional reforms and informality in post-Soviet spaces from several perspectives. How
and under what conditions do institutional changes, implemented with
the purpose of building democratic institutions, affect the informal
sphere? Do the reforms reduce the populations' and elites' reliance on informal practices? As Valerie Bunce argues, "New democracies often exhibit
a considerable gap between formal institutions, which meet democratic
standards, and informal practices, which do not."[18] How do formal institutions coexist with informal practices in the fSU? Do democratic institutional reforms weaken informality? What happens to informal practices
when institutional reforms succeed?

Following the consensus generally accepted in the literature on institution-building and democratization that formalization and institutional reforms undermine informality,[19] this study anticipates that the *strengthening of formal democratic institutions will lead to the weakening of informal practices.* Although many scholars have tested this hypothesis on different developing and postcommunist countries,[20] the literature has so far failed to produce a thorough analysis of the impact of institutional reforms on informality and in particular on informal practices outside of the informal economy in non-Baltic former Soviet states. More important, this book explains what happens to informal practices when institutional changes reform, decentralize, democratize, and increase the effectiveness of formal institutions. In contrast to previous studies, which have argued that strengthening democratic institutions weakens informal practices, this book demonstrates that strengthening formal institutions can have both positive and negative effects on their informal counterparts. In other words, while undermining negative aspects of informal institutions—such as nepotism and informal payments—might be important for the strengthening of formal rules, those can also be enhanced without eradicating the beneficial aspects of informality, such as networks that provide assistance and cooperation. Because some informal behaviors are not detrimental to democratic reforms, formal and informal institutions may also coexist harmoniously. As this book shows, reforming formal institutions is not necessarily associated with the weakening or disappearance of informal institutions. This hypothesis also serves as the basis for testing two additional hypotheses.

First, *in the process of institutional change, informal practices in post-Soviet regimes become absorbed into formal institutions, thereby blurring the boundaries between the formal and informal in a manner similar to institution-building processes in post-Soviet autocracies.* This synthesis of formal and informal institutions could either deformalize formal structures or, if democratic institutional reforms succeed, lead formal institutions to gradually transform informal practices and change the nature of informality. This hypothesis builds on two strands of literature. First, the assumption that informal practices infiltrate formal institutions and deformalize them comes from studies on informal political structures in postcommunist countries.[21] The key argument of this strand of literature is that informal institutions are widely used both by postcommunist elites, as mechanisms of institution-building, and by populations, as main private safety nets.[22] Although this pattern of formal-informal relations is typical for institution-building processes in au-

thoritarian post-Soviet regimes,[23] the relationship between democratic institutional reforms and a formal-informal equilibrium in transitional post-
Soviet regimes is still poorly understood.[24] Second, this hypothesis follows
discussions on neoinstitutional theory, arguing that informal practices may
coexist with formal institutions either by filling a void in areas neglected by
formal institutions or by complementing them.[25] In the course of democratic institutional reforms, therefore, the detrimental effects of informal
practices on formal institutions may be reduced. Since the post-Soviet region
has seen few attempts to implement democratic institutional changes and
even fewer successes, the literature is inconclusive regarding how informal
practices behave with regard to formal institutions.

The second hypothesis builds on arguments in the literature[26] suggesting
that informality in post-Soviet societies is not always a negative phenomenon, and *acknowledging the positive characteristics of informality might be instrumental to understanding the relationship between reforms and informality*. As
classical works on postcommunist informality argue,[27] informal practices
often provide social safety nets and offer populations a wide range of scarce
public goods, such as good jobs and access to better health care, education,
and communal services. In autocracies, informal practices allow citizens to
circumvent state bureaucracy and to access otherwise unavailable services or
public goods.[28] In hybrid regimes, informal institutions may lose some of
their functions as a result of democratic institutional changes but nevertheless still be needed to serve as support mechanisms and private safety nets. In
some cases, post-Soviet informal and formal spheres are presented as existing in a mutually dependent and beneficial symbiosis.[29] The population's
reliance on informality may therefore not necessarily be detrimental to
institution-building processes in hybrid regimes. Instead, as has often occurred in Central European[30] or Latin American[31] transitional regimes, informal institutions may simply fill the vacuum left by the often inevitable un-
derperformance of newly constructed or reformed institutions during the
early stages of transition without having detrimental effects on the process
of institutional change.

POST-SOVIET REGION

This book's theoretical framework, arguments, hypotheses, and research
methods are relevant for the broader disciplines of comparative politics, area

studies, social policy, and human geography. However, the volume focuses specifically on the postcommunist geopolitical region of the fSU to explain the remarkable association between institutional change and informality. The term *post-Soviet region* refers to a distinctive and coherent geopolitical region that encompasses the majority of former Soviet countries. The use of this term has geopolitical, geoeconomic, and sociocultural connotations.

Geopolitically, this book covers only those countries and regions that were originally part of the Union of Soviet Socialist Republics (USSR) and are not currently members of the European Union. This leaves out the Baltic states of Estonia, Latvia, and Lithuania as well as non-Soviet postcommunist countries such as Mongolia or Central European ex-socialist-bloc members and the Balkan states. For the purpose of this book, the geopolitical expanse of the post-Soviet region includes Eastern European former Soviet countries (Belarus, Moldova, Russia, and Ukraine), the South Caucasus (Armenia, Azerbaijan, and Georgia), and Central Asia (Kazakhstan, Kyrgyzstan, Tajikistan, Turkmenistan, and Uzbekistan). Though numerous similarities exist between the post-Soviet region and other postcommunist regions, this study specifically emphasizes the role of the Soviet legacy, defined by the impact of sovietization, in affecting the sociopolitical and socioeconomic spheres of the post-Soviet region.[32] In most communist regimes, political ideology had extensive influence on social traditions and organization. In contrast to other communist regimes, Soviet socialization had far greater impact in the Soviet socialist republics that experienced the decades of the Great Terror, forcible collectivization, and sociocultural standardization.[33] These historical developments, combined with severe economic shortages and high levels of political repression, have led to the spread and entrenchment of informality among the post-Soviet societies to a far greater extent than in most non-Soviet countries.[34]

For all of the post-Soviet non-Baltic states, the end of Soviet rule has not resulted in democratization. Throughout the 1990s, in contrast to their Central European neighbors or even Mongolia, the former Soviet states have either failed to implement democratic reforms or have purposefully retained and preserved the old autocratic forms of governance. Controlled succession of power and the entrenched authoritarianism remained a key characteristic of political regimes throughout Central Asia, the South Caucasus, and in most of the Eastern European former Soviet countries. The spread of color revolutions has brought political transitions to Georgia, Ukraine, and to a lesser extent Kyrgyzstan. The pace of democratic reforms in Moldova has been much slower. Today, the majority of post-Soviet countries are still undemocratic. In short, the geopolitical category of the post-Soviet region encompasses a group of countries that not only share a common history and therefore legacy but also have similarly designed political institutions.

Geoeconomically, in spite of the transition to market economy, most post-Soviet states have thus far failed to build functioning and efficient market economies. While the dependence on fossil fuels is a typical characteristic of most fast-growing, post-Soviet economies, rampant unemployment, systemic corruption, and social inequality are widespread.[35] Furthermore, in contrast to the expectations of transitology scholars, informality and other problems of postsocialism have not disappeared.[36] Instead, stalled economic transition continues to exacerbate socioeconomic underdevelopment inherited from the communist period.

Economic inequality and the lack of political transition, in conjunction with the enduring legacy of socialism, encouraged the continuity of sociocultural traditions, norms, and customs, and the reliance on informality in daily life is perhaps the most enduring sociocultural characteristic. It is shared by most post-Soviet societies, regardless of their geographical location, political system, and economic development. This is not to say, however, that the informal sphere is not important in other postcommunist or noncommunist developing regions of the world. However, informality has far greater importance for post-Soviet citizens than for citizens of other postcommunist regions. These distinctions indicate that classifying all postcommunist regimes into one broad category of "postsocialist" countries means ignoring inherent geopolitical, geoeconomic, and sociocultural differences. Such differences are of course also present among post-Soviet countries but are far more pronounced in distinctions between the post-Soviet region and other former socialist territories.

CASE STUDIES

This book examines the relationship between institutional change and informal practices in the post-Soviet region by analyzing case studies of Georgia, Moldova, and Ukraine. As a consequence of their inherent similarities and differences, these three countries serve as convenient laboratories for examining the effects of institutional transformation on informality among other post-Soviet states. Since the collapse of the USSR, Georgia, Moldova, and Ukraine have continuously experienced external pressure from both the West and Russia. Beginning in the mid-1990s, Georgia and Moldova—both facing a heavy burden of unresolved separatist conflicts—sought to counterbalance Russian political and economic pressure by pursuing European integration. These external factors, along with Russia's support for the breakaway Georgian regions of Abkhazia and South Ossetia as well as the Moldovan region of Transnistria, were instrumental in Georgia's and Moldova's efforts to reform and democratize their institutions. In contrast, Ukraine remained unaffected by separatist conflicts until the dramatic developments of early 2014. The annexation of Crimea by Russia and the pro-Russian separatist takeovers in the eastern regions of the country have now placed Ukraine on the list of post-Soviet countries affected by ethnoseparatist conflict.

All three countries experienced a series of initial openings for institutional transformation. In Georgia, the overthrow of Eduard Shevardnadze's regime following the victory of the 2003 Rose Revolution marked a fundamental step in the reform process. Additional steps occurred as the pro-reform government of Mikheil Saakashvili launched a series of comprehensive institutional reforms. The elites' support for institutional reforms, resulting in a reduction in corruption and notable improvements in state institutions, continued throughout Saakashvili's presidency and after the transfer of power from United National Movement (UNM) to the Georgian Dream coalition in 2013. In Moldova, the process of institutional change began in earnest after the end of nearly a decade of Communist Party domination and the transfer of power to the reformist pro-European coalition in 2009. Since then, the implementation of democratic reforms has been consistently—albeit with varying intensity and effectiveness—pursued by shifting camps of reformists. In 2015, intense intracoalition infighting strengthened the position of oligarchic elites within the reformist government and stalled reform progress. Moldova remains a hybrid regime with a formal commitment to democratization. In Ukraine, the victory of the 2005 Orange Revolution enabled the country to embark on a series of institutional reforms, but they were botched. Although Ukraine's democratization was reversed during the presidency of Viktor Yanukovich (2010–14), his overthrow in 2014 opened new prospects for institutional reforms. The extensive reform program aimed at thorough transformation of state institutions began to be implemented in 2015.

Georgia, Moldova, and Ukraine are the only transitional or hybrid regimes in the post-Soviet region. The current literature on democratization offers numerous competing definitions for transitional political regimes. While some scholars attribute the appearance of such regimes to the third wave of democratization,[37] others associate them and the series of color revolutions across postcommunist Eurasia with the "fourth wave"[38] of democratization. Similarly debatable are the various definitions of transitional regimes employed by scholars to describe those regimes that overthrew authoritarian rulers and embarked on democratic institution-building. From Steven Levitsky and Lucan A. Way's "competitive authoritarianism"[39] to Valerie Bunce and Sharon Wolchik's "mixed regimes,"[40] transitional regimes have been labeled *gray*, *hybrid*, or *electoral* regimes. Throughout this book, the terms *transitional regime* and *hybrid regime* are used interchangeably to refer to post-Soviet countries that consistently implemented effective institutional reforms to democratize, decentralize, and strengthen formal institutions. These regimes are neither full-fledged democracies nor semi-consolidated democratic states. Democratization was never completed in any of them, and all have serious deficiencies in democratic state-building.

Given that this book focuses on democratic institutional changes in the post-Soviet region, transitional regimes are selected based on two conditions. First, in the absence of participatory or representative democracies among the non-Baltic post-Soviet countries,[41] the presence of free, fair, and competitive elections is fundamental to classification a transitional regime. Although many scholars debate the significance of elections in nondemocratic or transitional regimes,[42] this book follows the voluminous literature on democratization that argues in favor of the positive role of elections during the transition.[43] Second, the process of institutional reform should be part of a coordinated, substantial, and longer-lasting reform effort. Reforms involving changes in the legislative and judiciary as well as executive branches must seek to eradicate corruption and promote democratic freedoms, civil society, and the free press along with economic sustainability. First and foremost, the effectiveness of reforms in reconstructing old institutions and creating new ones leads toward the transition to democracy.

The other important criterion for the selection of hybrid regimes is the continuity of democratic reforms. Among other post-Soviet states, Kyrgyzstan and Armenia[44] as well as Russia (though only for a short period)[45] were classified as hybrid regimes. Reforms in these countries have been short-lived and have had limited positive impact on institutional performance. Georgia, Moldova, and Ukraine thus constitute the only former Soviet countries that have retained (or repeatedly regained) the status of transitional regimes since the turn of the twenty-first century. For example, when comparing regime typology assigned to the former Soviet states by the Nations in Transit project,[46] it is evident that, except for Georgia, Moldova, and Ukraine, no other post-Soviet regime continuously maintained the pace of democratic institution-building (see table I.1).

Significant variation also exists among these three cases, however. First, the scope, extent, and continuity of institutional reforms are quite different across the three countries. For example, in contrast to the continuous and comprehensive reform process in Georgia, reforms in Ukraine stalled during Yanukovich's presidency. From 2009 to 2012, political turmoil also significantly retarded Moldovan institutional changes. Although democratic institutional changes began to take place after 2004 in all three cases, the types of reforms, their longevity, their continuity, and most of all their effectiveness differ markedly. The levels of influence on and support for institutional reforms by the European Union and other external actors also vary. These three case studies therefore present numerous convergences and divergences necessary for an in-depth analysis of different trajectories of institutional change in the post-Soviet context.

TABLE I.1. Nations in Transit Classification of Post-Soviet Regimes, 2004–2014

| Country | Year | | | | | | |
	2004	2006	2008	2010	2012	2014	Mean
Armenia	5.00	5.14	5.21	5.39	5.39	5.36	*5.25*
Azerbaijan	5.63	5.93	6.00	6.39	6.57	6.68	*6.13*
Belarus	6.54	6.71	6.71	6.50	6.68	6.71	*6.641*
Georgia	**4.83**	**4.86**	**4.79**	**4.93**	**4.82**	**4.75**	***4.83***
Kazakhstan	6.25	6.39	6.39	6.43	6.54	6.57	*6.43*
Kyrgyzstan	5.67	5.68	5.93	6.21	6.00	5.96	*5.91*
Moldova	**4.88**	**4.96**	**5.00**	**5.14**	**4.89**	**4.82**	***4.95***
Russia	5.25	5.75	5.96	6.14	6.18	6.21	*5.92*
Tajikistan	5.71	5.93	6.07	6.14	6.18	6.25	*6.05*
Turkmenistan	6.88	6.96	6.93	6.93	6.93	6.93	*6.93*
Ukraine	**4.88**	**4.21**	**4.25**	**4.39**	**4.82**	**4.86**	***4.57***
Uzbekistan	6.46	6.82	6.86	6.93	6.93	6.93	*6.82*

Note: NIT Democracy scores are a sum of political freedoms and civil rights.

6.00–7.00—Consolidated authoritarian regimes; 5.00–5.99—Semi-consolidated authoritarian regimes; 4.00–4.99—Transitional governments or hybrid regimes; 3.00–3.99—Semi-consolidated democracies; 1.00–2.99—Consolidated democracies.

Source: Freedom House, "Nations in Transit."

While democratic institutional changes distinguish Georgia, Moldova, and Ukraine from other post-Soviet regimes, the elites' and populations' continuous reliance on informality makes them quite similar to the rest of the fSU. Many studies have emphasized the widespread nature of informality in the post-Soviet region.[47] Moldova, Ukraine, and particularly Georgia did not constitute exceptions. As was typical in the former Soviet countries, the heavy reliance on informal practices in present-day transitional regimes makes these countries intriguing case studies of the relationship between institutional changes and informality.

All three countries embarked on democratic transition not from a consolidated authoritarian state but from a more ambiguous type of nondemocratic regime, an "informal state." This book defines an informal state as a political regime that (1) lacks a single power base, (2) relies heavily on informal constraints rather than on formal rules, and (3) fails to achieve the absolute monopoly on power necessary for authoritarian rule. Informal states are characterized by the prevalence and dominance of informal institutions over formal rules and by informality's supreme role in daily life. In contrast to hybrid regimes, ruling elites in informal states not only are content with the informal order but also work deliberately to sustain and strengthen it. The key difference between informal states and authoritarian regimes is that the former lack centralized vertical power structures typical of authoritarian states; instead, power is distributed among several informal power centers, some of which may harmoniously coexist with the incumbent while others may challenge the state's monopoly on power. Despite the incumbent's desire to centralize the reins of power, various factors, such as regional diversity or elite fragmentation, contribute to political pluralism and prevent the incumbent from realizing its goal. In informal states, informal institutions are not only sources of legitimacy for the ruling elite but also causes of their weaknesses. In other words, by either seeking to maintain the informal balance of power among various informal power brokers or by attempting to dominate other informal power centers, incumbents rely on informal rules rather than formal institutions. As a consequence of the weakness of (formal) state institutions, incumbents are unable to consolidate their rule and remain locked in a cycle of dependence on informal structures. Lacking effective mechanisms of coercion, the heads of informal states are vulnerable to elite defection and popular discontent. In stark contrast to authoritarian states, incumbents of informal states are reluctant to use excessive repression against their citizens for fear of a retaliatory backlash.

KEY TERMS

One term that frequently appears throughout this research is *democratic institutional reforms*. This term refers to institution-building processes that satisfy two basic conditions. First, democratic institutional reforms or changes are designed and implemented with the ultimate goal of creating democratic institutions—that is, institutions that facilitate societal access and therefore stand in contrast to authoritarian institutions that ensure acquiescence instead of access.[48] Although democratic institutional reforms do not necessarily result in the establishment of participatory or representative democracy, the process of institutional change is expected to formally pursue democratization as well as decentralization and formalization of formal state institutions. Institutional reforms can be considered democratic only if they result in the creation and establishment of transparent formal institutions that are accountable to the population and free of corruption. It is thus the final product of a given set of reforms that distinguishes democratic institutional reforms from those institutional changes and reforms that do not result in the emergence of the institutions of societal access in national and local governance, civil society, and mass media. Second, the process of democratic institutional reform must be implemented by popularly elected political actors and take place either in transitional (hybrid) regimes or in countries with recent or immediate experiences of transition from authoritarian or semiauthoritarian regimes to democratic institution-building. The current definition of institutional reforms thus excludes state-building processes in undemocratic regimes, including but not limited to facade electoral regimes or pseudodemocratic and electoral authoritarian state systems.[49]

Because hybrid regimes often have frail and unstable institutional frameworks, the reform processes in these countries often become stagnant or even fall backward. Alongside democratic institutional reforms, hybrid regimes may also enact reforms of an undemocratic nature, and the creation of democratic institutions might be accompanied by the strengthening or appearance of undemocratic structures, such as the buildup of patronage and clientelist networks. Bearing in mind these important caveats of the democratization processes in hybrid regimes, the effectiveness (or the lack thereof) of democratic institutional reforms must be understood not in absolute terms but rather as a fragile and inconsistent long-term process. Even if successfully built, democratic institutions of hybrid regimes may disappear or be reappropriated for undemocratic purposes. The institutional reform process in Saakashvili's Georgia, for example, was often accompanied by undemocratic reforms, including the monopolization of the executive branch, combined with various authoritarian efforts to control the media and civil society. In a similar vein, the Georgian Dream Coalition, democratically elected to succeed Saakashvili, continues to use charges of corruption to prosecute former regime officials and settle scores with the opposition.

Two other terms fundamental for this research are the interrelated concepts of *informality* and *informal practices*. The current scholarship on informality has tended to follow three rather similar approaches in studying the informal phenomenon. The first approach, favored in political science and institutional economics, centers on examining informality as based on distinctions between formal and informal institutions.[50] Encapsulated in Douglass C. North's presentation of institutions as either formal or informal constraints "that human beings devise to shape human interaction,"[51] informality is understood in terms of institutions that operate similarly to and often exist alongside of formal institutions. The second approach focuses on networks as structures engaged in informal activities. Informal networks, described as interpersonal, private, social, or strong- and weak-ties networks, are presented as structures that provide individuals with the organizational and operational means to engage in informal activities. Unlike institutions, networks are more intimate and individual-centered structures. The focus on networks therefore allows scholars to study specific aspects of informal practices at both the micro and macro levels. The third approach focuses on the broader concept of informal practices understood as a sum of informal activities conducted by either informal institutions or informal networks.

Numerous studies have, however, sought to merge institutional and networking approaches, incorporating different aspects of these two strands either to examine the role of networks in institutions or to explore informal institutions as consisting of networks.[52] More recent research on informality combines all three approaches.[53] Given that informal institutions are comprised of networks and that both the former and the latter employ informal practices to achieve their goals, this study understands informality as the process of the purposeful use of informal practices by informal institutions and networks.[54] Although this book builds on both the institutional and networking strands of the research on informality, it keeps a reserved distance either from structural (globalization-centered and neoliberalist) or dualist (presenting the informal sphere as the antithesis of the formal sphere) understanding of informality. Instead, informality is examined here as a process of sustaining and employing informal practices within (both formal and informal) institutions and networks: the latter are similar to informal institutions, since the distinction between informal networks and institutions is indeed more of a definitional disparity. In other words, both informal networks and institutions rely on informal practices to achieve their goals, and both are convergent with formal institutions.

Economic and noneconomic functions of informal practices are closely intertwined, which makes drawing boundaries between them very difficult. Although most informal practices are used with an ultimate goal of material gain and profit-seeking, they may also be used to achieve noneconomic goals. For example, informal practices are also used to gain access to political offices or to increase one's social standing. Yet examining informality beyond the informal economy requires distinguishing the economic, social, and political functions of informal practices. This book explains how institutional changes influence elites' and general populations' use of noneconomic informal practices—informal networking, the use of contacts and connections, (non)reciprocal exchanges of favors, and the population's reliance on private safety nets. The definition of informality used in this book therefore excludes such typical profit-seeking informal practices as moonlighting, black markets, informal self-employment, informal payments (envelope wages) at formal workplaces, cash-in-hand work, informal entrepreneurship, informal household incomes, informal profit-seeking enterprises of all types, underground markets, and other profit-generating forms of informal activities.

ORGANIZATION OF THE BOOK

This book examines the relationship between democratic institutional reforms and informal practices in post-Soviet spaces and therefore constructs theoretical, conceptual, and analytical frameworks that will be employed to investigate and interpret empirical data. Chapters 1, 2, and 3 are therefore primarily theoretical and conceptual. Chapters 4, 5, and 6 then provide an empirical examination of the case studies of Georgia, Moldova, and Ukraine.

Chapter 1 constructs a theoretical and conceptual baseline of informality that guides the rest of the book. After examining the history and development of the concept of informality, the chapter discusses the different uses of the concept in both economic and sociological connotations. The chapter then considers three interrelated terms encapsulated under the generic concept of informality: informal institutions, informal networks, and informal practices.

Chapter 2 delves into the specifics of informal practices across the world and in postcommunist countries in particular. It investigates distinctions between informality in post-Soviet states and in postcommunist non-Soviet countries of Central and Eastern Europe. It examines the structure and organization of informal circles and networks, explaining the dynamics of informal relations and the regional differences among informal practices employed by populations across the vast post-Soviet region. The chapter also discusses the relationships among informal economic and sociopolitical practices, informal practices, and corruption and explains relations between informal and formal institutions.

Chapter 3 provides the theoretical overview of the relationship between institutional change and informality. This chapter builds a theoretical framework for analyzing the association between democratic institutional reforms and informal practices in postsocialist countries. It characterizes, analyzes, and explains how, why, and under what circumstances informal institutions are influenced by institutional changes. Incorporating literature on the impact of democratic institution-building on the informal sphere, it explains a complex and uneasy relationship between democratic institutional change and informality. The comprehensive analysis of literature presented in this chapter engages with the new institutional theory as well as theories of postcommunist democratization and institutional transformation.

The second part of chapter 3 provides a brief empirical analysis of the history of democratic institutional reforms in the fSU, with a primary focus on the cases of failed democratization. This chapter concludes that both the initial openings for institutional reforms and the elites' willingness to embark on democratization processes were limited across the post-Soviet region. Following the observation that reform processes in undemocratic regimes are by design marred by informalization, the chapter opens the floor for empirical discussion of institutional reforms and informality in hybrid regimes.

Chapter 4 examines the Republic of Georgia. The first part of the chapter presents a detailed historical analysis of institutional reforms and informality in Georgia since the collapse of the Soviet Union. The second part of the chapter presents the book's empirical findings on institutional change and informality in Georgia.

Chapters 5 and 6 are dedicated to case studies of Moldova and Ukraine. Like chapter 4, these chapters begin with the analysis of institutional changes and the informal sphere before turning to a rigorous examination of empirical data pertinent to each of the cases. As with Georgia, these case studies demonstrate the association (or lack thereof) between institutional reforms and informal practices.

The book concludes by comparing the empirical evidence in support of the key hypotheses presented here. The conclusion offers a more comprehensive overview of the relationship between democratic institutional change and informality in the post-Soviet context and provides some analytical, comparative, and theoretical reflections and observations. Finally, it discusses the implications of these findings for the broader post-Soviet region.

CHAPTER I
Informality: Unraveling the Knot

ALTHOUGH THIS BOOK applies a thematic case study research design that focuses on institution-building, democratization, and the more general theme of postcommunist comparative politics, it is above all a study of informality. Like many other works on informality, this book pursues a multidisciplinary approach, synthesizing insights from politics, economics, anthropology, and sociology. While the book primarily emphasizes informal practices and institutions in the post-Soviet region, this chapter engages with the current literature on the topic of informality in its broadest form as a means of providing a theoretical grounding for the phenomenon of post-Soviet informality. The chapter therefore constructs the conceptual, analytical, and theoretical baselines that guide the empirical discussion that follows.

WHAT IS INFORMALITY?

Informality is perhaps one of the most heterogeneous and conceptually overloaded terms in social sciences. The current research on the issue of informality expands across a variety of disciplines, most prominently institutional and behavioral economics, developmental microeconomics, institutional politics, social anthropology, and sociology. As informality is itself a vague and amorphous phenomenon, the bulk of research on informality transcends disciplinary boundaries and encompasses two or more fields in the humanities and social sciences.

Informality in Economics

Since its inception in 1973, in Keith Hart's seminal study on household incomes in Ghana,[1] the term *informal* has become firmly lodged in develop-

mental economics.[2] Following Hart's division of economic activities into formal and informal, the perception of informality in economics was dominated
throughout the 1970s by the dualist model, which dichotomized all economic transactions as consisting of formal (legal) and underground (often
illicit). This approach was pioneered by W. Arthur Lewis[3] and further developed in studies such as those by John R. Harris and Michael P. Todaro.[4] However, the research on informal economy as a sector separate and in some accounts inferior to formal economy began in earnest only after Hart conceived
the term *informal sector*.[5] Many earlier studies on informal economy portrayed
the phenomenon as confined to the developing world. According to proponents of the dualist model, the lack of regulation and other malaises of economic underdevelopment in the developing world result in proliferation of
the informal economic sector, which "plagues" the formal economy in a variety of ways, destabilizing its performance and decreasing its efficiency.[6] The
negative perception of informality often stems from researchers' unwillingness to distinguish between the informal sectors of the developed North and
the developing South. Joseph P. Gaughan and Louis A. Ferman pointed out
that "the term 'informal economy' will mean different things in advanced
industrial nations from what it does in developing countries,"[7] and Klarita
Gërxhani concluded that "the distinction between the two types of countries
is of key importance" in research on informal economy.[8]

Comparison of informal sectors in developed and developing countries
eventually gave rise to the structuralist school of research on informal economy. Manuel Castells and Alejandro Portes were among the first to challenge
the dualist paradigm in studies of informal economy, arguing that as a consequence of the "moving boundaries of informal economy," formal industries and firms rely on informal practices as much as on formal rules and
regulations.[9] Furthermore, structuralists assert that informality is not a negative phenomenon but rather contributes to the improvement of living
standards in developing countries by providing access to public goods that
would otherwise be inaccessible for the majority of the population. In keep-
ing with this idea, informality is understood as structural (socially embedded) rather than transitional.

Somewhat similar to the structural school of research on the informal
sector is the voluntarist approach.[10] Proponents of this strand incorporate
elements of structuralist models but argue that the informal sector is essentially voluntary. This means that individuals engage in informal activities in
accordance with their own choices rather than being compelled to do so by

economic realities. Because individuals can always choose to remain formal, they participate in informal activities only when the benefits of informality outweigh its costs.

Unlike the individual-centered voluntarist school of informal economy, the legalist approach focuses on the role of institutions.[11] According to legalists, informality arises either from a lack of legal regulation or as a consequence of the weakness of legal institutions. The costs of legalizing economic activities and the benefits of remaining legal are decisive with regard to individuals' participation in informal economy.[12] Since the legalist understanding of the informal sphere builds on rational choice institutionalism and new institutional theories, it is to a certain degree synonymous with the meaning of the term *informal* in institutional economics. According to Douglass C. North's understanding, economic institutions consist of "formal constraints—such as rules that human beings devise" and "informal constraints—such as conventions and codes of behavior."[13] North's institutional approach to studying informal economy is just one step away from the voluminous body of research on informality in political science, which primarily follows institutionalist models of studying informality.

Informality in the Social Sciences and Humanities

Unlike economics—a discipline that both coined the term *informal economy* and monopolized the research on the informal sector and informality—a large and growing body of literature on the informal phenomenon in politics has thus far failed to produce a commonly accepted conceptualization of informality. As Gretchen Helmke and Steven Levitsky lament, the research on informality in politics encompasses a wide range of phenomena, including but not limited to clientelism, corruption, party politics, bureaucratic traditions, criminal groups, and informal power networks.[14] Although efforts are being made to limit the scope of informality in political science either to the realm of informal institutions[15] or to informal networks,[16] there is still little agreement among political scientists as to what exactly political informality is.

Informality also features prominently in social anthropology. In fact, Julius H. Boeke, a Dutch anthropologist, first suggested a "dualistic economic theory" in his book on the Indonesian economy.[17] Precipitously close to conceiving the term *informal economy*, Boeke emphasized the dichotomy between the formal market economy and "primitive economics" practiced by indigenous peasants. From Bronislaw Malinowski to Maurice Mauss, social anthropologists explored the issue of informality as a premodern, primordial, primitive, or prehistoric phenomenon, starkly contrasting Western and postmodernist forms of cultural and social organization. The informal character of human exchange and reciprocity was explored in studies by George C. Homans, Maria Emanuela Alberti and Serena Sabatini, Jonathan Parry and Maurice Blotch, and David Graeber.[18] Nevertheless, like the ambiguity and vagueness of informality in other disciplines, in social anthropology, "the terms 'informality' and 'formality' are inherently problematic because of their extensive and contradictory semantic fields whereby their meaning will vary in accordance with social context."[19]

No less amorphous is the understanding of informality in sociology. In her major theoretical work on informality as a sociological phenomenon, Barbara Misztal admitted that "the problem with the concept of informality is that it is a mundane term, difficult to define not only in sociological theories but also in everyday language."[20] Apart from Misztal's book, nuanced theoretically grounded studies on informality in sociology are scarce. Works by Homans, George Herbert Mead, Herbert Blunter, Erving Goffman, and Harold Garfinkel only occasionally cover the topic of formal-informal relations and the dichotomy of public and private spheres.[21] While the literature on social networks is rife with studies on informal networking,[22] the field of social networking studies extends well beyond the discipline of sociology and into research on economics, politics, business, and culture.[23] Although other disciplines still lack contextualized theoretical research on informality, there is a rich empirical literature on informal practices and institutions in ethnographic studies,[24] human geography,[25] and broader developmental studies.[26]

Defining Informality

Given this multiplicity of approaches and the interdisciplinary and heterogeneous nature of informality, definitions of the term are both manifold and discipline-specific. Even within the boundaries of economic studies, informal economy is difficult to define. According to Ana Maria Oviedo, Mark Roland Thomas, and Kamer Karakurum-Özdemir, in research on informal economy, "the hidden nature of informal activity has posed a significant challenge to defining and measuring it accurately."[27] Constructing an interdisciplinary definition of informality is even more challenging. For example, the International Labour Organization defines informality as an umbrella concept that "describes a variety of activities producing goods and services through which persons derive employment and incomes."[28] While such a definition cannot be easily employed outside of the field of economics, a sociological definition of informality that presents the phenomenon "as a form of interaction among partners enjoying relative freedom in interpretation of their roles' requirements"[29] is difficult to extend to economics, where the reliance on informality is often perceived not as a matter of choice but as a necessity. Misztal explained that in sociological texts the "concept [of informality] does not enjoy an independent standing but rather has the status of an ephemeral or residual concept."[30]

It is even more challenging to extract the definition of informality from political science. As much of the current literature on informality in politics is conceptually dominated by the research on informal institutions, informality as such is seen as an ambivalent network of relationships that "functions like a part of everyday social life and according to its mechanisms."[31] Regardless of the multitude of contrasting definitions, terminological ambiguity, and divergent interpretations surrounding the concept, informality has also acquired an array of similar characteristics across various disciplines.

First, informal is always presented in dichotomy with formal. In Alena Ledeneva's words, "everything that is not formal is considered to be informal."[32] According to József Böröcz, all forms of social behavior occurring outside of "professionally written, ritually accepted and publicly available—rules and regulations . . . qualify as *informal*."[33] In that light, informality is recognized as a feature of modernity and an inseparable attribute of a modern state. Since informal relations often remain beyond the boundaries of the state, the presence of the state with its institutions, norms, and regulations is fundamental for the existence of the informal sphere. Indeed, prior to the creation of states and the establishment of written laws and legally enforced rules, informality was the rule of the day for societies described by anthropologists as primitive, tribal, clannish, and most of all premodern. Even in anthropology, informality surfaces only with the onset of modernization and ensuing legalization and institutionalization of political, economic, and social life. Though many scholars agree that informality "precedes its formal counterpart . . . historically . . . , so most manifestations of informality constitute the natural pattern of social life,"[34] it is still understood that "informal processes refer to social interactions that occur [only] in formal contexts."[35] This dualist dichotomization of informal and formal spheres persists consistently across conceptual presentations of informality in economics, politics, sociology, and anthropology.

Second, formality and informality are by no means mutually exclusive, and theoretically, neither of the spheres can replace the other. Jack Knight argues that "informal rules are the foundation on which formal rules are built."[36] Ledeneva supported that opinion, emphasizing that despite clashes between formal and informal rules, these constraints exist in a state of symbiosis with each other.[37] Similar to other dichotomous sets of relationships, such as public and private, state and nonstate, legal and illegal, and so on, informality cannot exist and function in the absence of formality. Vladimir Gel'man supports that assumption, claiming that "formal and informal institutions are not alternatives; rather, each substitutes for the other from time to time to fill in gaps."[38] The synthesis of formality and informality is engrained in the inherent perception that "the roots of . . . informal systems are embedded in the formal organization itself and nurtured by the very formality of its arrangements."[39] Even Helmke and Levitsky's substitutive informal institutions function alongside (weak) formal institutions and not instead of them.[40]

As the initially dominant perception of informality as a pernicious, corrosive, and parasitic phenomenon began to recede, the existence of informality became accepted as normal. For example, Misztal argued that "'informalization' of formal organization is seen as a normal response to bureaucratization."[41] Although informalization causes "a higher level of structural insecurity,"[42] it also provides comfort and intimacy in interpersonal relations, allowing individuals to ease the burden of bureaucracy. Given that formality is inconceivable without informality, informal relations permeate all areas of human activity. Even in developed Western countries where the informal economy is reduced to a minimum and interpersonal relations in both the private and public spheres are formalized and legalized to a maximum, informality persists.[43] As a mode of exchange in interpersonal or social networks, informality is omnipresent—though not necessarily easily observable—in contemporary capitalist societies.[44] As a result of its ambivalent and secretive character, informality lurks on the fringes of the formal sphere, filling in niches untapped by formalization, such as family- and friendship-based relationships and other forms of interpersonal networking. Only with the retreat of formality, which often occurs hand in hand with the withdrawal of the state, does informality begin to expand and occupy areas traditionally reserved for the state and nonstate formal institutions, such as civil society.

Nevertheless, even after the withdrawal of the state and the spread of informality to some areas of the formal sphere, informalization does not lead to chaos and anarchy because informal institutions replace the formal ones by filling an institutional vacuum. As this book demonstrates, withdrawal of the state in post-Soviet regimes from certain areas of welfare provision and social security allocation did not result in disintegration of welfare services, which were overtaken by informal networks. In those cases, informalization serves as a "survival mechanism,"[45] and informal practices function as private safety nets, providing the population with public goods and services that either cannot be obtained formally or are in short supply. Although informalization usually results in the rise of corruption and clientelism,[46] formal institutions, particularly in weak or developing states, are also never entirely free of these pernicious practices. The debates in the literature on whether informality is good or bad are ongoing, and scholars seem to have reached no consensus.

The third cross-disciplinary characteristic intrinsic to informality is its individualistic and personalized nature, described by Homans as a "one-on-one relationship"[47] and termed by Misztal as "face-to-face interaction."[48] Unlike formal relations restricted by bureaucratic routine, informal relationships are embedded in privacy and based on mutual trust. Trust lies at the base of "informal socializing,"[49] and informal relations almost always depend on "face-to-face relations of family, friends and neighbours."[50] The personalized and covert nature of informality makes it preferable to formal relations. In contrast to formal constraints, informality functions on unwritten rules and mutually accepted pacts, which guide informal relations not only in reciprocal networking but also in clientelistic top-down relations. Face-to-face relationships are a definitive feature of informality that can be observed in most types of informal activities in economic, political, and social spheres. Apart from the personalization of the private sphere—such as of family and friendship circles—informality allows the deformalization of relations in the public sphere, including but not limited to communication with state officials and circumvention of formal rules and conventions. The reliance on informal channels, connections, and contacts allows individuals to personalize and humanize the bureaucracy by greasing its wheels with gifts, bribes, or reciprocal favors.[51] As a result, the generally unpleasant and intimidating experience of dealing with formal institutions is transformed into another form of interpersonal relationship.

Finally, there is a thin line between informality and illegality. Some informal activities, such as corruption and graft, may cross the border between informal and illegal behaviors. In addition, informal practices may consist of illicit activities such as bribery, blackmail, and extortion. Unlike these illegal activities, which are punishable by law, informal practices usually remain beyond the purview of criminal codes and legal persecution. When speaking about informal practices in Russia, Ledeneva points out that while bribery is criminally prosecuted, informal practices that often involve elements of bribery (gift-giving and unofficial payments) are not mentioned in legal statutes.[52] Notwithstanding the association between informal institutions and illicit activities, formal actors avoid criminalizing informal practices as a consequence of their ambiguous and all-inclusive nature. That being said, it is important to distinguish informal networks and institutions from criminal organizations (gangs and mafia networks), which frequently employ informal channels for their purposes.

Within the framework of this analysis, the concept of informality synthesizes all of these interdisciplinary characteristics. Informality exists and thrives alongside the formal sphere, yet the relationship between formal and informal is not antagonistic or competitively dualist. Rather, the formal-informal dichotomy is symbiotic, harmonious, and interdependent. While the retreat of the formal sphere results in the expansion of informality, the process of formalization and strengthening of formal institutions leads to the reduction of the informal sphere, but it never completely disappears. In addition, informality is always personalized and secretive. The face-to-face interaction, interpersonal trust (as opposed to generalized trust), covert pacts and agreements, and reciprocal or clientelist relationships are inseparable attributes of informal relations.

Building on Helmke and Levitsky's classical definition of informal institutions,[53] this book defines informality as *a sum of all relations, transactions, behaviors, and customs that occur in social, political, and economic spheres and that are unwritten and not legally binding*. This broad and all-encompassing definition covers a vast diversity of informal phenomena, excluding from the concept of informal sphere hardly anything except the formally chartered institution. Notwithstanding some important differences,[54] to reflect the multidisciplinary and highly heterogeneous character of informality, it is valuable to pull the different phenomena together under the concept of informality. Indeed, criminality is one of the few informal phenomena that this book purposefully excludes from the analysis, because informal practices are not always illegal. Having revisited normative characteristics of informality and examined diverse definitional and conceptual meanings of the term *informal* across various disciplines in social sciences and humanities, this chapter now turns to disentangling the complexity surrounding research methods and measurement indicators employed in studies on informality.

HOW CAN WE STUDY INFORMALITY?

Given the multiple definitions of informality and the cross-disciplinary nature of studies dealing with the issue, various methods of researching informality have evolved over the past several decades. Though there is no uniform approach to studying the informal sphere even within each of the previously discussed disciplines, a voluminous body of literature exploring the informal phenomena relies heavily on both quantitative and qualitative research methods. As Alice Sindzingre points out, in research on informality, "methods often construct the concept, which has contributed to the plurality of its meanings."[55] In the same vein, the vast majority of definitions of informal economy are constructed to ease the challenge of quantitative measurement of the informal sector.

Many scholars of informal economy rely on either *direct* or *indirect* methods of measuring informality in the economic sphere. The direct approach, more common in microeconomics, employs representative individual surveys, such as household and enterprise surveys, establishment-based surveys, and labor force surveys, to gauge the population's engagement in informal economic activities. The main shortcoming of this technique is that surveys, unless tailored to the specific needs of a particular research project, fail to capture the dynamics of informal activities. For example, cash-in-hand work done at one's formal place of employment is often coded in surveys as formal employment,[56] and the custom of gift-giving in return for preferential treatment—perceived in most postcommunist societies as part of social culture and a gesture of appreciation—is framed by many surveys as corruption.

In contrast, indirect measurement methods, widely employed in macroeconomics, are characterized by the reliance on sets of aggregate data used to compare discrepancies between individuals' declared income and expenditures (including overall household consumption), participation in formal and informal employment, and differences between the growth rate of the

gross domestic product and the growth rate of electricity consumption. Indirect methods also involve analysis of the characterization of economic
units, registration of economic units, and number of people engaged in formal employment. Indirect methods, however, may only be used to measure
the size and spread of informal economy; its composition and individuals'
reasons for participating in informal activities remain beyond the scope of
indirect techniques. Nevertheless, as indicated by the International Labour
Organization, the two "methods are not mutually exclusive,"[57] and researchers in the area of informal economy often simultaneously employ direct and
indirect measurement techniques.[58]

In contrast to research on informal economy, informality in political science, sociology, anthropology, and other humanities disciplines is primarily
analyzed qualitatively. Even after having narrowed down the definition of
informality to particular phenomena such as clientelism or corruption, researchers still face the challenge of producing quantifiable indicators and
reliable measurement criteria. Though large-n surveys are often used in research on political and social informality,[59] even surveys specifically designed to capture individual attitudes toward informal activities, like surveys
that measure informal economy, tend to produce inconclusive outcomes.
Because the perception of informal differs from one survey respondent to
another, representative surveys are prone to presenting informality as negative. A more common and arguably far more reliable approach to studying
informality is the use of small-n case studies, which may or may not be combined with the analysis of large-n survey data.

Bearing in mind the challenges and shortcomings of quantifying informality, many scholars have chosen to rely on qualitative participant interviews or ethnographic field observation.[60] These methods enable researchers to capture the microlevel dynamics on the ground and explore
participants' motivations and incentives for engaging in informal activities. In the words of Helmke and Levitsky, "Case-oriented ethnographic
research" is one of the most convenient methods of studying informal behaviors.[61] Hence, "ethnography is an important research tool in this
task."[62] The bulk of qualitative studies of informality, however, do not seek
to measure the informal phenomenon as such. Rather, qualitative research
on informality seeks to explain why informal activities exist and how they
function. The spread and scale of informal activities also elude efficient
measurement as a consequence of the lack of clearly identifiable boundaries between economic and noneconomic forms of informal activities. For
example, Jacques Rupnik and Jan Zielonka argue that in politics, "observa-

tory participation rather than the analysis of formal laws and documents"[63] is more suitable for research on informal institutions. Therefore, to study informality in politics, "cultural anthropologists are probably more suited than political scientists."[64]

Despite the absence of universally accepted measurement standards in mainstream research on informality, the plurality of studies on the informal sphere can be roughly divided in accordance with their choice of the units of analysis. Informal institutions, informal networks, and informal practices are the most widely used units of analysis in multidisciplinary research on informality (see table 1.1).[65]

Informal Institutions

The focus on informal institutions is perhaps the most dominant approach to studying informality in political science and, to a lesser extent, in economics. In institutional economics, North understood informal institutions in terms of informal constraints "embodied in customs, traditions, and codes of conduct"[66] that oppose, confront, and substitute for formal rules. Studies on informal economy from an institutionalist perspective are nevertheless scarce. In the discipline of institutional economics, informal institutions are still perceived through the dualist lenses, presenting informal institutions as constraints rather than as equivalent to formal institutions.[67] In contrast, political science research widely employs informal institutions as a unit of analysis. Although informal institutions had featured prominently in political studies for decades,[68] the seminal work by Helmke and Levitsky

TABLE 1.1. Informality: The Units of Analysis

	Informal Institutions	Informal Networks	Informal Practices
Defined by:	Constraints Rules	Interpersonal networks	Location-specific practices
Used in:	Political science, institutional economics	Behavioral economics, sociology, anthropology, ethnography	Sociology, anthropology
Advantages	Comparable to formal institutions	Perfect for individual-level analysis	Works best in multidisciplinary studies; emphasizes geographical diversity of informality
Disadvantages	Tend to disregard micro-level analysis	Challenging for macro-level (large-n) studies	Generalist and overstretched

firmly embedded the concept of informal institutions in the discipline of political science.[69]

In contrast to North's constraints-centered approach to understanding informal institutions, Helmke and Levitsky defined informal institutions in terms of informal rules that differ from their formal counterparts in context, presentation, substance, and enforcement.[70] This rules-based approach has since been broadly used in research on informal political institutions.[71] One of the key advantages of employing institutions as units of analysis of informal activities is the ability to then compare informal institutions with their formal counterparts. Approaching the analysis of informality through the framework of informal institutions enables researchers to identify differences between the effects of formal and informal rules. It also allows political scientists to portray such ambivalent and fuzzy phenomena as graft, clientelism, corruption, informal political brokerage, and the role of connections as informal institutions, which can be approximated—at least normatively and categorically—to formal structures.

Studying informality through the prism of informal institutions, however, runs the risk of institutionalizing a rather ambiguous set of phenomena. For example, the use of informal contacts and connections in politics is hard to categorize as an institution. Though the generic definition of institutions as "prescriptions that humans use to organize all forms of repetitive and structured interactions"[72] may accommodate many forms of informal activities, the bulk of informal relations function at the micro level of human interaction and tend to remain beyond the grasp of institutional analysis.

Informal Networks

To avoid the limitations imposed by institutional categories, another common economic and sociological strand of research on informality employs a networking approach. Åse Berit Grødeland broadly defines informal networks (also known as exchange networks, power networks, strong- and weak-tie networks, social networks, private networks, and network capital) as "informal circle[s] of people able and willing to help each other."[73] In research on informal economy, Larissa A. Lomnitz has promoted the emphasis on networks as units of analysis.[74] For example, she argues that informal "activities are not random and chaotic but are based on informal networks."[75] The networking model has, however, never been broadly applied in studies of informal economy, which focus on units that are easier to quantify than vaguely shaped and elusive informal networks. A far greater application of the networks-based models of analysis has occurred in sociology and its multiple subfields, such as political sociology and social communication studies. Mark S. Granovetter's revolutionary introduction of his theory on the "Strength of Weak Ties" established that "it is through . . . networks that small-scale interaction becomes translated into large-scale patterns, and that these, in turn, feed back into small groups."[76] Studies by Linton C. Freeman, Robert Putnam,[77] and others[78] have further cemented the role of networks in sociological analysis.

In research on political sociology and political science, the networking approach has been popular among scholars studying informality in postcommunist spaces. Scholars such as Ledeneva, William Mishler and Richard Rose, Endre Sik, James L. Gibson, and Markku Lonkila have thoroughly employed informal networks as primary units of inquiry in their research on informality in Russia and other postcommunist countries.[79] Stephen Weatherford and other political scientists have studied the role of informal networks in political processes such as voting behavior and political participation.[80] The emphasis on reciprocal or hierarchical networks of exchange has also been prominent in studies on anthropology. Informal networks as units of analysis in anthropological research on human modes of exchange and reciprocity featured notably in works by Malinowski[81] and other anthropologists.[82] Epitomized in Granovetter's strong- and weak-tie networks, the focus on networks presents researchers with an excellent opportunity to understand microcosms of social relationships remaining outside the reach of institutional approaches.

Informality, as seen through institutional frameworks, loses the individualism and personalized nature for which it is known in sociology, ethnography, and anthropology. The use of the networking approach, by contrast, enables the researcher to humanize and personalize informality and to explore specific features and components of informal activities impervious to institutional analysis. If used in macrolevel analyses, however, networking models tend to reduce informality to workings of narrowly defined interpersonal networks. The networks-centered approach is invaluable in the analysis of small-n cases but is rarely used in research dealing with larger datasets.

Informal Practices

Along with institutional and networking approaches, research on informality focuses on informal practices as a unit of analysis. While some scholars

understand informal practices as nearly synonymous or conflated with informal institutions,[83] a large and heretofore cluttered body of multidisciplinary literature categorizes most informal activities under the umbrella
term *informal practices*.[84] On the one hand, unlike institutions and networks,
the focus on practices provides researchers of informality with a broader
spectrum of analysis, enabling them to move beyond institutional boundaries and limitations of networks. Ledeneva describes informal practices "as
people's regular strategies to manipulate or exploit formal rules by enforcing
informal norms and personal obligations in formal contexts."[85] On the other
hand, such emphasis on practices enables more context-bound research. Be
it Russian *blat*, Chinese *guanxi*, or Mexican *palanca*, informal practices are
easily identified, categorized, and conceptualized. Well known to populations, informal practices such as *blat* are easier to measure through small-n
surveys specifically tailored to the target population or to capture in qualitative interviews.[86]

In addition to the context-bound research on selected types of informal
traditions, informal practices encompass a wide range of other phenomena.
Among these, informal payments, gift-giving, patron-client relations, informal employment, and many other forms of informal behavior have been
conveniently analyzed through the prism of informal practices. Indeed, the
all-encompassing scope of informal practices may seem to accommodate
nearly all forms of informal activities. Informal practices constitute an umbrella concept that incorporates both informal institutions and informal
networks. Informal practices such as *guanxi* and *wasta*, for example, rely on
the functioning of informal institutions (such as unofficial payments, gift-
giving, and corruption) and networks (patron-client, reciprocal, kinship,
and friendship). Unfortunately, this makes the practices-based approach so
overstretched and ambiguous that anything and everything defined under
the concept of informal practices becomes measurable and comparable.

To avoid becoming trapped in the limitations of these approaches to
studying informality, numerous studies—including this book—choose to
rely on a mixed design that combines institutional-, networking-, and
practices-based methods of researching informality. If anything, distinctions among informal institutions, informal networks, and informal practices are more discipline-bound than categorical. Indeed, it is difficult to argue that informal institutions cannot be made up of networks and that
informal practices are not employed by both the former and the latter. Consistent with this logic, this book presents informal institutions and networks

as organizational structures that rely on informal practices as means to achieve their goals. Conceptually and definition-wise, this book does not attempt to distinguish informal institutions from informal networks: institutions may or may not be made up of networks. The difference is in perception and is grounded largely in research design and research objectives. In some cases involving networks of connections or colleagues, it is reasonable to refer to informal structures as networks. In other cases, when informal structures are more amorphous and difficult to grasp in microanalyses, informality can be perceived in institutional categories. The need to reach beyond categorical disparities existing between institutional-, networking-, and practices-centered approaches emanates from the necessity of studying informality as a multidisciplinary phenomenon. Expanding the research beyond economic and political perceptions of informality requires researchers to traverse institutions, networks, and practices and present the informal sphere as a combination of all these categories. Indeed, informality—with its ambiguous and ambivalent nature—is an exceptionally diverse and multidimensional phenomenon that manifests itself through a myriad of informal practices and behaviors around the world.

SUMMARY

Informality, a term with multiple definitions and countless connotations across a number of disciplines, refers to a sphere that lies outside of formal, legally bound, and defined spheres of human activity. Almost always remaining on the margins of mainstream research, the topic of informality has been lurking in the shadows of many prominent theories and approaches in institutional economics, political science, political sociology, and other major disciplines in the humanities and social sciences. The methods and approaches to studying informality therefore became context-bound and discipline-specific—strictly qualitative in sociology and anthropology while heavily quantitative in economics. In addition, the problems of distinguishing informal institutions from informal networks and informal practices have for decades puzzled researchers. Although this book does not solve the definitional and conceptual challenges in research on informality, it does untangle the confusion.

CHAPTER 2

Mapping Informality

To CONCEPTUALIZE INFORMALITY beyond the normative limits of informal economy and informal political institutions, this chapter provides a rigorous theoretical examination of the phenomenon of informality in postcommunist and particularly post-Soviet contexts. Postsocialist informality is presented neither as transitional nor as a temporary postcommunist phenomenon; rather, it is a coping mechanism embedded in the social culture of postsocialism sustained by a combination of the Soviet legacy and such challenges as the withdrawal of the state and the weakness of formal institutions.

THE MANY NAMES OF INFORMALITY

Informal institutions, networks, and practices are known by many names. Although a detailed analysis of different manifestations of informality around the globe is well beyond the scope and aims of this book, a concise overview of the most well-known informal practices is essential to understanding informality in post-Soviet spaces. To that end, prior to analyzing the Russian-Soviet practice of *blat* and other postcommunist informal practices, this section introduces specific informal behaviors presently thriving among various societies.

The most widely studied informal practice in the world is the Chinese *guanxi*. Translated as "relationship(s)," *guanxi* (pronounced *guan-shee*) has been the subject of a voluminous body of research over the past two decades. In her seminal 1994 book, Mayfair Yang defined the phenomenon as "dyadic relationships that are based implicitly (rather than explicitly) on mutual interest and benefit."[1] Countless studies have since explored *guanxi*'s functions in social relations, business environments, the public sphere, and politics.[2] In

Thomas Gold, Doug Guthrie, and David Wank's explanation, "Conventional wisdom among Chinese and foreigners holds that in the People's Republic of China (PRC), *guanxi* is absolutely essential to successfully complete any task in virtually all spheres of social life."[3] Embedded in Confucian principles of social organization, *guanxi* became an inextricable part of Chinese society under communism, allowing lower classes to build social bridges connecting them to higher cadres.[4] Though "*guanxi* relationships are by definition un-equal,"[5] *guanxi*, like many other informal practices, is mutually beneficial and reciprocal. Many scholars have noted that *guanxi* is more than just a system of interpersonal exchange networks; it is, rather, a part of Chinese culture.[6] As Gold, Guthrie, and Wank explain, "Some Chinese engage in the practice of *guanxi* for the intrinsic enjoyment of the ongoing personal relationship it-self."[7] *Guanxi* is widespread not only in mainland China but also in Taiwan[8] and Hong Kong[9] and among ethnic Chinese communities (Singapore and Malaysia) and émigrés in many parts of the world.[10] In fact, the Korean prac-tice of *gwangye* (connections), which like *guanxi* traces its origins to the Con-fucian social order, is a heretofore unstudied offshoot of *guanxi*. The equally obscure Japanese practice of *amakudari* and South Korean "parachute ap-pointments" are also rooted in Confucian sociocultural traditions.[11]

An Arab equivalent of *guanxi* is *wasta*. The term, derived from the word *waseet*, meaning "middleman" or "intermediary," refers to interpersonal networks, connections, and informal influence. Research on *wasta* began to grow in popularity only about a decade ago, and the phenomenon was pre-viously largely unknown to outsiders. In Arab societies across the Middle East and North Africa, *wasta* is "an ever-present part of life."[12] According to Hayfaa Tlaiss and Saleema Kauser, familiarity with the workings of *wasta* "is crucial for understanding how decisions are made in this region because it permeates the culture of all Arab countries and is a force in every significant decision."[13] *Wasta* prospered in Arab societies for centuries and is as a social phenomenon ingrained in tribal traditions. The sociocultural significance of *wasta* is immense. In the words of Andy Barnett, Bruce Yandle, and George Naufal, *wasta* "practices are an integral part of lengthy social processes that generate order within and across all societies."[14] While some research on *wasta* depicts the phenomenon as nepotistic and even parasitic,[15] other stud-ies present *wasta* in more neutral tones. Empirical studies by Gary D. Gold and Naufal and by Deborah C. Bailey conclude that *wasta* has both positive and negative characteristics and is understood accordingly by the plurality of the population in Arab countries.[16] Studies that have sought to compare *wasta* to *guanxi* have found that they share numerous similarities in their functions and operational patterns.[17] Differences between these two informal practices are observable primarily in how they manifest themselves in business environments. *Protektzia*, a practice similar to *wasta*, flourishes in Israel.[18] Unlike *wasta*, which is deeply embedded in clan structures, *protektzia* is more of an urban practice, thriving among middle and upper classes of the Jewish state.

Another internationally well-known informal practice is the Brazilian *jeitinho* (pronounced *jay-tcheen-yoo*), translated as a "little way around." *Jeitinho* is omnipresent in Brazilian society as a problem-solving mechanism that functions in a variety of settings. Gelles Amado and Haroldo Vinagre Brasil describe *jeitinho* as "a typical cultural feature" of Brazilian daily life and as a means of overcoming and circumventing formal bureaucracy.[19] Though the research on *jeitinho* dates back to the early 1990s,[20] only a handful of studies have specifically addressed the phenomenon, and empirical research on *jeitinho* beyond business and management studies remains scarce.[21] Nevertheless, in spite of its features typical for Brazilian society, such as intimacy, vibrancy, and sociality, *jeitinho* is based on sustaining interpersonal networks and contacts. This makes it similar to other informal practices such as Mexican *palanca* practices[22] and Chilean *confianza*,[23] neither of which differs significantly from *jeitinho* in functions, operational structure, or societal embeddedness.

Although a number of scholars have argued that the spread and importance of informal practices and institutions in the developing world has resulted from the lack of social security and the weakness of formal institutions, informal practices also exist among developed Western societies. Perhaps the most widely known informal practice in Western European societies is the British practice of "pulling strings."[24] Though the absence of research on pulling strings is noteworthy, Peter B. Smith and his coauthors' comparative study of differences among informal practices around the world describes the British phenomenon as being used for "obtaining favours particularly through links with influential persons."[25] More institutionalized and networked than pulling strings are "old-boys" or "good ol' boys" networks or clubs. These networks-centered informal practices are widespread not only in the United Kingdom but also in Canada, Australia, New Zealand, and the United States.[26] Informal behaviors known as skimming and gypping are practiced in the United States.[27] The well-known yet far-too-little-researched French practice of *piston* serves as an equivalent of pulling strings.

Numerous informal practices also exist in other European societies.[28] Cologne, Germany, has become noted for its informal practices in public administration and other areas, and those practices are described with the well-known local term *Kölner Klüngel*.[29]

Regardless of their various names and forms, informal behaviors practiced by various societies around the globe do not fundamentally differ from each other in terms of the functions they perform and the means they employ to achieve their ends. First, they are all used to circumvent formal procedures. They compete with, complement, accommodate, and even substitute for formal institutions. Legal and illegal functions and activities practiced by these various informal structures are frequently employed alongside each other. Such symbiosis is usually perceived as normal, and most of these behaviors rely on dyadic, triadic, and occasionally polyadic types of interpersonal relationships. Although informal practices are thought to be more widespread and omnipresent in the developing world, existing research shows that even developed capitalist societies are not bereft of informality. As József Böröcz suggests, "Social life is simply impossible, even in the West, without a serious, reliable and comfortably available informal component."[30] Informal practices in Western European and North American contexts, however, manifest themselves in a less explicit manner and are less prevalent and important than in more economically underprivileged parts of the world. As confirmed by a comparison of *guanxi*, *wasta*, *jeitinho*, *blat*, and pulling strings in international business settings, the "informal influence varies between nations more in amount than in its specific qualities."[31] If the "amount" of informality is taken as a unit of measurement, no other part of the world is more notorious for the spread and significance of informality than the postcommunist region as well as China and Arab countries.

COMMUNIST-ERA INFORMALITY AND ITS LEGACY

Though informal practices were widespread in the region even prior to the establishment of socialist order in present-day postcommunist European countries, the decades of communist rule produced a unique sociocultural microcosm that became innate to the region.[32] There is a large volume of published studies describing the role of the communist state in the spread of informality in Central and Eastern Europe (CEE) and the former Yugoslavia.[33] Traditional arguments have held that informalization of these communist states followed two interrelated and mutually reinforcing pathways. Chronic shortages, economic mismanagement, and the overall inefficiency of planned or command socialist economies led to the rise and proliferation of the second economy, which functioned on informal modes of exchange. Sustained by a myriad of dyadic and triadic interpersonal networks, the second economy penetrated virtually every area of economic activity, creating additional sources of income for citizens of socialist states.

The functioning of the second economy rested on complex supporting mechanisms extending well beyond economic institutions and into political offices. As a result, informalization of communist societies also occurred outside of the economic sphere. To keep the second economy running, connections and networks in government institutions were indispensable in greasing the wheels of the communist bureaucracy. The processes of de-bureaucratization and informalization of state institutions—accompanied by extreme patronage, nepotism, and rampant corruption—grew to immense proportions across the socialist bloc. As Barbara Misztal explains, "In the context of the authorities' control over public communication, an open exchange of values and opinions was limited to one's own small informal circles."[34] These informal circles were equally important in economic and social spheres, and the contacts used to earn the "parallel" (informal) income often were also part of an individual's social circles. Informality was the main mode of communication not only between elites and commoners but also among elites themselves.[35] During the communist period, CEE informal practices began to flourish. Such informal practices as *vruzki* in Bulgaria and *veze* in Serbia (both translated as "connections") and Poland's *zalatwic´ sprawy* ("to arrange something") grew increasingly important under communist rule.[36] According to Adrian Smith and Alison Stenning, *zalatwic´ sprawy* was an "everyday practice founded on the networks of friends and family who made up one's s´*rodowisko* or circle."[37]

As a consequence of the restrictiveness of the communist rulers of CEE states and Yugoslavia, research on postcommunist informality beyond the second economy was scarce until after the fall of the Iron Curtain, when scholars began to explore different sociopolitical aspects of postcommunist informality.[38] The 1989 collapse of state communism among Eastern Bloc countries enabled the newly forged CEE governments to embark on the transition to democracy and a market economy. This, however, did not lead to the decline of informality. On the contrary, the ambiguity of the transitional period and hardships of the immediate postcommunist decade resulted in the continuous reliance on informal practices across the entire former socialist bloc. Judging by the size of the informal economy in Hungary, which replaced the second economy after the fall of communism, Endre Sik argued that informality became even more widespread "under post-communism than under communism."[39] More than half a decade later, in his seminal article on informality in Hungary, Böröcz lamented that informality permeated all areas of political life during the immediate postcommunist period: "Informality is so widespread in the post-state-socialist societies of Central Europe today that conducting any business, economic or otherwise, is virtually impossible without bowing, or even succumbing, to it."[40]

Bearing in mind that Hungary is widely considered a success story of postcommunist transformation,[41] informality is even more common in Southeastern Europe and the Balkans. As Åse Berit Grødeland observed in her work on the use of informal contacts and networks among postcommunist elites, informal practices appear to be more widespread and pervasive in Southeastern Europe and the Balkans than in Central European states.[42] Research by Mishler and Rose and other scholars as well as reports by international organizations demonstrate that informal behaviors are more widespread in southern postcommunist countries, particularly in Balkan states.[43] Informality has far greater importance for postcommunist countries than for other European regions well known for the dominance of informal relations, such as Greece and Italy. Today, nearly three decades after the end of state communism, even those postcommunist European states that have succeeded in democratic institution-building and transitioning to market economy as well as in joining the European Union (EU) are still affected by informality.[44] In contrast to expectations of transitologists,[45] who assumed that informality is a transitional phenomenon,[46] informal practices have not disappeared or receded since the end of state communism; instead, they "could serve as a possible mapping of the futures of many developed countries' economies."[47]

In the assessment of the European Bank for Reconstruction and Development, for example, the reliance on private safety nets such as informal networks among new EU members and Balkan countries during and after the global economic crisis (2008–10) was 10–15 percent higher than in Western European countries.[48] Despite the austerity reforms enacted in many of the EU southern states and the growing reliance on informal practices as a result of those measures, informality remained more widespread and important in new EU members from among CEE countries than in Southern Europe.[49] Adrian Smith therefore contends that the evidence from the first postcommunist decade suggests that informality in ex-socialist countries is not a temporary or transitional phenomenon but rather a tradition with "longstanding cultural and economic significance."[50] With all their institutional weaknesses and the seemingly perpetual entrenchment of informality, the CEE and many Balkan countries are nevertheless incomparably more successful in their democratization and transition to market economy than the former Soviet states to the east.

If totalitarian legacies and side effects of command economy are to be held accountable for the entrenchment of informality in CEE, the Balkans, and even in still formally communist China as well as North Korea,[51] no other part of Eurasia (with the exception of North Korea) has been under both the iron grip of totalitarian rule and tight control of planned economy longer than the former Soviet Union (fSU). Given that this book is a study of informal practices of post-Soviet countries, understanding post-Soviet informality—its characteristics, functions, and distinctions from and similarities with informal behaviors elsewhere, particularly in other postcommunist countries—might be fundamental to understanding the relationship between democratic institutional reforms and informal practices. This book supports an assumption that informal structures of post-Soviet states differ notably from informality in other parts of the world and that this difference is expressed in the spread and importance of informal practices, institutions, and networks. Although many different variables influence the prominence of informality, the impact of the Soviet legacy and problems of postcommunism have shaped the contours of post-Soviet informality.

No study of post-Soviet informal practices can ignore *blat*, a ubiquitous and omnipresent Soviet-Russian practice born out of decades of economic shortages, political repression, and the complete absence of independence from the communist party public sphere. To gain preferential access to commodities in short supply and inaccessible services, *blat* was widely used in Soviet times to circumvent the notoriously rigid and impenetrable communist bureaucracy. Alena Ledeneva defines *blat* practices as "the use of personal networks and informal contacts to obtain goods and services in short supply and to find a way around formal procedures."[52] She also presents *blat* as an "economy of favours" and "a distinctive form of non-monetary exchange, a kind of barter based on personal relationship."[53] Sheila Fitzpatrick describes *blat* "as a system of reciprocal relationships involving goods and favors that, in contrast to patronage relations, entail equals and are nonhier-archical."[54] Although *blat* performs functions similar to other informal prac-tices around the globe,[55] unlike Chinese *guanxi*, which has evolved from Confucian principles, and Arab *wasta*, engendered in centuries-long tribal and clannish traditions, *blat* is a by-product of communism.

The informal networks and behaviors that became clustered under the generic term *blat* during the Soviet period no doubt existed prior to the Bol-sheviks' ascent to power in the 1920s.[56] However, *blat* became an inseparable part of popular culture in the milieu of Soviet urbanization, standardization, and industrialization.[57] The term *blat* entered the Russian lexicon from the German word *die Blatte* (paper note), widely used in German camps for Rus-sian prisoners during World War I. As a form of encouragement for hard work, prisoners were given paper notes that they could exchange for food items and cigarettes.[58] Prior to the 1920s, the word *blat* was mainly used in the Russian criminal jargon to refer to individual protection (*krysha*) or to a person of one's personal circle (*svoi chelovek*). A decade later, *blat* "was not often used" but nevertheless "was practised by all social groups."[59] During the hardships of Stalinism in the 1930s, *blat* entered the daily language of the Soviet population. In the following decades, *blat* became an inseparable part—albeit well hidden from outsiders' eyes—of the daily lives of Soviet citizens. After World War II, "it was impossible to avoid becoming involved to some degree in relationships based on *blat*."[60] Ledeneva describes Soviet *blat* as a dyadic, reciprocal, and nonhierarchical informal practice offering individuals access to goods and services in accordance with their "personal qualities and occupational opportunity."[61] Though *blat* remained largely un-noticed by Westerners and was therefore ignored by Sovietologists, the broadly accepted consensus in literature on Soviet society was that "in the Soviet Union, a 'society of connections,' whom you know will dictate how well you are housed, what food you eat, what clothing you wear and what theatre tickets you can get."[62]

With the end of Soviet rule and relaxation of the economic shortages characteristic of the Soviet economy, *blat* started to lose its function of pro-viding commodities in short supply, but it still remains in high demand in the search for jobs and in accessing health care and education services as well as in many other areas.[63] As the barren shop shelves that sustained the importance of *blat* connections during the Soviet period are no longer the case in postcommunist Russia, money has acquired a much higher value than under communism. In the new post-Soviet Russia, the old Russian proverb "Better a hundred friends than a hundred rubles," which essentially epitomized the importance of *blat* in Soviet society, began to lose its value. As the levels of individual social trust decreased,[64] monetized interpersonal relationships began to be favored over reciprocal friendship networks, and a hundred rubles became far more valuable and trustworthy than a hundred friends. Nevertheless, *blat* did not disappear, and it retains its access-granting function not only in economic and interpersonal relations but also in politics. Defined by Ledeneva as *sistema* networks, informal power institutions operate at different levels of present-day Russia's state apparatus and "impose certain norms of reciprocity and informal constraints on people in official positions."[65] Recent research on postcommunist *blat* presents it as an extremely diverse phenomenon that manifests itself in a wide variety of forms across the vast expanse of the Russian Federation.[66] To the plurality of individual informants interviewed by scholars of Russian informality, *blat* is the sum of informal institutions and personal networks widely employed in public and private spheres.[67]

As in Russia, *blat* is widespread in Ukraine, Belarus, and Moldova.[68] This confirms the hypothesis, suggested by Richard Rose, that informality in Russian and Ukrainian societies does not fundamentally differ: "In both societies the most frequently recommended tactic to get a flat, a government permit, or prompt hospital treatment, is anti-modern, such as a cash payment to officials or using connections."[69] In line with Ledeneva's assessment of *blat* practices in present-day Russia,[70] a study by Olga Onoshchenko and Colin C. Williams reveals the importance of *blat* in Ukraine and confirms that Ukrainians, like Russians, employ *blat* to secure access to services and use it interchangeably with money.[71] Similarly, Catherine Wanner and Alexander Tymczuk found that *blat* in post-Soviet Ukraine is based not only on favor-centered reciprocal exchanges but also on cash-based transactions.[72]

Regardless of the relatively successful transition to market economy, democratization, and accession to the EU observed in Estonia, Latvia, and Lithuania, informal practices functionally similar to *blat* prosper in the Baltic countries.[73] Although often described in literature as part of CEE or as new EU members, the Baltic republics differ from both CEE and fSU in that informality in these countries is more widespread than in most of CEE apart from Romania and Bulgaria[74] but remains below the scale of the fSU. Informal employment,[75] envelope wages,[76] and out-of-pocket payments are reportedly used in Baltic republics much more often than in many other new EU member states.[77]

Informal institutions and practices also differ across the former Soviet region. Although *blat* is well known and widely used in many post-Soviet societies, in non-Slavic territories it often acquires different functions and characteristics. In the South Caucasus, *blat* is well known and practiced in Armenia
and Azerbaijan. In both countries, however, local terms such as *tapsh* or *hor-
met* in Azerbaijan are used more commonly than *blat* to describe favor-based
informal networks and practices.[78] The scarce literature on informality in Armenia[79] and Azerbaijan[80] has demonstrated that the Soviet-age norms of reciprocal informal networking became intertwined with local traditions of relying on extended families and kinship structures.[81] The reciprocal character
of Russian *blat* in the South Caucasus often comprises honor-based family
commitments requiring distribution of nonreciprocal favors and prioritiza-
tion of hierarchical kinship-centered homogenous networks over moderately
more open informal institutions than exist in Russia and Ukraine.[82] Like Russia's *sistema* networks, informal institutions in Armenia and Azerbaijan play
an important role in politics. Instead of using formal institutions, these countries' political elites rely heavily on informal networks.[83] In Georgia, as numerous studies document,[84] informal institutions and practices flourished
throughout the Soviet period. Among other Soviet socialist republics, Georgia's informal sphere was known for its immense scale and its exceptional significance for the population.[85] The political and economic instability that
followed the breakup of the USSR further increased the importance of informal practices, defined by the Georgian term *krtami*, and encouraged the
spread of informal networks (*natsnoboba*).[86] Although less hierarchical and
homogenous than those in Azerbaijan and Armenia, Georgia's informal institutions are also heavily centered on family and immediate kinship circles.[87]
This distinguishes them from the networks focused on friends and acquaintances that prevail in the Eastern European fSU.

Central Asia's informal institutions are both different from and similar to
their counterparts in the Caucasus. As Johan Rasanayagam argues in his account of informality in Uzbekistan, informal institutions penetrate all areas
of public and private life and constitute an important part of people's daily
lives.[88] Victoria Koroteyeva and Ekaterina Makarova draw similar conclusions, while in Gerald Mars and Yochanan Altman's observations, Uzbekistan's informal institutions encompass broader circles of individuals than
do Georgia's more intimate and kinship-centered informal networks, so that
"individuals react individually in the exploitation of their environment."[89]
Uzbekistan's networks are therefore more based on interests rather than kin-

ship and more closely resemble Russia's *blat* networks. Rustamjon Urinboyev notes that different types of informal relations in Uzbekistan function under the framework of indigenous *mahalla* communities, a claim that Kobil Ruziev and Peter Midmore have substantiated empirically.[90] Edward Schatz insists that informal institutions in Kazakhstan as well as in other Central Asian republics are deeply entangled with clan politics.[91] Clan association also plays an important role in the informal distribution of resources. Kathleen Collins advances this argument further, suggesting that "clans in fact serve as an alternative to formal market institutions and official bureaucracies."[92] Given the symbiosis between formal and informal spheres, Central Asian clans that function as semiformal and in some countries formal institutions differ markedly from the informal institutions observed in the Caucasus and the Eastern European fSU.

Other scholars argue that informality in Central Asian republics penetrates formal spheres and informalizes them to such degree that "the informal is all that there is."[93] As Rico Isaacs describes, in Kazakhstan, "informal networks are understood to be the arenas in which real political power and decision making occurs, rather than in the formal institutional realm."[94] Like other informal behaviors in the fSU, informal practices in Central Asian states are deeply embedded in social culture and traditions.[95] For example, Cynthia Werner makes the case that Kazakhstan's *para* (informal practices based on the exchanges of gifts and favors of both a monetary and a nonmonetary nature) are part of traditional culture.[96] Although reinforced by economic shortages and the state bureaucracy during the Soviet period, *para* are seen as a Kazakh custom. Unlike informal institutions in the South Caucasus, where *blat* and other similar practices became associated with concepts of family honor and kinship obligations, or those of Russia, where *blat* is seen not only as a means of circumventing formal institutions but also as social and political leverage,[97] in Central Asia, "*blat* took root on the [population's] desire to have additional means, additional produce [*produkty*]."[98] Perhaps Central Asian countries have preserved their traditional clan-based forms of social organization, sustaining and reinforcing the culture of informality, in part as a consequence of the relatively low levels of Soviet social standardization experienced by that region.[99]

The informal practices deployed across the post-Soviet space have similarities as well as differences. In parts of the South Caucasus and Central Asia, various pre-Soviet traditions and the indigenous forms of social capital became embedded in the broader culture of informality under Soviet rule. On the one hand, this process created country-specific types of post-Soviet informal practices. On the other hand, it led to the establishment of a uniform culture of informality across the entire post-Soviet region. Despite regional differences, these informal practices and institutions are nevertheless very similar in structure and function, scale and scope, and importance for the population. Over the decades of Soviet rule, traditional forms of favor exchanges and reciprocal networks endemic to the ethnic groups of the fSU were heavily affected by the spread of *blat* culture. These characteristics distinguish post-Soviet informality from the informal sectors of other postsocialist regions where the spread of informal practices remained limited as well as from informality in other parts of the world where the importance of informal practices and institutions is often mitigated by institutional constraints or by cultural boundaries.[100]

In spite of the scarcity of studies comparing informality in CEE and the fSU, researchers have nevertheless confirmed that informal behaviors are more widespread and important among post-Soviet societies than in other postsocialist contexts.[101] A 2011 report by the European Bank for Reconstruction and Development (compiled after the 2008–10 global financial crisis), for example, showed that while only 30 percent of the population in CEE and 35 percent in the Balkan countries relied on private safety nets on a daily basis, more than 60 percent of the population in the fSU employed informal networks in their day-to-day life during the crisis years.[102] As John Round and Colin C. Williams point out, "Of course, such [informal] practices occur the world over; what is different in the post-Soviet context is their importance to everyday life."[103] Having employed representative survey data collected by the Centre for the Study of Public Policy, Rose compared informal behaviors of Russians and Ukrainians with those of Czechs and concluded that residents of former Soviet republics are several times more likely to rely on informal practices than are Czechs.[104] Rose's assumed that these divergences do not simply result from differing social or cultural characteristics and that "the distinctiveness of Czechs is not a consequence of passivity"; rather, "Czechs are more likely to rely on the market or to personalize and plead with bureaucrats to expedite their demands."[105] By contrast, "few Russians and Ukrainians think that nothing can be done when formal organizations fail; four-fifths have some sort of network to invoke in every situation."[106]

Informality in post-Soviet spaces thus must be distinguished from informal behaviors and traditions elsewhere in postsocialist societies. These differences emanate from the historical conditions that led to the emergence and expansion of informal practices and institutions in the fSU. The challenges of postcommunist transition, such as the lack of democratic transformation and the failure of transition to market economy, have further cemented the continuity and preservation of informal behaviors.

Soviet Legacies

A large and growing body of literature in political science, political economy, and political sociology has explored the communist legacy in postsocialist societies.[107] Since the 1989–92 dissolution of the socialist bloc, not only scholars of path-dependency but also scholars who sought to explain the inherent differences between postsocialist societies and their neighbors in the West have turned to analyzing postcommunist politics and societies through the lenses of the region's communist past.[108] This trend is encapsulated in Rose's claim that "ignoring the past encourages a misunderstanding of the present."[109]

Throughout the 1990s, the term *Leninist legacies*, coined by Kenneth Jowitt, featured prominently in research on the communist aftermath and its effects on postcommunist societies and politics.[110] Grzegorz Ekiert and Stephen E. Hanson have clarified that Jowitt's phrase refers "to the specific impacts on postcommunist societies of the particular forms of institutional standardization that were characteristic (in ideal-typical terms) of all countries in the communist world."[111] The concept of Leninist legacies has been broadly applied to the entire postcommunist space stretching from East Germany in the west to Mongolia in the east.[112] Although proponents of Leninist legacy theories made some efforts to differentiate between those countries that were part of the socialist bloc in CEE and their neighbors incorporated into the Soviet Union, the general consensus was based on an assumption that regardless of the regime-specific differences, all socialist regimes were "strictly authoritarian."[113] With all postsocialist regimes lumped together into one category broadly defined as "postcommunist states," divergences in post-1989 democratization and the transition to market economy were explained in terms of commonalities and differences in cultural, religious, and institutional backgrounds.[114] In more simplistic terms, Ekiert and Hanson explained that "countries that are situated closer to the West" were more successful in their political and economic transformation.[115] Adding a legacy dimension to Jeffrey S. Kopstein and David A. Reilly's "crude model" of "distance from the West," Grigore Pop-Eleches proposed that the difference in democratization

and transition pathways among postcommunist regimes resulted from the
different types of legacies affecting these processes.[116] He further suggested
distinguishing among "five key legacy dimensions for ex-communist countries": geography, cultural/religious heritage, economic, social condition/
modernization, and institutional legacies.[117] If applied to explain the differences in the spread of informality in CEE and the fSU, this categorization of
the Leninist legacy provides no answers regarding why informal traditions
are less widespread in Muslim Balkan countries than in Christian Russia or
Ukraine. It also fails to explain why the highly industrialized countries of the
fSU have relied more heavily on informal institutions and practices than far
less industrially developed Slovakia or Macedonia.

The argument that different types of communist regimes account for different trajectories of postcommunist development has gained wide usage in

Herbert Kitschelt was one of the first to argue that a common "Leninist
legacy" does not explain the diversity of postcommunist regimes.[118] In his
earlier work, Kitschelt suggested dividing communist regimes into three major types: patrimonial, bureaucratic-authoritarian, and national-consensus.[119] Along with the former Yugoslavia, Romania, and Bulgaria, he proposed including all ex-Soviet republics in the category of regimes that were
governed during the communist period by patrimonial communism.[120] This
type of communist regime was characterized by a hierarchy of patronal relations between the leadership and the elites distributed through widespread
patron-client networks.[121] Czechoslovakia and East Germany (the German
Democratic Republic) were classified as slightly more liberal but highly bu-
reaucratized bureaucratic-authoritarian communist regimes. Finally, Poland
and Hungary were presented as examples of a national-consensus type of
communist regime in which local elites sought to maintain distance from
the Soviet *nomenklatura*.[122]

The argument that different types of communist regimes account for different trajectories of postcommunist development has gained wide usage in
studies of postcommunist politics and societies.[123] For example, in their research on party patronage in postcommunist countries, Petr Kopecký and
Maria Spirova suggest that ex-socialist regimes were governed by a "plurality
of communist regimes, rather than [one] communist regime."[124] Similarly,
Tatjana Thelen asserts that postcommunist societies "demonstrated the
presence of a variety of socialisms, particularly in the rural areas."[125] Hence,
Valentina Dimitrova-Grajzl and Eszter Simon insist that "putting all former
socialist regimes in one category can be misleading."[126]

While all the details and nuances of the causal linkage between legacies
of communist regime types and postcommunist informality have not been

systematically explored, many researchers have noted the existence of a connection between these two phenomena. Indeed, the impact of the Soviet patrimonial type of communist regime on the emergence and spread of informal practices and institutions among the diverse societies of the USSR is hard to ignore. If Kitschelt's patrimonial communist regimes were rather similar in their political composition and bureaucratic functioning, the effect of sovietization—and in particular of Soviet sociocultural standardization unique to the Soviet Union—created inherent distinctions in the societal development of Soviet and non-Soviet patrimonial regimes and their successor states. Though Kitschelt's typology of communist regimes offers a point of departure for the analysis of the communist legacy's impact on postsocialist informality in the fSU, distinguishing between the Soviet and non-Soviet legacies becomes fundamental.[127] Citing New Democracies Barometer surveys, Rose contends that the "Soviet experience [was] most likely to foster" the spread of informal networks.[128] In a similar vein, Gel'man has written that "the Soviet legacy has developed a sustainable dominance of informal institutions both on the level of policy making and in the everyday life of ordinary citizens."[129] As a result of socialization enforced over most aspects of daily life in the Soviet socialist republics, "informal practices were an extremely important part of everyday life and were culturally different to informal practices in market economies."[130] Soviet sociocultural standardization was echoed by a socioeconomic environment unique to the Soviet command economy. Both the former and the latter were often combined in such policies as collectivization (the creation of work *kollektivs*), a typically Soviet form of workforce organization.[131] The Soviet *kollektiv* is just one of the examples of how "the formal and the informal were organically linked within the everyday lives of Soviet citizens."[132] As a direct outcome of Soviet sociocultural standardization, "the functioning of informal contacts and connections was predicated upon the structural characteristics of the Soviet-type system."[133] Some scholars have even argued that the present-day omnipresence of informality is a historical phenomenon that is only circumstantially influenced by "contemporary institutional factors."[134]

The emergence and proliferation of informal practices and institutions in Soviet societies is also closely associated with the economic shortages particularly characteristic of the command economy during the first two decades of Soviet rule.[135] More generally, it is assumed that as a result of economic challenges such as shortages of consumer goods and the limited availability of communal services, postcommunist societies are riddled by complex interpersonal networks employed by the population to access public goods and consumer items in short supply.[136] This economic dimension of the informal sphere was irrevocably associated with and embedded in the sociopolitical environment of oppressive Soviet society, which Rose describes as an "hour-glass society."[137]

These factors created enormous differences between informal behaviors in Soviet societies and societies of noncommunist regimes. According to Colin C. Williams, John Round, and Peter Rodgers, the "difference between informal practices in Soviet compared with Western economies was its omnipresent nature."[138] Despite Soviet advances in industrialization, urbanization, education, and health care, Soviet society lagged behind capitalist states in terms of modernization.[139] Not only did immense differences exist between Soviet and Western European and North American capitalist societies, but significant structural divides also separated Soviet societies from other socialist bloc countries.[140] Rose's comparison of Russians', Ukrainians', and Czechs' use of informal practices and institutions reveals that a "dual society" where informality replaced formal rules existed longer in the Soviet Union than in other CEE communist states.[141]

Soviet informality, which emerged during and became firmly rooted under communism, therefore laid the groundwork for post-Soviet informal practices and institutions. The pervasiveness and importance of informal behaviors among post-Soviet societies cannot result solely from Soviet legacies. The omnipresence and indispensability of post-Soviet informality is also rooted in issues of postcommunist transition.

Problems of Postsocialism

Despite the decisive importance of the Soviet legacy, it would be too simplistic to assume that the current scale and pervasiveness of informality in the fSU results solely from the historical divergences between ex-Soviet societies and other postsocialist or developing countries. Armed with the experience of postauthoritarian transitions in Latin America, parts of Asia, Southern Europe, and CEE, Western policymakers and former Sovietologists widely expected that, as Williams, Round, and Rodgers have observed, postcommunist challenges in the fSU would "only be temporary and that economic growth would bring prosperity to the majority in a short space of time."[142] Indeed, the overly optimistic expectation boldly proposed by the adherents of the transition paradigm was based on an assumption that the post-Soviet

region would gradually follow in the steps of CEE, with the individual countries transforming into democratically governed market economies.[143] The
authors argued that reforms in the fSU "introduced in a blanket fashion," as
well as the general failure of transition, which became obvious during the
first postcommunist decade, increased the importance of informal channels.[144] Round and Williams further suggested associating the omnipresence
of post-Soviet informality with the failure of economic transition, contend-
ing that informal practices and institutions "have greater importance [in the
fSU] than in more mature economies because of the severity and longevity of
economic marginalization . . . and the rent-seeking nature of many of their
state officials."[145]

The failure of the postsocialist political and economic transition has
been accompanied by the lack of social transformation. As Rose has argued,
Russian society as well as the societies of all other non-Baltic states of the fSU
remained "anti-modern."[146] Characterized by low levels of individual and
institutional trust,[147] such societies continued to harness the power of informal connections mostly because these informal institutions remained the
most adequate alternatives to incapable and weak state institutions. As Abel
Polese has keenly observed, the reliance on informal institutions in postcommunist societies is prominent in sectors "where the state fails to secure
basic needs for their citizens," and the informal practice therefore "makes up
for the incapacity of the state."[148] This situation has been endemic to post-
Soviet societies .

Given that in most societies, "an ongoing *failing statehood* (not to be confused with *failed state*) leads to the emergence and proliferation of informality,"[149] the lack of transparent and efficient governance was one of the definitive features of the Soviet system of governance that inevitably transferred
to post-Soviet regimes. Under such circumstances, the reliance on informality was inevitable primarily because informal networks provided the population with higher levels of social security than did the state or formal institutions.[150] As a consequence, the dominance of informality in the everyday
lives of post-Soviet citizens has led to the creation of an environment unique
to the fSU in that informal work and informal transactions not only replaced
their formal equivalents but also "become central to everyday life."[151]Apart
from a series of democratic institutional reforms implemented in a handful
of hybrid or transitional post-Soviet regimes, most ex-Soviet countries have
failed to embark on democratization since the dissolution of the USSR.
Throughout the 1990s and 2000s, the majority of these countries were gov-

erned by a variety of authoritarian and semiauthoritarian regimes. By 2015, nearly two and a half decades after the end of state communism, authoritarianism had become further entrenched across the post-Soviet space.[152] A successful transition to market economy also has not occurred in most of the fSU.[153] In Ekrem Karakoç's observation, rather than leading to improved living standards in the fSU, the process of transition to market economy "has transformed the region from one of substantial equality [during communist period] to one of high inequality."[154] Economic crises of the first postcommunist decade, industrial stagnation, and the failure of the Washington Consensus were blamed for the surge in unemployment rates, which almost tripled between 1989 to 1998.[155]

The second postcommunist decade, however, did not bring either successful transition to market economy or improvements in economic equality. Between 1990 and 2000, "income inequality [in the fSU] increased on average by 45%. [In contrast,] other Third Wave democracies in Europe, such as Spain and Portugal, experienced an increase of only about 10%."[156] Those few post-Soviet economies—Russia (during the first decade of the twenty-first century), Azerbaijan, Kazakhstan, and Turkmenistan—that managed to recover and grow have done so primarily by relying heavily on natural resources. In fact, the "resource curse" not only has prevented diversification of economies in resource-rich post-Soviet states but also seems to be directly associated with the lack of democratization in these countries.

Informality has retained its importance precisely as a result of the range of problems of postsocialism endemic to the fSU. These problems of transition have collectively created sociopolitical and socioeconomic conditions unique to the post-Soviet region, distinguishing it from CEE or the Balkans, though the latter have also experienced many of these malaises. While Jeremy Morris and Abel Polese maintain that "social and economic transformation does not necessarily mean convergence with a western 'model,'" neither social nor economic transition has succeeded in the post-Soviet context.[157] Not surprisingly, the reliance on informality in fSU states is markedly higher than in other ex-socialist countries. For example, as the European Bank for Research and Development has reported, while less than 5 percent of CEE's population (8–10 percent in Balkan countries) encountered the issue of unofficial payments and gift-giving at public institutions, at least 20 percent of the population in fSU countries reported such experiences.[158]

Some scholars have argued that informal practices and institutions, sustained and empowered by the problems of postcommunism, further obstruct democratization and effective transition to market economy.[159] While chapter 3 discusses in more detail the impact of informality on institutional reforms (not to be confused with the impact of institutional reforms on informality) in the fSU, this book maintains that informality as such is neither negative nor positive; rather, some byproducts of informal practices—such as clientelism, nepotism, corruption, or patronage networks—can be seen as negative. Nevertheless, even in light of these generally detrimental and malevolent side effects, the popular perception of informal practices in the fSU often differs from that of populations (and elites) in other parts of the world. This observation points to the larger debate about the relationship between informality and corruption or bribery.

INFORMALITY AND CORRUPTION

Informal practices and institutions are by definition often understood as either corrupt or closely associated with corruption.[160] The association between informality and corruption is nevertheless ambiguous and often depends on the definition of corruption applied. In Western European societies as well as developing countries, corruption is not necessarily perceived as negative.[161] For instance, Geetanee Napal details, in Mauritius, "the practice of bribery provides an easy way out and is viewed as acceptable."[162] In the post-Soviet context, the relationships among bribery, gift-giving, and reciprocity are complex and multidimensional. While the majority of ex-Soviet countries firmly occupy the lower end of international corruption rankings, popular perceptions of what constitutes corruption and bribery are so ambivalent that scholars continue to struggle with a proper definition for the phenomenon. Terms such as "out-of-pocket," unofficial payments, and "under-the-table" transactions are used alongside more conventional representations of corruption ingrained in definitions assigned to it by international organizations.[163] Though some scholars have seen corruption in the fSU as an attribute of postcommunist transition that will decrease over time, recent studies suggest that corruption is not going to disappear easily.[164]

One of the biggest problems surrounding the perception of corruption in post-Soviet countries is a lack of distinction between corruption/bribery and gifts. A number of studies have demonstrated that acts normally considered bribery in Western societies are seen as "signs of attention" or as reciprocal gifts in post-Soviet spaces.[165]

A number of scholars have therefore insisted on distinguishing informality from corruption.[166] Polese argues that "gift and corruption are not objective; they do depend on the context and the same definition is not applicable everywhere. Offering a box of chocolates to a teacher, therefore, does not have the same meaning in Odessa and London."[167] Most post-Soviet citizens understand this culture of gift-giving or gift exchanges (both monetary and nonmonetary), like informality, as part of popular culture and as a daily reality. Polese further insists that "in Ukraine, the word *vzyatka* [bribe] is not a taboo . . . and people increasingly tend to use it when talking of their own actions."[168] In his anthropological research on informal payments in Ukrainian universities and hospitals, Polese has found that informal "exchange—be this called bribe or gift—is at the base of the Ukrainian society."[169] Wanner has made a similar observation in her research on the meaning and significance of gifts in post-Soviet Ukraine.[170] Whereas Westerners may see informal transactions with money changing hands as corrupt and morally reproachable, citizens of post-Soviet countries perceive these transactions as common and time-tested forms of reciprocal exchanges. Other scholars have argued that since the Soviet period, informal payments to public officials have come to be seen as morally justifiable and acceptable.[171] For example, Misztal explains that under communism, although corruption among high-ranking Communist Party officials was disapproved by the masses, lower-level bribery was often seen as a means of circumventing the bureaucracy.[172]

In the postcommunist period, informal exchanges of monetary gifts and other types of informal practices became an inextricable component of the formal bureaucracy, which on many occasions simply cannot function without relying on informal rules.[173] This blurring of the boundary between gifts and bribes as well as between the formal and informal is endemic to the post-Soviet region as a consequence not only of the Soviet legacy, which made informal monetary transactions morally acceptable and socially embedded, but also of the problems of postcommunism. Morris and Polese argue that the state, which they dub "an 'absentee landlord' in many spaces, sectors and institutions," is most to blame for the monetization of gift exchanges and the perception of such practices as ordinary and acceptable.[174] Although the bulk of informal transactions involving exchanges of money or other material gifts are defined by international organizations as corruption,[175] in practice, monetary "gifts" are often used to pave the way for future reciprocal networking.

There is no question, however, that informal practices differ from corruption and bribery, mainly because nearly all informal practices in the fSU and elsewhere are based on mutually accepted cooperation. Many forms of informal relationships are not one-off transactions—unlike corruption—but rather continuous and meticulously sustained interpersonal relationships. Informal practices—whether *blat* or its equivalents in the Caucasus and Central Asia—are embedded into kinship, friendship, and solidarity-based relationships. Informal practices have many functions and depend on the workings of numerous informal or semiformal institutions, including corruption and bribery. Informal practices cannot avoid relying on exchanges of monetary gifts and one-off "out-of-pocket" payments, which in certain contexts may or may not be described as corruption and bribery.[176] If corruption is based on money or on the exchange of material gifts, then the role of short-term financial exchanges in informal practices is secondary to long-term reciprocal or hierarchical networking. Since a great number of informal transactions and exchanges do not involve money changing hands and function more as barter or a reciprocal exchange of services and favors, it is very difficult to categorize post-Soviet informality as corrupt. Ledeneva consequently warns against confusing informal practices with corruption because, for example, *blat* is thought to be "more legitimate [than corruption], since it is oriented to satisfying everyday needs and basic necessities."[177]

Thus, informality and corruption exist in symbiosis in post-Soviet spaces. Bribes and corruption are often indistinguishable from gifts and "signs of attention" and are used alongside other forms of exchanges to both reciprocate for a favor and gain preferential access to formal institutions. As Polese has demonstrated in his case study of gift exchanges in Ukrainian institutions, public officials believe that "If I receive it, it is a gift; if I demand it, then it is a bribe."[178] Attitudes toward corruption and perceptions of bribes in the fSU are manifestly context-bound, and although receiving or offering a monetary gift is a necessary part of an informal relationship in some situations, on other occasions it is a form of institutional corruption. In other words, post-Soviet informality is only as corrupt as most of those who rely on it think it is.

BEYOND INFORMAL ECONOMY

One of the biggest challenges facing any interdisciplinary researcher of informality is to differentiate between informal economic and noneconomic (political and social) functions of informal practices and institutions. It is not difficult to observe that many forms of informal economic activities—employment, black markets, and other forms of entrepreneurship—depend on the functioning of informal networks of contacts and connections and are therefore deeply embedded in social contexts. Indeed, the functioning of an informal economy would be unimaginable without the framework of interpersonal relations that underlies informal economic activity.

This sort of symmetrical relationship, though often ignored by scholars of informal economy, is nevertheless acknowledged as essential for the informal economy.[179] As Alice Sindzingre admits, the effectiveness of the informal economy depends on the "fundamental social relationships" between network members.[180] Ledeneva points out that studies on the informal economy often generalize *blat* as a component of the Soviet "second economy."[181] Smith and Stenning argue that postsocialist economies, both formal and informal, must be seen in terms of "interwoven sets of economic practices" that manifest themselves in the social, cultural, and political spheres as well as in the economic sphere.[182]

More commonly, however, informal practices and institutions are understood not merely in terms of being economic and noneconomic but as encompassing the political, economic, and social spheres. As Janine R. Wedel posits, "Informal groups and networks operate in the multiple domains of politics, economics and law. They are not confined to any one domain, but traverse them."[183] According to Smith and Stenning, informality in postcommunist spaces provides individuals not only with economic spaces but also with social life, which often becomes embedded in economic activities.[184] Round, Williams, and Rodgers argue that postsocialist informality "cannot be placed into binary divisions" that distinguish between the informal economy and all other forms of informal activities.[185] Informal practices and institutions in the fSU extend well beyond the economic sphere as a result of their embeddedness in historical legacies, local culture, and power relations.[186] Similarly, in Ledeneva's view, students of informal practices must expand the scope of the analysis beyond the boundaries of the informal economy to adopt a more multidisciplinary approach.[187]

Other scholars have presented postsocialist informality as a "survival strategy" operating across several spheres, including economic, political, and sociocultural activities.[188] Morris and Polese thus believe that postcommunist informal practices are better understood as "embedded in social life rather than part of a rationalist economic reasoning; informality is often about 'poaching' opportunities and utilizing the rules, and the gaps therein, of the formal."[189] Although most studies on the informal "second" economy of the USSR have focused exclusively on economic dimensions of informal behaviors,[190] some scholars have noted that sustaining a complex system of underground economy required reliance on a myriad of networks that provided political cover (*krysha*) and social support.[191] Understanding post-Soviet informality, which has developed within specific sociohistorical conditions, requires expanding the definition of informality to include not only binary distinctions between formal and informal but also distinctions between economic and noneconomic relations.

While this book does not focus on economic activities of post-Soviet informal practices and institutions, which have already been thoroughly explored,[192] it does acknowledge that post-Soviet informality must be understood as extending across economics, politics, culture, and society. In contrast to the economic functions of informal practices, which almost always draw their support from vast networks of social and political connections, informal institutions and networks operating in political and social spheres do not necessarily engage in economic activities. For example, patronage or clientelistic networks might be essential to certain underground economic activities (for example, black markets) but do not always participate in the informal economy. Rather, they operate by exchanging nonmaterial favors or by involvement in corruption and earning income from unofficial payments. As a result, while political and social informal institutions, operating as a part of informal practices, do not need to be part of the informal economy, that economy inevitably depends on underlying systems of networks and connections, many of which do not participate in economic transactions, directly or otherwise. This is not to say, however, that informal economic behaviors are secondary. The role of informal economic (for-profit) institutions and networks operating within frameworks of certain informal practices is context-bound and depends on specific circumstances and sociohistorical conditions on the ground.

SUMMARY

Informal practices and institutions have been observed in nearly all societies throughout human history, but particularly widespread and pervasive forms of informality emerge and proliferate only under specific socioeconomic and sociopolitical conditions. In contemporary history, these conditions were the effects of totalitarianism and planned economies, both of which are inherent characteristics of socialist bloc countries. While informality was omnipresent in all communist regimes, the Soviet Union was home to the most deeply rooted and resilient informal practices and institutions. A combination of the Soviet Marxist-Leninist legacy and the enormous challenges of postsocialist transformation ensured the survival of communist-era informal behaviors and encouraged their continuity and evolution. The final product of these conditions, post-Soviet informality, is both more widespread and more important (for both the elites and populations at large) than informal behaviors in those parts of the world that never experienced a prolonged experience of either totalitarianism or a command economy.

CHAPTER 3
Institutional Reforms and Informality

THIS CHAPTER PRESENTS a theoretically informed analysis of the relationship between institutional reforms and informality. In addition to explaining the complex and multifaceted association between institutional change and informality, the chapter is concerned with developing an analytical framework that will help in understanding why, when, and under what circumstances democratic institutional reforms affect informality. This chapter theoretically grounds the relationship between institutional change and informality. In an effort to narrow the general theme of institutional change to focus specifically on democratic institutional reforms, this chapter weaves together theories of democratization and strands of literature on democratic institutional reforms with the topic of informality. Finally, the chapter explains the contentious relationship between post-Soviet informality and postcommunist reforms by examining lessons learned from the experience of institutional reforms across the post-Soviet region.

INSTITUTIONAL CHANGE AND INFORMALITY

Over the past half century, political scientists and economists alike have insisted that institutional change has a major impact on various forms of human behavior.[1] The informal sphere is by no means less susceptible to the effects of institutional transformation than other spheres, and whether seen through the lens of institutional analysis or in terms of informal networking and practices, the informal sphere is intimately interconnected with its formal counterpart. As part of the formal/informal equilibrium, "formal institutions and informal institutional arrangements are built up and change in co-evolution."[2] Some scholars have even insisted that formal and informal institutions are so dependent on each other that unless formal institutions are "able to rely on informal personal loyalty, they are doomed."[3]

More commonly, however, informal institutions are understood as providing "templates and substitutes for formal choices."[4] Formal rules and conventions are both influenced by and exert continuous influence on informal institutions and practices. The process of informal interactions within any society is also a process of continuous transformation and adaptation of informal institutions to their ever-changing environment. Informal practices emerge, expand, wither away, and disappear over time. In such a relationship, a change to the status quo may occur only with the change of formal institutions. Provided that informality exists in symbiosis with the formal sphere, informal practices and institutions rarely change as a result of endogenous processes. While it is not unusual for informal practices to transform from within, most notable changes involve external pressures, such as the transformation of a given operational environment. For example, the Russian practice of *blat* has lost its function of procuring deficit goods and commodities, primarily as a consequence of the collapse of the command economy and the economic liberalization that ensued in the postcommunist period. This is a case of an informal practice changing, or losing some of its functions, to adapt to transformations in its environment.

Unlike many formal institutions, informal practices emerge spontaneously. They are not centrally controlled, and the role of agents or actors is that of participants, not of purposeful institutional creators and guarantors of their stability.[5] Even the most hierarchical informal political institutions usually lack central coordination and planning, emerging instead in response to external changes. Despite their self-enforcing nature, informal practices and institutions are highly susceptible to changes in their environment and transformations of external conditions. In addition to being spontaneous and erratic, informal practices and institutions are also ambivalent and elusive. Informal structures consequently have limited opportunities to consciously and harmoniously facilitate an endogenous transformation. As rational players, individuals engaged in informal practices may wish to reshape and change these institutions. As a result of the lack of centralized mechanisms of control and coordination, however, individual agents cannot consciously "reform" informal institutions. According to the consensus in the literature, the change of informal structures occurs primarily under the impact of exogenous shocks. These exogenous "concussions" are typically caused by the influence exerted by formal institutions on informal structures. Scholars posit that the change of formal institutions is implemented with the main goal of changing informal rules, with Jack Knight asserting that "the formal rules are established as a way of stabilizing or changing existing informal rules."[6] The change may occur when old institutions are displaced or layered by new ones or when brand new institutions emerge.

All cataclysmic transformations of formal institutions—such as revolutions, economic crises, or regime changes—may be expected to affect informal institutions to the point of their disappearance. More commonly, however, formal institutions influence informality as a result of institutional reforms, implemented with the aim of changing or shifting the priorities and purposes of formal institutions by strengthening, reorganizing, modernizing, and improving them. Institutional reforms not only have a direct impact on agents but also influence the structure and environment in which informal practices function.

With regard to economic reforms, "governments can have a major impact on informal institutions based on the capacity and willingness of a government to enforce its will."[7] A number of studies on the effects of reforms on informal economies have concluded that institutional reforms affect not only the performance of informal institutions but also the formal/informal equilibrium.[8] If, for example, ineffective reforms may strengthen and spread informality, a successful reform process is expected to undermine informal practices. A similar line of argument has been adopted in political science. Janine R. Wedel has hypothesized that the state has a crucial impact on the transformation of informal rules.[9] Knight writes that "when the relationship between formal and informal rules is considered, the main focus is from the top down: the effects of the state's formal institutions on informal rules and conventions."[10] Similarly, Gretchen Helmke and Steven Levitsky identify the process of "formal institutional change" as the most important source of informal institutions' change.[11] They propose that informal institutional change occurs primarily as a consequence of (1) change in formal institutional design and (2) change in formal institutional strength and effectiveness. Informal institutions and practices, the functioning of which is associated with or affected by formal institutions, become inadvertently transformed as a result of changes in the design of formal institutions. In particular, "changes in the level of enforcement of formal rules alter the costs and benefits adhering to informal institutions that compete with or substitute for those rules."[12]

Clientelism, patronage, corruption, and other parasitic forms of informal institutions closely dependent on their formal counterparts would be most affected by changes in institutional design. Change in institutional design may be especially critical for those informal practices that thrive on weaknesses and deficiencies in formal institutions. In such instances, the strengthening and improvement of formal institutions as a result of reforms may deliver a fatal blow to informal practices surviving solely as a result of flaws of formal institutions. Helmke and Levitsky explain that "when the credibility of previously ineffective formal structures is enhanced, the benefits associated with the use of substitutive institutions may diminish, potentially to the point of their dispensability."[13] In both cases, informal institutions are affected by reform processes aimed at improving or redesigning formal institutions. Though formal institutions may also affect informal structures without undergoing a process of institutional transformation—for example, by gradually evolving—formal structures usually influence informality after (or during) the process of institutional change. Some scholars have even argued that since "informal institutions are dependent upon the existence of formal institutions," formal institutional change inevitably influences informal rules.[14]

While different schools of new institutionalism developed their own interpretations of the relationship between formal institutional change and informal institutions, this process has so far received little attention in either strand of institutionalism. As Lucan A. Way has noted, for scholars of institutionalism, "it is always much easier to focus critiques on formal institutional design rather than on informal practice, which is by definition harder to figure out."[15] Given that sociological institutionalism, among other schools of new institutionalism, employs fairly broad definitions that tend to describe institutions in terms not only of rules and constraints but also of social and cultural norms, the impact of institutional change on informal behaviors is seen as "slow and incremental."[16] In contrast to formal institutions, which in accordance with sociological institutionalism may change relatively quickly, "cultural norms are slow-moving institutions," and changes in informal behavior can therefore span generations.[17] As Svetozar Pejovich has pointed out, informal cultural institutions "change primarily through their erosion, which is a slow and time-consuming process."[18]

As a result of the lack of clear-cut distinctions between formal and informal institutions in sociological institutionalism, the same institution may perform both formal and informal functions, thereby complicating the process of delineating formal and informal institutional changes. From a sociological perspective, for example, political parties engage in both formal and informal politics. A change in either formal or informal rules must therefore be accompanied by a change in the sociocultural background from which these rules originated. The importance of sociocultural background for institutional change is also seen as path-dependent or ingrained in historical processes. As Chavance explains, "Cultural change, extinction, revival and creation are dependent on the historical context."[19] The emphasis on the historical origins of institutional change in sociological institutionalism is an area in which it converges with historical institutionalism's perspective on informal institutional change.

Historical institutionalists believe that informal institutions change under the influence of formal institutional changes through the process of "critical junctures." Following the punctuated equilibrium model of institutional change, informal institutions change together with formal rules. According to Douglass C. North, "Usually, the norms (informal constraints) that have evolved to supplement formal rules persist in periods of stability, but get overturned by new formal rules in periods of change."[20] Like formal institutions, informal practices remain unchanged during periods of stasis and transform as a result of developments within formal institutions. Changes to formal rules and constraints have an inevitable impact on informal institutions. In North's view, formal and informal structures are mutually interdependent, meaning that a "new informal equilibrium will evolve gradually after a change in the formal rules."[21] Given the lack of theoretically grounded explanations of how exactly formal institutional change affects informal institutions, the interaction between formal and informal institutions in historical institutionalism, which is usually seen through the prism of path-dependency, remains rather ambiguous.

Regardless of the differences in views among scholars of institutionalism, the relationship between formal institutional change and informal practices and institutions across different strands of new institutionalism is viewed as driven by rational motivations. Even the incremental process of change in historical institutionalism rests on the assumption that formal institutions embark on the process of changing informal rules only when the two types of institutions become locked in conflict over resources or interests, a conflict that rationalizes the change. North argues that changing informal constraints "will usually require substantial resources or at the very least overcoming the free-rider problem"; the process of change is thus initiated only when formal institutions have no other alternatives.[22] Knight supports this opinion by suggesting that a "major challenge to the stability of informal rules comes from the apparent incentives provided by noncompliance" with formal institutions.[23] Indeed, the failure of informal structures to comply with formal rules or to maintain a status quo creates an inherent conflict.

Even in the absence of obvious conflicts between formal institutions and informal practices, the process of formal institutional change exerts such a powerful influence on informal behaviors that they have no other choice but to transform. If agents benefiting from informal institutions have limited centralized control over such structures, then the agents in charge of formal institutions may choose to redesign or reform their rules to transform informal practices if they become redundant. These changes are not necessarily aimed at strengthening or improving formal institutions. For example, petty corruption of government officials undermines the revenue that state institutions generate from service fees and in transitional and authoritarian regimes prevents higher-ranking officials from benefiting from the spoils of corruption. Tackling low-level bribery is in the interests not only of the state but also of the elites in charge of such institutions. In light of this fact, measures undertaken by transitional or autocratic regimes to tackle petty corruption as well as the institutional support harnessed in favor of such measures do not necessarily reflect the agents' willingness to construct transparent and corruption-free institutions. As rational actors, major institutional stakeholders, such as ruling elites, choose to "reform" only those informal institutions that are seen as redundant or harmful to their purposes.

Numerous anticorruption campaigns in post-Soviet countries not only resulted in the reduction of petty corruption but also led to an increase in corruption in higher echelons of power. With the will and resources necessary to transform informal institutions by reforming formal rules and constraints, formal institutions may seem to possess an insurmountable advantage over informal practices. Formal institutions' centralized control mechanisms and ability to self-reform often lead to the perception that they are superior to informal rules.[24] Nevertheless, neither the capacity of formal institutions to achieve consensus on rational actions nor their direct or indirect ability to influence informal practices and institutions can guarantee the success of efforts to reform informality.

As Indra de Soysa and Johanns Jütting warn, "There are also strong limitations to the role that the government can play in changing informal institutions."[25] These limitations emerge as a consequence of informal actors' unwillingness to accept changes. Knight insists that it is inevitable that "informal rules persist when efforts at formal change are attempted."[26] Way hints that when the work of formal institutions does not interfere or overlap with informal practices, "formal institutional reform [may] be irrelevant."[27] Regardless of agents' rationale for implementing reforms targeting informality, informal practices may still be favored by the individuals who sustain them. North explains that regardless of a "wholesale change" of formal constraints, informal rules may persist and overcome the transformation "because they still resolve basic exchange problems among the participants, be they social, political, or economic."[28]

Some scholars have argued that formal institutional change can weaken informal institutions but cannot change them completely.[29] Agents who lack centralized control mechanisms over informal institutions but still rely on them for benefits may continue to use these practices regardless of exogenous shocks. In that case, efforts by formal institutions to eradicate or transform informal institutions may face staunch resistance from those actors who still view informal behaviors as rational. Knight observes that "much of the resistance to intentional change can be explained by distributional factors, but some of the persistence of informal social rules in the face of intentional change and external enforcement can be traced to ideological and cognitive factors."[30] These ideological and cognitive factors may be analyzed from both sociological and rational choice perspectives.

According to sociological interpretations, informal institutions resist change and may survive reform because they are culturally embedded. The vast majority of post-Soviet citizens understand informal practices such as gift-giving and unofficial payments at formal institutions in return for preferential treatment, for example, as a part of popular culture. Attempts to eradicate such practices through administrative reform may come to naught simply because these practices are still perceived as morally acceptable and culturally appropriate. Reform, therefore, should start at the sociocultural level and target the attitudinal-perceptional premises of such practices. Sociocultural embeddedness may enable informal practices not only to persist through numerous reform efforts but also to overrun the formal institutions that attempted to eradicate them. For example, in spite of efforts to undermine the USSR's culture of *blat* by labeling it "an anti-Soviet phenomenon deriving from the moral perversion of some individuals," Soviet officials were simply unable and unwilling to "eliminate what in effect supported them and what they were coupled with."[31] Although communist elites at the top of the party saw *blat* as detrimental to the system, both the population and numerous low- and mid-ranking government officials saw *blat* as a culturally acceptable and inseparable part of everyday life. As practice demonstrates, however, even attempts to socioculturally reform informality may run aground as long as informal practices and institutions perform their functions well and fulfill the expectations of their beneficiaries.

From a rational choice perspective, although the reform in question might be in the interests of actors in charge of "reformist" institutions, these actors may not understand whether these reforms can realistically succeed. As Paul Pierson explains, "Actors may be motivated more by conceptions of what is appropriate than by conceptions of what would be effective."[32] As a consequence, by attempting to reform something that is either beyond their ability to reform or does not need to be eliminated, actors may embark on a process of change that is doomed. Despite being rational actors, the drivers of institutional change also may be shortsighted.[33] Seeking to change the rules and institutions that indirectly and stealthily hold the foundations of their own power bases, actors engage in a zero-sum game. Even when perceived as rational, change in fact may not be in the interests of "reformists." For example, *blat* networks were important to the same communist institutions that have sought to eradicate *blat*.

At times, institutional actors may not realize that the existence of informal practices, both within and beyond formal institutions, enables the actors to control these structures and reap benefits from them. More often, however, elite "reformist" actors are well aware of the benefits of informal channels but face pressure from domestic or international actors to implement democratic reforms and seek to enact surface-only changes. As Tanja A. Börzel and Yasemin Pamuk describe, for example, anticorruption reforms in Armenia and Azerbaijan implemented from 2003 to 2010 under pressure from the European Union have "cleansed" state institutions of unwanted officials—removed on corruption charges—but replaced them with proregime individuals who continued to rely on informal practices.[34] As a result, the vicious cycle of patronage and clientelism within these institutions remained uninterrupted. Thus, although institutionalists consider informal behaviors precarious and inferior to formal institutions, those behaviors have the potential to resist reforms and pervade and weaken formal institutions in the process of reform.

Indeed, while a voluminous body of literature investigates how and under what conditions formal institutions affect informal practices, informal institutions—particularly in transitional settings—are also expected to have an effect on formal institutional change and reform.[35] Wedel explains that "much evidence worldwide suggests that informal groups and networks facilitate, inhibit, or otherwise alter the institutions and processes of industrialization, urbanization, bureaucratization and democratization."[36] As the case of the former Soviet Union demonstrates, informal structures not only complement, accommodate, substitute, and compete with formal institutions but also infiltrate, strengthen, replace, and incapacitate them.[37] Anna Grzymala-Busse argues that in postcommunist contexts, regardless of formal institutions' capacity, they can be replaced, weakened or reinforced by informal constraints.[38] Henry A. Hale has raised a similar argument in his attempts to understand how the workings of informal institutions affect institution-building in post-Soviet countries.[39] Both Alena Ledeneva and Vladimir Gel'man have noted that in the context of Russian institution-building, power networks have pervaded all functions of formal institutions.[40] As a result of this "informalization" of formal institutions, institutional reforms lead not to the dismantling of informal systems of control (known as *sistema*) but rather to their strengthening at the expense of institutional transparency and efficiency. When formal institutions become deformalized, every effort to reform and formalize them further strengthens informal rules. In other words, to address the collective action problems that pose barriers to reform, reformists must rely on informal networks.

Having employed these informal networks to enable institutional change, reformists unwittingly strengthen informal institutions, thereby allowing them to hijack the reform process. The case of Russian *sistema* networks again provides a good example of how reform efforts aimed at undermining *sistema* fail because the leadership's capacity and political will are restricted by their reliance on *sistema* networks.[41] Even in the more stable institutional environments of developed economies, "existing informal rules can limit the extent of formal institutional change through the effects of enduring expectations on the formal recognition process."[42] As Knight emphasizes, state officials and other institutional stakeholders may create, legalize, and adopt formal rules as part of institutional practice. These rules, however, become part of the established institutional practice only after informal recognition—that is, after they are accepted and approved by "various social actors," many of which are informal interest groups.[43] Such recognition becomes much less straightforward in nondemocratic settings, where informal recognition is more important than formal. For an institutional change to be recognized in societies dominated by informality, the approval of the change by informal stakeholders becomes even more important than its legalization and institutionalization. As a consequence of the ubiquitous nature of informal practices in postcommunist societies and their symbiotic relationship with formal institutions, as Wedel posits, any reform effort will be influenced by informal constraints.[44]

In autocratic regimes, which intentionally harness the power of informal institutions for their own purposes, such as strengthening and centralizing the presidential apparatus, reforms are usually cosmetic in that they are not directed against informal practices but are instead aimed at further deformalizing the decision-making process. In hybrid regimes, which seek to formalize their institutions, "the lack of attention to informal systems can produce unanticipated and undesired outcomes in reform."[45] Ignoring informal institutions can lead informal actors to undermine the reform process, which in turn can delegitimize the regime and lead to its weakening and ultimate demise. For example, the failure of Viktor Yushchenko's government in post–Orange Revolution Ukraine to take into consideration informal stakeholders to a certain degree led to the failure of the reform process and the delegitimization of the hybrid regime. Yushchenko then lost popularity and failed to win election to a second term in office.

Notwithstanding the fact that informal practices and institutions may exert tangible influence on formal institutions, sometimes even forcing them to reform and change, formal institutions can have a more robust and transformative impact on informality. The retreat of informality in the face of effective institutional reforms was evident not only in Central and Eastern Europe (CEE) but also in Latin America.[46] Empirical studies on the effects of reforms on informality have cemented an academic consensus that successful institutional reforms weaken informal practices and institutions.[47] Informal rules that directly contradict formal constraints are least likely to survive the initial stage of reform.[48] On the theoretical level, as Åse Berit Grødeland hypothesizes, if informality "is a response to the institutional and legislative disruptions initially brought about by transition—then one may expect it to gradually wither away as 'chaos' is replaced by institutional order and clear rules and regulations allowing for the formal solution of problems."[49] On the empirical level, effective institutional reforms in democratic or transitional regimes have a strong potential to reduce negative effects of informality, dismantle patronage and clientelistic networks, and eradicate corruption and other forms of unofficial payments.[50] The fact that nearly all successful examples of the impact of institutional reforms on informality occur in democratic settings suggests that regime type as well as the format and design of reforms (such as democratic versus undemocratic), are crucial criteria for analyzing the relationship between institutional change and informality.

DEMOCRATIC INSTITUTIONAL REFORMS AND INFORMALITY

This book is primarily concerned with the analysis of one particular type of institutional change, democratic reforms—institutional transformations implemented with the ultimate goal of creating transparent, inclusive, egalitarian, and corruption-free formal institutions. Democratic institutional reforms differ from all other types of institutional changes in that their ultimate goal is the establishment of democratic institutions. As Guillermo A. O'Donnell acknowledges, the definition of democratic institutions "is elusive."[51] Although O'Donnell maintains that "democratic institutions are political institutions," the process of democratic institution-building may also involve the creation of economic and social institutions such as civil society.[52] According to O'Donnell, the term *democratic institutions* covers an array of structures, some of which "are formal organizations belonging to the constitutional network of a polyarchy: these include congress, the judiciary, and political parties. Others, such as fair elections, have an intermittent organizational embodiment but are no less indispensable."[53] The term *democratic institutional reforms* can refer to political institutions as well as to neoliberal economic reforms and the liberalization of social policies. As this book primarily focuses on the political and social spheres of post-Soviet countries, economic reforms therefore lie outside the scope of this analysis.

Bearing in mind that institutionalization does not equal democratization and that an undemocratic regime may construct corruption-free and inclusive institutions, it is fundamental to differentiate democratic institutions from all other types of institutions. Among the numerous criteria that researchers of democracy attribute to democratic institutions, the most essential is "horizontal accountability."[54] In full-scale democracies such as the United States, this system is known as checks and balances or "the controls that state agencies are supposed to exercise over other state agencies."[55] In other words, democratic institutional reforms are expected to produce not just one democratic institution but an ensemble of such institutions that will in turn ensure each other's accountability and transparency. Institutional reforms in established democracies pursue the goal of improving the quality of democracy and strengthening existing democratic institutions; in transitional regimes, such reforms seek to create democratic institutions, often from scratch. As the examples of Western European and North American democratization illustrate, democratic reforms need not be associated with a regime change or "modular democratic revolution."[56] Nevertheless, the vast majority of recent attempts to construct democratic institutions have occurred in the aftermath of regime change or at least as a result of major policy transformations.[57]

The process of democratic institutionalization is known as democratization.[58] As the introduction details, democratization may not result in the establishment and consolidation of either participatory or representative democracy but its ultimate goal is expected to be the creation of stable and functional democratic governance. Even the political and economic reforms implemented under Mikhail Gorbachev's perestroika arguably were not bereft of democratic elements.[59] Nevertheless, these and many other reform processes in the regimes that succeeded the USSR had no ultimate goal of democratizing, decentralizing, and liberalizing formal institutions.

The discussion in political science on what attributes democratization should have spans a number of dominant theories and schools of thought. The sizable literature on democratization, particularly pertaining to post-communist studies, is dominated by two theoretical schools of thought—transitology and modernization theory.[60] *Modernization* theory is perhaps less suited for the analysis of the association between democratization and informality. The key premise of modernization theory rests on an assumption that economic development and all societal processes associated with it eventually and irrevocably lead to the emergence and consolidation of democratic institutions.[61] In the words of Ronald Inglehart and Christian Welzel, economic development framed by industrialization and market economy creates "a self-reinforcing process that transforms social life and political institutions, bringing rising mass participation in politics and in the long run making the establishment of democratic political institutions increasingly likely."[62] Valerie Bunce explains that according to the proponents of modernization theory, "although democracy can be introduced in poor as well as rich countries, its prospects for enduring increase substantially at high levels of economic development."[63]

Although institutional design, such as the existence of a parliamentary rather than presidential system, is also instrumental for the effectiveness of democratization, economic progress is its main prerequisite. As Seymour

Martin Lipset summarizes, "If [political actors] can take the high road to economic development, they can keep their political houses in order."[64] Advocates of modernization have presented extensive empirical evidence in support of this assumption but have often failed to consider the emergence of many new democracies, such as postcommunist transformations or democratizing processes in Latin America.[65] Herbert Kitschelt reminds us that "differences in economic wealth and development cannot account for the observed pattern in postcommunist Europe and Central Asia."[66] Empirically, Stephen White demonstrates that modernization theory can neither explain democratization in CEE—which was not accompanied by economic growth—nor account for Eurasia's color revolutions.[67] More important for this book, modernization scholars have largely ignored the role of informal practices and institutions in the process of democratization. If informal political and social institutions were either completely omitted from the analyses of modernization-centered democratization or presented as "vestiges" of incomplete institutionalization, then informal economy was seen as detrimental and backward.[68]

The second prominent strand of democratization theory is the *transition paradigm*, also known as transitology, contingent choice theory, or agency-focused democratization. Pioneered by Dankwart A. Rustow, the transition paradigm is not a uniform theoretical school but instead consists of many different strands and approaches to understanding democratization.[69] Michael McFaul observes that "no single theory of transition has been universally recognized."[70] Born out of studies on a series of successful democratic transitions in Latin America and Southern Europe, transitology, in contrast to structural modernization theory, is primarily an agent-focused approach.[71] In his major critique of transitology, Thomas Carothers lists five core assumptions of this theoretical school, ranging from the essential need to end dictatorial rule in a country that intends to embark on democratization to the existence of a functional state.[72] More generally, however, Rustow's key criteria for successful transition to democracy are the existence of democratically minded elites and opportunities for an elite consensus or "pact."[73] Unlike modernization theory, which insists that democratization is path-dependent and develops as a historical process, Rustow identifies only "a single back-ground condition—national unity" as necessary for democratization.[74] For elite pacts to succeed, "a transition from dictatorship to democracy seems to depend heavily on the interests, values, and actions of political leaders."[75]

The need to explain many recent transitions away from authoritarianism has given rise to "wave theories" of democratization.[76] According to wave theorists, the early Western European transitions to democracy constitute the first and second waves, Southern European (Spain, Portugal, and Greece) transitions make up the third wave, and the collapse of communism in CEE brought about the fourth wave of democratization.[77] As McFaul explains, the wave theory of democratization prioritizes actors over structure. Indeed, when applied to post-1989 transitions to democracy in CEE, "actor-centric, cooperative approaches to democratization offer a useful starting point for explaining postcommunist regime transformations."[78] In all CEE countries, transition occurred as a result of elite bargaining and consensus among various prodemocratic forces. Such pacts and agreements among elites led to rapid democratization in Hungary, Poland, the Czech Republic, and Slovakia. Nevertheless, the failure of the majority of post-Soviet states to democratize and the lack of elite consensus among the fourth wave of transitions—which occurred as a result of color revolutions spreading across postcommunist Eurasia in the early 2000s—increased opposition to the transition paradigm.

The critique of transitology is both voluminous and multidimensional, and its key point in relation to postcommunist regions is that "pacted transition" is not possible in post-Soviet contexts.[79] As Gel'man argues, "Principal sources of political contestation in post-Soviet societies are intra-elite conflicts rather than 'pacts.'"[80] A more recent generation of transitologists has critiqued wave theorists for having abandoned the ground principles of transition paradigm, such as the focus on "transition from authoritarianism," in favor of a more "objectivist" and "anticipatory" tone of "transition to democracy."[81]

Apart from O'Donnell, who wrote about the importance of informal rules in the process of democratic consolidation, transitologists have so far paid little attention to the relationship between democratic institution-building and informal practices.[82] The major works of transitology, such as studies by the founding fathers of the transition paradigm, Terry L. Karl and Philippe C. Schmitter, make no reference to informal institutions.[83] Although both Juan J. Linz and Adam Przeworski mention other "relevant forces" in democratization processes, neither details the role of informal rules.[84] In contrast, O'Donnell insists that "the lack of fit between formal rules and observed behavior" defined by informal constraints is crucial for the effectiveness of democratization.[85] According to O'Donnell, "When informal rules are widely shared and deeply rooted," they present a particularly tough challenge for the agents of democratization.[86] Transitologists have, however, refrained from drawing further connections between democratization and informality, notwithstanding O'Donnell's contributions to defining the role of informal institutions in transitioning to democracy.

With the growing critique of transitology in postcommunist studies, some scholars of democratization have proposed "reframing" transitology into synonymous approaches.[87] For example, the observation that democratization "exhibits strong regional effects" led Bunce to propose a "diffusion" theory.[88] In accordance with that approach, democratization spreads not just in waves but as a process of cross-national diffusion.[89] The emphasis on the external dimension of democratization in diffusion theory relates it to theories of conditionality democratization, which argue for the importance of outside forces.[90] Given that authoritarian states usually have only a limited willingness and resolve to create transparent, corruption-free institutions that are accountable to their beneficiaries and efficient in providing services and other public goods, scholars have argued that an external "push" is crucial for pressuring autocratic leaders to either embrace democratization or step down.[91] Lucan A. Way and Steven Levitsky describe that "push" as "Western leverage."[92] The proponents of "external" democratization, however, warn that "international factors should be perceived as facilitating conditions, not as causes determining specific outcomes."[93] Among the strands of democratization theories, two others stand out as particularly noteworthy: institutional design theory, which associates the success of democratization with the parliamentary form of government; and political cultural theory, which prioritizes the impact of political culture on democracy.[94] But both of these theories as well as the school of "external" democratization leave little room for informality. If the institutional design and conditionality strands of democratization see informal institutions as having only marginal significance, then political cultural theory perceives informality primarily through the lens of "civic" culture.[95]

The fundamental assumption that "transitions did not always lead to democracy" has haunted advocates of all strands of democratization theories since the start of widespread failures in democratic transition across the post-Soviet region and sub-Saharan Africa.[96] Whereas researchers of Latin American democratization anticipated that once a country embarked on a transition from a dictatorial regime, it would remain on the path to democratization, in the postcommunist region, "countries that by 1994 were more democratic have stayed that way. Countries that were authoritarian have not reversed course and become democratic."[97] As Grzegorz Ekiert, Jan Kubik, and Milada Anna Vachudova observe, "In the majority of former communist states, political transformations have either lost their momentum and re-sulted in partially democratic systems or have been reversed and brought new authoritarian regimes."[98] Larry J. Diamond offers a more precise obser-vation, suggesting that "one of the most striking features of the 'late period' of the third wave has been the unprecedented growth in the number of re-gimes that are neither clearly democratic nor conventionally authoritar-ian."[99] This unexpected "diversity" of transitional regimes validated Jowitt's somber prediction during the first years of postcommunism that "most of the Eastern Europe of the future is likely to resemble the Latin America of the recent past more than the Western Europe of the present."[100] Bunce, McFaul, and Kathryn Stoner-Weiss conclude that the end of authoritarianism led not to "the rise of democracy" but, rather, to "the formation of regimes that are located in the middle of a continuum anchored by democracy at one pole and dictatorship at the other."[101]

The emergence of regimes that do not fit into the definitions of democra-cies and nondemocracies clearly delineated in the existing literature has led to the proliferation of countless new definitions for such countries.[102] By adding adjectives to either *democracy* or *authoritarianism*, political scientists have designated such regimes *semi-*, or *pseudo-*, delegative, illiberal, partial, or incomplete democracies, electoral and competitive authoritarian regimes, or simply mixed regimes.[103] The main problem with this definitional diver-sity is that while some of these definitions are too broad, others are too spe-cific. For example, O'Donnell's delegative democracies "rest *on* the premise that whoever wins election to the presidency is thereby entitled to govern as he or she sees fit, constrained only by the hard facts of existing power rela-tions and by a constitutionally limited term of office."[104] According to this definition, delegative democracies differ from authoritarian states only by possessing a commitment to free and fair elections. This classification does not take into account the resolve and willingness of such regimes to embark on democratic institution-building.

In a similar vein, Levitsky and Way define competitive authoritarian re-gimes as "civilian regimes in which formal democratic institutions exist and are widely viewed as the primary means of gaining power, but in which in-cumbents' abuse of the state places them at a significant advantage vis-à-vis their opponents."[105] Although closer to democratic regimes than delegative democracies, competitive authoritarian regimes are described as such because the competition for office in these regimes is "heavily skewed in favor of incumbents," which makes it "real but unfair."[106] Levitsky and Way further specify that competitive authoritarian states fail to democratize because they are incapable of either conducting free elections or protecting civil liberties.[107] As a result, unlike O'Donnell's concept of delegative democracy, which he applied primarily to Latin American states, the key characteristics of competitive authoritarianism can be ascribed to a vast array of political regimes. Not surprisingly, Levitsky and Way use this term to describe both Belarus, a consolidated authoritarian regime with no recent experience of free elections, and far more liberal Georgia.[108] Levitsky and Way present informal institutions as essentially detrimental to democratization and conducive to the entrenchment of competitive authoritarianism.[109]

To provide some structure in the midst of such definitional ambiguity, some studies, including this book, employ the much simpler terms of *hybrid* and *transitional regimes* when referring to states that are neither full-scale democracies nor consolidated autocracies.[110] Graeme B. Robertson explains that the term *hybrid regimes* "covers a broad range of regimes in which at least some legitimate and public political competition coexists with an organizational and institutional playing field that renders this competition unfair."[111] Carothers describes "any formerly authoritarian country that was attempting some political liberalization as a 'transitional country.'"[112] In the words of Leah Gilbert and Payam Mohseni, "This general name [*hybrid regimes*] without reference to authoritarianism or democracy is appropriate because it prevents conceptual confusion and conceptual stretching."[113] The use of such general terms as *hybrid* or *transitional regimes* is favored over more specific definitions because these regimes are as far from democracy as they are from authoritarianism. Unlike competitive authoritarianism, hybrid regimes "do not represent a single regime type but rather a range of types" that differ from each other in terms not only of their attributes and features but also in their geography-specific characteristics.[114]

In the post-Soviet context, while some hybrid regimes have bounced back to authoritarianism (Kyrgyzstan) or carried out democratic institutional reforms (Georgia), others have remained nearly static in their transition (Ukraine). The lack of transition "toward or away from ideal-type endpoints like democracy or autocracy" among post-Soviet hybrid regimes has led some scholars to believe that these regimes are not exactly transitional or hybrid but rather that they follow "cyclical phases of elite contestation and consolidation," which Hale has dubbed "patronal politics."[115] According to

Hale, "What may appear to be a country's strong shift from autocracy toward democracy at a given moment, therefore, may not be part of a 'transition' or 'trajectory' at all, because the observed shift may simply be just another swing in a fairly regular cyclical process."[116] Hale presents his concept of patronal politics as a framework of informal relationships "organized around the personalized exchange of concrete rewards and punishments through chains of actual acquaintances."[117]

The concept of patronal politics that leads to "regime cycles" echoes O'Donnell's concept of "protracted unconsolidation," which he declares took place across Latin America and Southern Europe after the third wave of democratization.[118] Both Hale and O'Donnell argue that hybrid regimes boast informal politics to their core. As O'Donnell explains, "Actors are as rational in these settings as in highly formalized ones, but the contours of their rationality cannot be traced without knowing the actual rules, and the common knowledge of these rules, that they follow."[119] These "actual" rules are usually informal constraints that define the political behavior of the elites. Bearing in mind that, as Gel'man notes, the mode of interaction among post-Soviet elites is not pacts but conflicts, informal contestation is ongoing between those elites who favor democratic changes and those who insist on maintaining the status quo.[120] Elites in charge of hybrid regimes move back and forth in their democratization efforts precisely because of these conflicts.

Contrary to transitologists' expectations, many hybrid regimes make little effort to follow the traditional "trajectory" of democratization, which Samuel P. Huntington predicts will lead to the consolidation of liberal democracy.[121] As Richard Rose and Doh Chull Shin observe, many hybrid regimes tend to introduce "competitive elections before establishing basic institutions of a modern state such as the rule of law, institutions of civil society and the accountability of governors."[122] As a consequence, democratic institutional reforms in hybrid regimes differ from institutional changes in consolidated democracies. Many of these reforms may be ushered in by informal actors who are driven by rational interests yet have only a limited understanding of effective institution-building. In addition, the concept of effective institution-building may have an entirely different interpretation among the elites in charge of these reforms in hybrid regimes. Nevertheless, one important caveat pertaining to regime cycles is that consolidated hybrid regimes rarely fall back to full-scale authoritarianism. Although the reforms may be flawed and incomplete, the actors' willingness to decentralize and formalize institutions is often sufficient to keep their countries from regressing to authoritarian states. Unlike consolidated democracies, with their relatively clearly demarcated borders between formal and informal spheres, institutional reforms in hybrid regimes depend on the formal-informal balance, leading to the contentious and ambiguous relationship between democratization and informality.

Although many existing studies on democratization prioritize formal state institutions as the key actors in democratic institutional reforms, a small but growing body of literature also emphasizes the significance of informal practices and institutions for democratization. As Helmke and Levitsky state, "Successful formal institutional engineering requires understanding the incentives and constraints that existing informal institutions impose."[123] To date, however, the literature on democratization presents the role of informal practices and institutions in the process of democratization as mainly detrimental.[124] For example, Diamond observes that even established parliamentary democracies are not entirely free of informal politics: "Democratic regimes are also 'mixed' forms of government, not only in the ways they empower institutions intentionally placed beyond the reach of elected officials (such as constitutional courts or central banks), but in less desirable respects as well."[125]

Informality in studies on democratization is usually portrayed as hidden, often illegal and illicit, and almost always negative. The irresistible yet sinful appeal of relying on informal practices seems to haunt participants in democratization at all major stages of the process. Levitsky and Way suggest "that actors frequently employ informal institutions as a 'second-best' strategy when they cannot achieve their goals through formal institutions but find the cost of changing those institutions to be prohibitive."[126] Having once used informal channels to achieve their goals, elites promoting democratic reforms can no longer resist the temptation of informality. Anna Grzymala-Busse and Pauline Jones Luong caution that if "competing elites rely primarily on informal institutions, elite turnover and succession will not occur at regularized intervals."[127] With formal institutions and the entire process of democratization disempowered and derailed, informal institutions will take over policymaking and resource distribution mechanisms.

Though seldom mentioned in classical works on democratization, informality is characterized as one of the major nemeses of democracy and as needing to be undermined for democratic institutions to exist and function effectively.[128] Once the process of democratic institutional reform is initiated, informal institutions are expected to oppose it vehemently, creating obstacles and derailing the progress of democratization. Giuseppe Di Palma asserts that "the more the reforms inch toward democratization, the more a bandwagon effect may take hold."[129] Given that informal practices and institutions serve as fundamental mechanisms of governance in autocratic regimes, sometimes occupying and dominating many areas of the public and private spheres, regime change and consequent institutional reforms cannot be expected to eradicate the behaviors and traditions inherited from the ancien régime overnight.

In many if not all undemocratic regimes, "the rule of law is replaced by the rule of informal ad hoc arrangements orchestrated by people who have no accountability operating in a mode of dirty togetherness."[130] In that light, informality may persist and continue to pervade formal institutions for decades after the beginning of the transition from dictatorship to democracy. For example, Helmke and Levitsky as well as O'Donnell note that in Latin America and Northeast Asia, informal institutions endured well after the start of democratization and that although some informal practices disappeared over time, others continue to exist.[131] The Mexican informal practice of *dedazo* (big finger), which involves the informal selection of presidential candidates and other top-ranking politicians by their predecessors, survived well after the start of democratization and did not disappear until decades later.[132] Both the Japanese practice of *amakudari* and the South Korean "parachute appointments," which allocate top positions in private companies to retired high-ranking politicians, have never been fully eradicated.[133]

In ex-socialist countries, "informal institutions and practices appear to be equally important in shaping and in some cases eroding democracy."[134] As Grzymala-Busse details, informal practices and institutions continue to perform countless functions in party politics of postcommunist democracies.[135] Jacques Rupnik and Jan Zielonka illustrate that even after Bulgaria and Romania's joined the European Union, "formal democratic institutions have continued to work in the shadow of informal 'networks' and persistent patterns of political culture."[136] In other cases, such as Poland, prodemocratization actors "managed to divert [the] democratic agenda from reforming the formal institutions to haunting informal networks: 'układ' as they call it in Polish."[137]

Because most successful cases of democratization in postcommunist Europe occurred either in CEE or among Baltic republics, Grzymala-Busse and Luong suggest that in those ex-socialist countries "where formal state structures were more developed"—Poland, Hungary, and the Czech Republic— "informal institutions augmented the formal."[138] On the contrary, those postcommunist regimes "where the central state apparatus was not well-developed," such as in most post-Soviet countries, "traditional patronage networks developed under Soviet rule came to define the political and economic system itself."[139] Even in those postcommunist countries that boast successful transformation, however, "building informal alliances and coalitions is the daily bread of democratic politics. Lobbying by NGOs or interest groups also tends to be informal."[140] In this light, notwithstanding occasional references to informality's neutral or positive effects on democratization in new postcommunist democracies, most scholars remain cautious and distrustful of the role of informal practices and institutions in democratic institution-building.

The literature addressing the relationship between democratization and informality in tones less hostile toward informality is much smaller. O'Donnell was among the first to suggest that unlike formal rules that exist on paper, informal rules in new democracies are the "actual rules" that work.[141] Though Hans-Joachim Lauth describes the relationship between formal and informal instructions over the course of democratization as that of competition (with one type of institution replacing the other) and of conflict, he also acknowledges that informal rules may complement formal ones.[142] Helmke and Levitsky support that opinion, pointing out that "informal institutions merit our attention because they shape how democracy works—for both good and ill."[143] They argue that "informal rules shape how democratic institutions work" in several areas of democratic politics, among them political representation, democratic accountability, democratic governance, and the rule of law.[144] The key argument proposed by those who view informality as not necessarily or exclusively negative for democratization is that informal rules work in the shadow of formal ones and thus have effects that are often hidden from observers. Applying empirically rich evidence from numerous Latin American cases, Helmke and Levitsky hypothesize that in those areas of governance "where formal state and regime institutions are weak, ineffective, or insufficiently democratic, informal rules may enhance the performance and stability of democracy."[145]

Nevertheless, this argument has thus far received little support from scholars of post-Soviet societies, who maintain almost unequivocally that informal practices and institutions across the ex-Soviet space have been anything but conducive to democratization.[146] In reality, however, post-Soviet

informal practices and institutions may not be more pernicious than informal structures in Latin American countries or in other case studies of successful democratization. Like other developing regions of the world, ex-
Soviet autocracies and hybrid regimes alike employ informal channels as
"actual rules" that work as the second-best alternative to nonexistent or
weak democratic institutions. For example, Wedel theorizes that rather than
being perceived as detrimental to democratic institution-building, "informal groups and networks that functioned under communism and helped to
ensure stability . . . could become crucial instruments of change" during
postcommunist institutionalization.[147] The most obvious divergence between many Latin American countries and the post-Soviet region lies not in
the degree of informality's maliciousness but in the lack of efforts to implement democratic institutional changes. Post-Soviet elites' attempts to democratically reform their institutions, decentralize, liberalize, and formalize
formal structures were few and far between.

DEMOCRATIC INSTITUTIONAL REFORMS
IN THE POST-SOVIET REGION

With few exceptions, such as the cases of Georgia, Moldova, and Ukraine,
democratic institutional reforms in non-Baltic successor states of the former
Soviet Union were never an elite priority. Apart from a few examples of "color
revolutions," such as the Georgian Rose Revolution and Ukrainian Orange
Revolution as well as the more recent Ukrainian Euromaidan and Kyrgyz Tulip Revolution, the initial openings needed for the initiation of democratic
institutional reforms never occurred. Controlled regime succession, elite
continuity, rigged elections, persecution of opposition forces, and many
other typical characteristics of authoritarianism became firmly established
in a majority of former Soviet republics.

One post-Soviet region that has appeared particularly impervious to democratization is Central Asia, with the exception of Kyrgyzstan. The other
four Central Asian republics—Kazakhstan, Tajikistan, Turkmenistan, and
Uzbekistan—are among the most entrenched cases of authoritarianism in
the world. Turkmenistan has been the least affected by either external or internal democratization since independence from the Soviet Union in 1991.
The 2006 death of Saparmurat Niyazov, the country's former communist
leader, and his replacement by Gurbanguly Berdimuhamedov has brought

no notable changes with the regard to democratic institution-building. Lu-ong describes the pace of economic reform in Turkmenistan as perhaps the slowest in the former Soviet Union (fSU).[148] Similarly, Tajikistan has been controlled by its former communist leader, Emomali Rakhmonov, since 1992, and he has made no effort to reform state institutions. In Uzbekistan, too, the president, Islam Karimov, is a former communist leader who has re-mained in power since the dissolution of the USSR. As Kathleen Collins notes, "Democratization and economic reform" have not been on his agenda.[149] Amid the failure of anticorruption reform, Uzbekistan continues to occupy the lowest positions on international corruption ratings.[150] In a similar vein, the reform of local government resulted in centralization of lo-cal communities (*mahallas*) and their complete dependence on the incum-bent.[151] Kazakhstan, which implemented "extensive market reforms," is also ruled by a former communist apparatchik, Nursultan Nazarbayev, who has been in power since the country's independence from the USSR.[152] Despite Nazarbayev's success in modernizing Kazakhstan's oil- and gas-dependent economy, the country has not promoted democratic political reforms and a transition to market economy, though it also has not openly rejected democ-ratization.[153] As in other Central Asian republics, anticorruption campaigns have thus far been largely ineffective in Kazakhstan.[154]

The Central Asian regimes (with the exception of Tajikistan) have re-mained highly dependent on energy rents by either relying on their fairly extensive deposits of fossil fuels or serving as energy transit routes. The re-sult, as Collins observes, has been "limited liberalization of the economy."[155] Freedom House's Nations in Transit project ranks all four countries as con-solidated authoritarian states, defined by unconditional dominance of a "su-perpresidential" executive branch dependent on regional power bases and by the prevalence of informal politics and the complete lack of institutional checks and balances.[156] Collins observes that since Kazakhstan, Tajikistan, and Uzbekistan gained independence in 1992, "behind their formal facades, all three Central Asian regimes are moving toward government by roughly the same kind of informal politics."[157] Although these regimes have formally adopted democratic rhetoric and pledged commitment to democratic re-forms, Kazakh, Tajik, and Uzbek elites favor democratic reforms only as long as they benefit from "distributive gains."[158] For incumbents in Turkmeni-stan, Kazakhstan, Uzbekistan, and Tajikistan, democratizing their state insti-tutions would mean the loss of control over the networks of resource distri-bution and their ultimate removal from the political scene.

Belarus under Aleksandr Lukashenka has been branded "Europe's last dictatorship," and like the four Central Asian republics remains resistant to democratic institutional changes.[159] After an initial opening in 1994 when Lukashenka came to power as a result of relatively free and fair elections, he replaced the parliamentary system with a superpresidential and centralized executive branch.[160] With Belarus's economy crippled since the financial crisis of 2008–9 and in a bid to move away from its growing economic and political dependency on Russia, Lukashenka has on a number of occasions indicated his willingness to launch political liberalization to receive assistance from the West. But despite his eloquent 2013 announcement that "the period of dictatorship is over; we are transforming to democracy from next year," no efforts to reform the country's formal institutions have occurred.[161]

Not far from Belarus in terms of democratic institutional reforms is the South Caucasian republic of Azerbaijan. Like Belarus, Azerbaijan had an initial opening for democratization in 1993, when the former head of the communist government, Heydar Aliyev, ousted nationalist leader Abulfaz Elchibey.[162] Democratically elected as the second president of Azerbaijan, Aliyev, however, continued to rely on his communist-era patronage networks to strengthen the presidential apparatus. As Bunce and Sharon Wolchik describe, democratic politics have not taken root in postcommunist Azerbaijan.[163] Aliyev died in 2003 and was succeeded by his son, Ilham Aliyev, who continued the country's autocratic modes of governance. Under the Aliyevs' rule, Azerbaijan has formally pursued a democratic reform agenda. However, Azerbaijan's "national strategy is still *de facto* not oriented toward democratization."[164] Börzel and Pamuk find that "the efforts of Azerbaijan's authorities to fight corruption have focused on strengthening the state apparatus, expanding its control over society and fostering the power of the incumbents."[165]

As a result of anticorruption reforms that purged unreliable officials by replacing them with proregime proxies, "political corruption has gained [more] prominence."[166] Irrespective of formal commitments to democracy and occasional cleanups of state institutions, "tightly organized patronage networks permeate the public sphere and help sustain a stable equilibrium of informal institutions."[167] According to Bunce and Wolchik, the Azerbaijani regime's stability and survival are based in the continuity of informal networks "because those involved in these networks, which reach down to the lower layers of the apparatus and permeate all sectors of the economy, realize that all will lose if the regime changes."[168] Described by Hale as a typical example of patronal politics, Ilham Aliyev's regime depends on informal clientelistic networks in a way that is likely to prevent any democratic institution-building in the near future.[169]

Unlike these ex-Soviet regimes, which are defined as well-entrenched authoritarian states, the South Caucasian republic of Armenia is classified as a semiconsolidated authoritarian or partly free regime.[170] Following the collapse of the USSR, a former dissident and prodemocracy activist, Levon Ter-Petrosian, was popularly elected as the first president of Armenia. Notwithstanding this initial opening and his officially prodemocratic stance, democratization has failed to occur, with Ter-Petrosian widely accused of harassing free media, civil society, and opposition parties.[171] Attempts to implement institutional reforms were informal pacts made by the elites. As Babken Babajanian describes, the Armenian government since the 1990s has pursued active decentralization policies targeting not only the economic sector but also social welfare and the construction of institutions of local governance.[172] Nevertheless, the reforms have failed to encourage democratization and instead have contributed to the further growth of informal institutions.[173] In Babajanian's assessment, rather than resulting in the creation of a functional welfare system, neoliberal reforms increased the population's use of informal channels for welfare distribution.[174] And as with welfare reforms, efforts to implement institutional changes in other sectors have led to the establishment of "two parallel systems of governance"— one formal (framed by the state) and one informal (clientelistic networks that holds the "actual power" in both the allocation of economic resources and in political decision-making).[175] Amid widespread protests, Ter-Petrosian won a second term in rigged 1996 presidential elections; however, a loss of support in parliament and popular disapproval forced him to resign by late the following year.

The 1998 presidential elections that brought to power former prime minister Robert Kocharian were neither free nor fair. Over Kocharian's two terms in office, the presidential apparatus further strengthened, and Armenia steadily transformed from a semipresidential regime to a superpresidential regime. Anticorruption reforms during this period were largely ineffective and served "as an instrument of internal power struggle," allowing ruling elites to strengthen their control over both formal and informal institutions.[176] In 2008, Kocharian's handpicked successor, Serzh Sarkisian, won election to the presidency.

That election and Sarkisian's successful 2013 bid for a second term in office as well as the intervening parliamentary elections have been described as generally "well-administered" but filled with widespread irregularities and electoral fraud.[177] Despite two openings for democratization (in 1992 and 1998) and the presence of relatively free civil society and independent mass media, Armenian elites' have shown little willingness to implement democratic institutional reforms. Regardless of Armenia's formal support for democratization, all of the country's governments have continued to rely heavily on informal modes of governance. As a result, every attempt to reform state institutions was either cosmetic—designed to please the European Union and other international actors and thus secure much-needed economic cooperation—or directed at strengthening informal channels.

In contrast, the main successor of the Soviet Union, the Russian Federation, has undergone a lengthy institutional metamorphosis during which it regressed from a hybrid state or even a semiconsolidated democracy into a consolidated authoritarian regime. Widely termed a "managed democracy" under Boris Yeltsin, a "sovereign democracy" during Vladimir Putin's first term in office, and a hybrid regime under Dmitry Medvedev, the Russian Federation is currently classified as a full-scale autocracy.[178] On its road to authoritarianism, Russia passed through numerous openings for democratization, which made many scholars believe that the country was indeed on its way to building a democracy.[179] The ascent to power of Yeltsin, a democrat who promised to build a democracy and a market economy on the ashes of the Soviet empire, was followed by neoliberal "shock therapy" reforms unprecedented for the fSU. Yeltsin's administration planned key measures to liberalize the Russian economy, among them mass privatization, large-scale liberalization of the private sector, and significant budgetary constraints on state enterprises.[180]

A voluminous body of literature discusses the scope and scale of democratic institutional reforms in Yeltsin's Russia, and further exploration of the subject lies beyond the limits of this book. Noteworthy here, however, nearly all major institutional changes either purposefully or accidentally led to the decline of institutional quality and deterioration of the rule of law, and Russia's state institutions failed to become either more formalized or more liberal. As Hale describes, all of Yeltsin's major economic and political institutional reforms—privatization, decentralization and semipresidentialism—were mismanaged and led to the deformalization of the state.[181] If poorly coordinated mass privatization encouraged the appearance of oligarchs, then regional autonomy increased the powers of governors and regional administrators who had limited accountability to the federal center. Instead of decentralizing the executive branch, Yeltsin's experiments with semipresidentialism ended with the conversion of a parliamentary-presidential regime into a superpresidential regime.

In 2000, when the reins of power were transferred to Yeltsin's chosen successor, Vladimir Putin, Russia's political system, though disorderly, remained geared toward democratic state-building. But unlike Yeltsin's botched efforts, particularly during his first term in office, to liberalize and decentralize Russia's institutions, Putin has worked to centralize the unmanageable institutional scene, constructing his own "vertical of power" (*vertikal' vlasti*). Reconstructing the judiciary, strengthening coordination between federal and regional legislation, and centralizing and monopolizing the executive branch at the expense of legislative and media freedom were among the main components of Putin's institutional reform.

The ensuing inevitable confrontation with oligarchs has ended in the "purge" of Boris Berezovsky, Vladimir Gusinsky, Mikhail Khodorkovsky, and many other oligarchs unwilling to comply with the Kremlin.[182] The appointment of federal envoys to control the newly created federal districts (*okrugs*) curbed regional autonomy.[183] In the aftermath of the 2004 Beslan school massacre, the law on direct election of regional governors was scrapped in favor of a direct appointment system controlled by the president.[184] The recentralization aimed at disempowering of regional centers was accompanied by the strengthening of power ministries (*siloviki*) and the buildup of power networks (*sistema*). Of all the major institutional changes implemented during Putin's first presidency, the 2004 administrative reform to reduce the number of state bureaucrats was deemed to be the most democratic.[185]

Nevertheless, the rise of informal governance—crucial to Putin's control over formal institutions—occurred alongside democratic reforms. As Ledeneva observes, by the end of Putin's second term in office, "it had become clear that the World Bank–backed administrative reforms, which aimed to reduce and restructure the role of the state, had proved ineffective against the network-driven growth of bureaucracy."[186] Instead of formalizing Russia's state institutions, as Regina Smyth, Anna Lowry, and Brandon Wilkening note, "the Kremlin's reform program brought formal institutions in line with coercive informal institutions."[187] Though Putin's institutional reforms undoubtedly strengthened and modernized frail formal institutions, Russian institution-building was never aimed at either formalizing or liberalizing institutions. In contrast, the informal institutions and networks that the

Russian government employed "to promote its modernisation agenda" have played a prominent role in Russia's institutional reform.[188] Not surprisingly, as Ledeneva notes, the ruling elites have had "no strategic plan or practical capacity to reform" the *sistema* networks.[189] In Putin's Russia, both formal and informal institutions are managed and regulated by the state, creating a formal/informal symbiosis that Smyth, Lowry, and Wilkening label "two different sets of rules."[190] Sakwa consequently hypothesizes that Russia has two types of state order: one is based on "the formal constitutional order, what we call the *normative state*," while the other functions on informal clientelistic networks that ensure the smooth functioning, accountability, and subordination of formal institutions to the presidential apparatus.[191]

This formal-informal dualism, however, is not unique to Russia.[192] It is also widely present in most other ex-Soviet autocracies, where formal state institutions are informalized to the degree that their work depends on an underlying ensemble of informal networks. Given that political elites purposefully install and integrate informal institutions into their formal counterparts, the post-Soviet dual state differs from the institutional dualism of the Soviet Union. If Soviet authorities saw informality as pernicious for their institutions and had limited mechanisms to control it, then post-Soviet autocracies calculatingly harness and sustain informal institutions to maintain the loyalty and accountability of formal institutions. Gel'man explains that this system of mutual codependence has enabled informal institutions to dominate Russian politics "both by design and by default."[193]

By 2008, when Putin bequeathed his institutional framework to his chosen successor, Dmitry Medvedev, who was elected in one of the "free but unfair elections" typical under Putinism, informal institutionalization of the state was close to completion.[194] Though viewed by some as another opening for democratization, Medvedev's presidency has been marked by the continuity of rules of institutional conduct established under Putin.[195] As Gel'man argues, "'Informal institutionalisation' deserves to be viewed not as a temporary 'defect' of post-Soviet democracy . . . but rather as a long-term principal feature of Russia's political regime."[196]

Since the start of Putin's third presidency in 2012, and particularly after the imposition of Western sanctions on Russia after the annexation of Crimea and Russian actions in eastern Ukraine in 2014, no attempts to implement liberal institutional reforms have occurred. As Thomas Ambrosio describes, measures undertaken by Putin's administration to "insulate" itself from external democratization or the "negative" influence of color revolutions in neighboring post-Soviet republics include a standard authoritarian "tool-set" that combines repressive policies against civil society and free mass media with an increase in proregime propaganda.[197] Both the former and the latter have been implemented in conjunction with a further strengthening of the presidential apparatus, leading to the gradual transformation into absolute superpresidentialism. Following Russian involvement in Ukraine, the Putin regime's growing insecurity at home and increasing isolation abroad have prompted the regime to tighten its control over both formal and informal (*sistema*) institutions. As detailed in the 2014 report by the Nations in Transit project, Russia experienced institutional deterioration not only in areas of national and local governance, which have declined steadily since the mid-2000s, but also in terms of the openness and independence of the judicial framework and freedom of association.

Finally, more than any of these other ex-Soviet countries, Kyrgyzstan has bounced back and forth in its democratic institution-building since the end of Soviet rule. The only post-Soviet regime other than Georgia and Ukraine to experience a successful color revolution, Kyrgyzstan is currently just one step away from becoming a hybrid regime. To date, however, the formal-informal institutional balance in Kyrgyzstan has not favored democratization. Kyrgyzstan differs from its Central Asian neighbors not only because the dissolution of the USSR brought to power a former dissident and prodemocracy advocate, Askar Akayev, but also because Akayev's regime—at least during its early years—pursued an agenda of active democratic reform. Whereas the other Central Asian republics have opposed democratization and been exceptionally slow to embark on the transition to market economy, Kyrgyzstan "rapidly adopted democratic and market reforms."[198] Brought to power as a result of free and fair elections, Akayev's government adopted a liberal constitution, ensured separation of powers, and established transparent electoral laws. Massive decentralization of regional administration was accompanied by the rapid expansion of independent civil society and relatively free mass media.[199]

As a consequence of these rather extensive (by fSU standards) institutional reforms during the first years of Akayev's presidency, "a far-reaching *process* of democratization did get under way" in Kyrgyzstan.[200] Nevertheless, that process was flawed. Akayev's autocratic tendencies began surfacing early in his efforts to consolidate presidential powers. Regional decentralization was achieved not so much through the empowerment of regional administrations as through pacts with regional elites, who received greater shares of resource distribution in return for supporting the regime. Under Akayev, both political offices and financial assets were distributed through patronage networks associated with clans, ethnic Kyrgyz elites, and regional power centers. It soon became obvious that in the absence of attempts to break up the clientilistic networks that formed Akayev's power base, institutional reforms would remain ineffective. As Collins observes, "The rise of vested clan interests has blocked or corrupted economic reforms, and has blocked further political reforms that might benefit society but undo their economic gains."[201] As Bunce and Wolchik point out, by the mid-1990s, Akayev no longer had any interest in conducting free and fair elections.[202] In the late 1990s, amid rampant corruption and institutional informalization, the regime's commitment to democratic institution-building began to wane. After his victory in the 2000 presidential elections—achieved mainly through intimidation of opposition and ballot rigging—Akayev lost support from the majority of his patronage networks. According to Luong, "Regional leaders' growing influence over political and economic reform made them confident that they would ultimately be successful in establishing the electoral law that they preferred."[203] Some scholars argue that the Tulip Revolution—mass protests that followed fraudulent 2005 parliamentary elections that ousted Akayev from power—were organized by the political opposition and civil society.[204] However, a compelling body of evidence suggests that the key organizers of anti-Akayev protests were regional elites dissatisfied with the results of the parliamentary elections who sought to remove the president as a means of gaining access to government positions that they had previously been denied.[205]

Akayev's successor, Kurmanbek Bakiyev, was elected president in 2005, receiving 89 percent of the vote in elections praised as free and transparent. Despite this second opening for democratization, Bakiyev was even less interested in conducting institutional reforms than his predecessor. Redistribution of government offices and a struggle over control of profitable industries marked Bakiyev's first years in office. In 2006–7, a series of opposition-organized rallies demanding Bakiyev's resignation led only to a further consolidation of the presidential powers.[206] In 2007, under pressure from the political opposition, Bakiyev adopted constitutional amendments designed to allocate more powers to parliament. By formally limiting the executive branch, however, he continued to further expand informal power networks. In Hale's observation, the "electoral process, media independence, democratic governance, and judicial independence were all as bad or worse by 2009 than they had been immediately before the Tulip Revolution."[207] After violent demonstrations, Bakiyev fled the country in 2010, and an interim government held a referendum proposing extensive constitutional changes. A new constitution adopted that year allocated greater powers to parliament, thereby transforming the country into a parliamentary republic.

The Kyrgyz government continues to pursue an active institutional reform program enshrined in the 2010 constitution. A series of administrative changes that includes land, police, and judicial reforms is ongoing.[208] Unlike the ex-Soviet regimes examined here, Kyrgyzstan currently has a functional albeit flawed parliamentary system and regularly holds free and competitive elections. Notwithstanding the government's efforts to introduce legislation curbing free mass media and restricting the work of foreign-funded civil society organizations, the country has a far more liberal civil sector than its Central Asian neighbors do. Nevertheless, the process of democratic institutional reforms remains sluggish and inefficient. Despite some improvements in local and national democratic governance, rampant corruption and nepotism as well as public officials' widespread use of informal institutions still pose crucial obstacles to the reform process. The newly created parliamentary system remains in competition with the executive office, occupied by Almazbek Atambayev. The president's informal efforts to influence parliamentary decisions continued throughout 2013–14.[209] As the formalization of state institutions has not been systematically implemented, formal institutions are still weak and plagued by graft, nepotism, and patronage. The actual power centers remain in regional elites rather than in formal institutions. Representatives of these regional power bases in parliament fail to represent the interests of their constituencies but rather continue to prioritize the interests of the clans and cliques that helped them get elected. Kyrgyzstan thus remains a semiconsolidated authoritarian regime. In contrast to the superpresidential autocracies of other Central Asian republics, Azerbaijan, Belarus, and Russia, Kyrgyzstan is a unique case of "clannish-parliamentary" authoritarianism.

Among the undemocratic and nonhybrid ex-Soviet regimes, Kyrgyzstan not only had the largest number of initial openings but also—unlike Russia and Armenia—made good use of these opportunities to advance toward democratization. Provided that the Kyrgyz elites continue to pursue ongoing democratic institutional reforms and emphasize institutional liberalization and modernization, the country might be expected to transform into a hybrid regime in the near future. However, the limited scope and lack of efficiency of post-2010 institutional reforms mean that discussion of the relationship between democratic reforms and informality in Kyrgyzstan is unlikely at this time to produce valuable insights into the causal connection between democratization and informalization of post-Soviet institutions. As in Russia, institutionalization in Kyrgyzstan has been closely followed by uninterrupted informalization of formal institutions, which have become purposefully integrated with and homogenized into informal structures. In such semiformal regimes, the functioning of formal facade institutions, their accountability to political elites, and the rationale for their existence depend on the less visible but omnipresent entourage of informal networks and practices. As with formal-informal institutional relations in full-scale authoritarian regimes, informal institutions in semiconsolidated autocracies sustain, reinforce, and insulate formal institutions. Planned and institutionalized efforts to separate formal governance from informal networking have not yet been attempted either in Kyrgyzstan or in other semiconsolidated autocracies.

Thus, semiauthoritarian regimes, with their ad hoc (Kyrgyzstan) or facade (Armenia) reform processes, are poorly suited for analysis of the impact of democratic institutional change on informal practices and institutions. In other words, regardless of the formal commitment to institutional reforms, the "reformist" elements among the ruling elites of semiautocratic regimes are either too fragmented to effectively conduct the reforms or are simply determined to implement cosmetic reforms aimed at satisfying international donors and legitimizing the regimes. On the contrary, the stronger commitments to formalizing and liberalizing formal institutions evidenced in hybrid regimes make them convenient laboratories for the analysis of democratization's impact on informality.

SUMMARY

The topic of institutional change has occupied a prominent place in recent research on institutions in political science and economics alike. The association between institutional transformation and informality nevertheless remains underinvestigated. While the dominant strands of institutional theories maintain differing approaches to understanding the process of institutional change and its association with informal structures, they generally agree that institutional transformation and informality are closely intertwined.

Although the relationship between democratic reforms and informal rules is not easily discerned, in transitional contexts, informal institutions and practices exert a powerful and often decisive influence on the outcomes of democratization. Notwithstanding the widespread bias against informality among scholars of democratization, the relationship between democratic institutional change and informal institutions and practices is context-bound and filtered through a number of intervening variables. Of these, the regime type and elites' commitment to reforms are among the key factors behind the impact of democratization on informality.

Because many post-Soviet regimes have made little or no attempts to formalize their institutions and have instead continued to foster and enhance informal structures, investigation of institutional reforms' impact on informality in undemocratic regimes cannot explain causal connections between democratization and informality. Consequently, this book examines only those ex-Soviet countries classified as hybrid regimes—that is, those that have systematically and purposefully sought to formalize, liberalize, and decentralize their state institutions.

CHAPTER 4

Georgia: Reforming an Informal State into a Hybrid Regime

THIS CHAPTER EXAMINES the first of the three case studies that empirically explore the relationship between democratic institutional change and informality in post-Soviet regimes. In its modern history, the small South Caucasian Republic of Georgia has transformed from a textbook case study of one of the most corrupt and informal socialist societies into a role model of post-Soviet institution-building and an example of the most successful anticorruption campaign in the post-Soviet space. As a consequence of the complex formal-informal synthesis that accompanied Georgia's miraculous transformations, Georgian institutional reforms illustrate an institutional metamorphosis. Georgia was notorious as one of the most informal Soviet republics, and it remained highly affected by informality since the demise of the USSR. In addition, the Republic of Georgia also became the first post-Soviet state to purposefully attempt to reform informal institutions. This chapter explores the informal practices and institutions of Georgia from the Soviet period, through Eduard Shevardnadze's and Mikheil Saakashvili's presidencies. This empirical examination of Georgia's informal sphere is a first-of-its-kind research effort to map Georgian informality beyond the realms of informal economy. The chapter begins with a comprehensive analysis of the country's contemporary informal institutions before examining the impact of institutional reforms on informal practices and institutions.

THE ROOTS OF INFORMALITY

Informality has for centuries been an inextricable part of Georgians' political, economic, and social life. Bounded by the southern edge of the Greater

93

Caucasus range, the northern foothills of the Lesser Caucasus, and the Black Sea in the west, the Republic of Georgia is inhabited by numerous ethnic subgroups of Kartvelian people collectively known as Georgians.[1] Despite the strong regional identities of Georgian subgroups and the variety of dialects spoken across contemporary Georgia, Georgian subgroups share similar culture, history, and religion (predominantly Orthodox Christianity). A nation of only 3.7 million people, Georgia has produced not only a few notorious historical figures such as Joseph Stalin but also internationally acknowledged artists such as Niko Pirosmani. Like other ethnic groups in the wider Caucasus region but unlike Russians and other Central and Eastern European nations, Georgians have traditionally lived in tightly knit patriarchal kinship groups that value family honor and intragroup bonding.

The reliance on informal networks—based on immediate family and blood kinship—cemented by traditional gatherings or feasts involving family and friends (*supra*), has always been part of Georgian culture.[2] This deeply entrenched sociocultural tradition of bonding social capital and fostering informal networks has historically led to the belief that Georgians favor informality over formal institutions.[3] Many scholars have often associated extensive informal economy, high levels of corruption, and endemic disregard of formal institutions—intrinsic to Georgians throughout the communist and immediate postcommunist periods—with tightly knit nuclear families and a highly developed culture of interpersonal networking.[4] Other scholars have argued that the entrenchment of informality and the disdain for state institutions among Georgians are a direct result of the centuries-long foreign domination of the Georgian state.[5] Georgia has had only limited modern experience with independent statehood—less than four years between the Bolshevik Revolution and its incorporation into the USSR in 1921. Before the dissolution of the Soviet Union, "the state was never seen as constituted by or for the people but was instead a force imposed from the outside."[6] Since Georgia's incorporation into the Russian Empire in the early nineteenth century, Georgians mistrusted and disrespected first tsarist and later Soviet state institutions.

However, associating the emergence of Georgia's culture of informality with the country's reliance on kinship networks and historical disdain of alien institutions is insufficient to explain either the persistence of informality after the fall of the USSR or the effectiveness of formalization under Saakashvili. Therefore, a more nuanced analysis of Georgian informality is required to understand why Georgian society has remained informal for generations and why the institutional reforms implemented in the aftermath of the Rose Revolution have specifically targeted the culture of informality.

Soviet Georgia

Informal institutions and practices flourished in Georgia for centuries, but Georgians did not engage extensively in developing informal networks until after the Georgian kingdoms and principalities became incorporated into the Russian Empire. The main venue for networking and the generation of vibrant social capital were the lavish and luxurious traditional feasts. These *supra* provided family and individual prestige for Georgians, lasting for several days and requiring substantial financial investments.[7] Along with magnifying a person's reputation among friends and kin members, *supra* could provide new contacts, offer opportunities to seal business deals, and cement personal networks. According to one expert on Georgian society, "With the end of feudal warfare and relative economic stability, building up interpersonal networks and feasting became most cherished occupations for Georgians."[8]

The October 1917 Bolshevik Revolution and subsequent collapse of tsarist administration in the Caucasus brought enormous changes to Georgia. Though Bolshevik-era purges and the persecution of anti-Soviet dissent were less brutal in Georgia than in other parts of the Caucasus, Stalin and his right-hand man, Lavrentiy Beria, who was in charge of the republic, kept an iron grip on Georgia during the 1930s and 1940s. Nevertheless, as Stalin's native republic, Georgia continued to enjoy a special status—and to receive lavish subsidies and massive investments—until the Soviet leader's death in 1953. During Stalin's tenure, Georgia developed from a backward colonial province of the tsarist empire into one of the most vibrant Soviet republics.[9] Even under Stalin, however, Georgians and the other ethnic groups that inhabited the Caucasus fiercely opposed the Soviet policy of collectivization, which sought to organize peasants into farming communities, kolkhozy.[10] Nikita Khrushchev's 1956 denunciation of Stalinism signaled the start of Georgian alienation from the Soviet Union.[11] Georgians' disillusionment with communism became evident in a systemic disregard for tenets of Marxism-Leninism and en masse subversion of the Soviet command economy. The end of Stalin's era both weakened Georgians' sense of Soviet identity and decreased the likelihood of brutal repressions and purges. According to Louise Shelley, Georgians "ethnic identity, family and immediate community became central, a tradition that fostered nepotism."[12] It is, however, unclear when exactly Georgia became "arguably the most corrupt Soviet republic" and the hotbed of the socialist informal economy.[13] Nonetheless, most communist-era records date the informalization of the Georgian Soviet Socialist Republic to the early 1950s.[14] Following Beria's 1953 arrest and execution, Khrushchev's *nomenklatura* cleansed the Georgian administration of Stalin's cadres and appointed Khrushchev's protégé, Vasil Mzhavanadze, as first secretary of the Communist Party of the Georgian Soviet Socialist Republic.

During Mzhavanadze's almost two decades as first secretary, the republic's formal economy posted a rather unremarkable performance. Between the 1950s and 1960s, Moscow invested billions of rubles into developing Georgia. However, a great share of the money settled in the pockets of corrupt officials at all administrative levels.[15] As Alexander Kupatadze details, throughout the 1960s, Georgia's national income remained one of the lowest in the USSR, yet "the average Georgian savings account was nearly twice as large as the Soviet average."[16] The informal economy was flourishing in Georgia on a scale unknown and unimaginable in other Soviet republics. For example, more than half of Georgia's cattle were in private households, as was more than 70 percent of the construction industry, home repairs, and furniture production.[17] Almost half of agricultural production on kolkhoz lands was done privately, and many Georgian farmers cultivated private patches.

J. W. R. Parsons has commented that "yields on private plots are twice as high and it is widely acknowledged that the quality of privately grown produce is far superior."[18] Enjoying the advantage of subtropical climate near the Black Sea, Georgian farmers reaped enormous profits from informal exports of citrus fruits, which were scarce in the USSR. In David Law's assessment, "The extent of private trade in Georgian fruit across the USSR [was] infamous."[19] According to Shelley, "Enriched by the sale of their sought-after citrus fruits, ordinary Georgian farmers often enjoyed incomes 10 times those of the average Soviet worker."[20] Since private produce—exported by Georgians with the help of interpersonal networks to Russia—exceeded officially produced goods, Georgia's standard of living improved.

Georgians were not only richer than other Soviet nations but also more educated.[21] Whereas 25 percent of Russians, 23 percent of Ukrainians, and 10 percent of Moldavians completed secondary education, more than 40 percent of Georgians did so.[22] While long waiting lists for state-built apartments prevented millions of people in the rest of the USSR from having their own flats, Georgian officials illegally established apartment buildings and distributed apartments as they saw fit.[23] Hundreds of luxurious private mansions mushroomed along the Georgian Black Sea coast. As Parsons wrote in 1982, "The scope [that informality] achieved in Georgia in the 1960s remains unrivalled."[24] Not surprisingly, during the 1960s and 1970s, Western economists used Soviet Georgia as a classic case study of the informal economy, and Sovietologists portrayed Georgia as an example of the failure of Soviet Marxism-Leninism.[25]

The efficient functioning of an informal economy on such an immense scale would have been impossible without participation of state and party officials. Soviet Georgia had what were arguably the USSR's highest levels of nepotism and political corruption. As Fyodor Razzakov points out, positions within the Communist Party of the Soviet Union (CPSU) or in ministries sold for between one hundred thousand and five hundred thousand rubles, depending on the type of job.[26] Corruption thrived at all administrative levels, both within and outside of the CPSU, and reached all the way up to Mzhavanadze's office, which collected the highest bribes. In complete contradiction to communist dogmas, everything was for sale in Soviet Georgia: positions, property, real estate, educational credentials, and even entire industries.[27] As Parsons outlines, "Such was the extent of corruption in the administration and the economy that many in the USSR began to question whether Soviet power still existed in Georgia."[28]

Although the bulk of research on Georgian informality focuses on the scale and specifics of the informal economy and corruption, scholars have also acknowledged that the prevalence of informality is ingrained in Georgia's sociocultural organization. For example, Gerald Mars and Yochanan Altman argue that the Georgian informal economy thrived on a complex network of interpersonal relations, which the authors define as the "cultural bases" of the informal economy.[29] In Altman's observation, Soviet Georgia possessed two types of informal networks, social and resource networks.[30] Whereas social networks were confined to family circles, resource networks extended into work *kollektivs* and were primarily employed to gain access to resources unavailable within social networks. Networks were carefully maintained and developed, and contacts and connections were passed from one generation to another. In Mars and Altman's view, a Georgian "man's personal support network is his most important social resource; the means by which bureaucracies are circumvented, through which significant contacts are effected and deals arranged."[31]

Accumulation of personal wealth, access to imported luxury goods, and the ability to organize impressive feasts were central to the Georgian social culture under Soviet rule. During the decades of "Brezhnev's stasis," well-off Georgians engaged in unprecedented attempts to display personal wealth and influence, competing to organize the most extravagant *supra*, with some items shipped directly from Moscow or even from beyond the Iron Curtain.[32]

Unlike informal actors in Central Asia, who engaged in illicit trade and in informal employment to provide sustenance to their large kinship groups, those Georgians who sustained the thriving informal sphere were "gambling entrepreneurs concerned to spend and to display."[33] Acquiring and displaying wealth were a means of increasing one's family status and therefore involved issues of family and individual honor. Under such circumstances, "decisions are submitted to honour commitments" and "every role holder is network-bounded," making engagement in informal practices essential for all household members.[34] Hence, masses of Georgians relied on informal channels not necessarily out of material need; rather, "the degree to which networks in Georgia are institutionalized as a means of linking individuals through trust-based honour commitments" conditioned popular participation in informal activities in all areas of daily life.[35]

Parsons explains the rise of informality in Georgia as encouraged by the lack of legal opportunities to accumulate wealth in the Soviet Union.[36] However, both corruption and the informal economy thrived in Georgia not only because of officials' and individuals' interest in amassing private wealth but also because of the population's intrinsic desire to exploit the Soviet system. Shelley contends that "Georgians thrived in a culture of rule evasion" that not only condoned expropriation, theft, and embezzlement of Soviet property but also encouraged such behavior.[37] According to Mars and Altman, nepotism was seen as "a moral duty," and "hierarchical official relations [were] resented and resisted and [were] the source of perpetual conflict."[38] For more than two decades after the Stalin's death, the Georgian masses' disillusionment and disappointment with the Soviet state became synthesized with the traditional Georgian reliance on kinship networking. Under Mzhavanadze, "the individual Georgian [saw] honour accruing to families and [saw] families linked by a common honour. In such a context there [was] little role for the state or for any centrally organized hierarchy."[39] In more critical terms, Roy Godson and his coauthors insist that in Georgia, "corrupt attitudes and practices arise from, and flourish in, a *culture* in which corruption is normalized and honesty is marginalized."[40] Thus, the culture of informality was legitimized and institutionalized among both Georgian elites and the public.

Nepotism and corruption existed in all Soviet republics, including the Russian Soviet Federative Socialist Republic. Yet, unlike many other corrupt Soviet administrators, who shared their spoils with patrons from higher echelons of communist *nomenklatura* in the Kremlin, Georgian officials had little desire to pay tributes to Moscow. As black markets and criminality prospered across the republic, enriching broader circles of Georgians, the Kremlin's control over Georgia steadily waned.[41] In this environment, the Kremlin appointed a young and ambitious police official, Eduard Shevardnadze, as minister of internal affairs in the late 1960s as part of an effort to restore Moscow's control over the informalization of Georgian institutions. Shevardnadze built up a strong case (*kompromat*) against Mzhavanadze and his officials. Shevardnadze's growing influence as Moscow's man in Tbilisi, ultimately forced Mzhavanadze to retire from all the major posts he held in the CPSU, including the position of first secretary of the Georgian Communist Party.

In 1972, Shevardnadze replaced his former boss and nemesis as first secretary. During his first six months as head of the Georgian Soviet Socialist Republic, twenty ministers and members of the CPSU's Central Committee, hundreds of party secretaries on the regional and oblast levels, and dozens of town majors were arrested and expelled from the party.[42] Over a five-year period, Shevardnadze's anticorruption campaign led to thirty thousand arrests and to the dismissal of more than forty thousand public and party officials.[43] Those dismissed from their positions included the rector of the Tbilisi Medical Institute, deans and professors from Tbilisi State University, and hundreds of other officials in the education, health care, and service-provision sectors.

This massive cleanup delivered a serious blow to political corruption and favoritism, both of which had previously remained outside of Moscow's control, and brought Georgia closer to the Kremlin. However, Shevardnadze's anticorruption crusade—widely publicized in Soviet mass media—was aimed neither at formalizing Georgian institutions nor at cleansing them of nepotism and bribery. Rather, the Kremlin's key goal had been restoring its control over the Georgian Communist Party. Shevardnadze's "publicized efforts to fight crime and corruption often promoted personal and political objectives rather than addressing the core problem."[44] Like the Georgian politicians who both preceded and succeeded him, Shevardnadze, too, depended on informal clientelistic networks of support. While some of these networks functioned through kinship ties, others were comprised of members of the elite who disapproved of the previous administration.

The wave of arrests and dismissals allowed Shevardnadze to replace the informal power bases of his predecessor with his own informal actors. As Law explains, "The cause of exposure was more likely the result of an inter-elite struggle with motives less noble than the establishment of honesty and goodness."[45] Since only those corrupt officials who opposed the new first secretary were purged, Shevardnadze's campaign of formalization amounted to nothing more than "political infighting" that resulted when "some unspoken rule of rent-seeking had been breached."[46] More important, Shevardnadze's reforms did not target the informal institutions at the base of Georgian society. Having removed from their positions several hundred officials, the new administration left the culture of informality intact. Mars and Altman explain that the system remained unaffected by reforms because

> in a network-based culture, though a person can be replaced, networks continue to exist. Persons will use personal support networks to try to find a lead to the new appointee, or if he proves too difficult to deal with, find a way to get rid of him or make his task impossible by limiting access to the social resources he needs.[47]

In a similar vein, Parsons argues that the eradication of endemic bribery and the formalization of state-society relations are challenged by "the all-pervasiveness of family ties, and the cult of megobroba, or friendship, often apparent in relations between Georgian men, stressing the virtue of loyalty in all circumstances."[48] Instead of dismantling the cult of *vory-v-zakone*, Shevardnadze's administration often used connections within the criminal underground to achieve political goals or to control political dissent.[49] In contrast to Mzhavanadze's period, when vast numbers of public servants or ordinary citizens could benefit from clientelistic networks and the culture of nepotism, under Shevardnadze, the spoils of bribery settled in pockets of narrow circles of chosen elite members, leading to the "steady growth of a clan-based corruption culture."[50]

By the end of the 1970s, Georgia had the highest population density in the USSR.[51] Farming of citrus fruits and the prosperous wine industry also gave Georgia the Soviet Union's largest rural population. Encouraged by informal economic profits, kinship networks—largely unperturbed by sovietization—continued to thrive across Georgia during Shevardnadze's period. With the start of perestroika and Shevardnadze's promotion to serve as the USSR's minister of foreign affairs, little changed in terms of the prevalence of informality in Georgia. As Richard Sakwa wrote in 1998, "Lacking the ability to introduce substantive political reforms, the political and economic elites . . . were purged and purged again."[52] The political and cultural liberalization brought by glasnost and perestroika gave rise to dissident and secessionist movements. By 1989, inspired by the growth of nationalism elsewhere across the USSR, such nationalist organizations as the Il'ia Chavchavadze Society became more active and vocal.

The 1992 breakup of the Soviet Union found Georgia torn between warring camps of nationalists, secessionist rebels, and semicriminal militias. Nationalist leader Zviad Gamsakhurdia won election to the Georgian presidency in 1991. Despite his extensive experience as a political dissident, Gamsakhurdia appeared incapable of coming to an arrangement with either the mutinous ethnic minorities in Abkhazia, South Ossetia, and Ajaria or the leaders of the semiformal but heavily armed paramilitary groups. These groups, the largest and most powerful of which was the Mkhedrioni (Horsemen), founded by a notorious *vor-v-zakone*, Djaba Ioseliani, controlled vast swaths of Georgian territory.[53] Less than a year after his election, Gamsakhurdia was overthrown by a coalition of militia leaders and former members of the government disappointed by his failure to consolidate the independent Georgian state. According to Ghia Nodia, "Gamsakhurdia failed because he could not live up to his image."[54] As Georgia was turning into a failed state and none of the opposition leaders proved able to assume leadership, the anti-Gamsakhurdia coalition invited Shevardnadze to return.

INFORMALITY AND REFORMS UNDER SHEVARDNADZE

Upon his return in 1992, Shevardnadze found the Georgian state in complete chaos. As Shalva Machavariani has observed, "At the time of the Soviet Union's collapse, Georgia was one of the richest republics in the Soviet Union," but the Georgian economy collapsed during the early 1990s, and its GDP dropped by 78 percent from its pre-1991 level.[55] The informal economy accounted for 70 percent of all economic production.[56] Secessionist conflicts in Abkhazia and South Ossetia as well as large numbers of armed militias threatened political stability. The formal institutions that Shevardnadze had inherited from Gamsakhurdia were overtaken by informality and sometimes functioned entirely on informal rules. For example, boundaries between state security forces and semilegal militias were blurred, and the Mkhedrioni and other less prominent paramilitary groups were deployed alongside regular forces during Georgia's conflict with Abkhazia. To restore law and order in an informal state, Shevardnadze, like the leaders of other post-Soviet republics, relied heavily on informal institutions.[57] This formal-informal synthesis resulted in the establishment of a semiformal state in which informal institutions and actors wielded actual power and functioned alongside or instead of their formal counterparts. During his two (incomplete) terms in office, Shevardnadze never had complete control of state institutions.

The need to bargain control of the state and share power with informal actors both within the Georgian government and in the country's regions prevented Shevardnadze from consolidating a centralized authoritarian state system similar to Heydar Aliyev's Azerbaijan or Vladimir Putin's Russia. Nevertheless, as a shrewd and experienced politician who enjoyed the support of informal networks forged in Soviet times, particularly during his first presidency, Shevardnadze wrestled power from some of his informal opponents. Thus, the Georgian military fiasco in Abkhazia led not only to the region's de facto independence but also to the weakening of the Mkhedrioni, which suffered significant losses during the Georgian-Abkhazian war. Shevardnadze subsequently consolidated his control over power ministries.[58] He legalized the Mkhedrioni and incorporated them into the National Guard, granting their leader, Jaba Ioseliani, a ministerial position. During the mid-1990s, Shevardnadze relied on the Mkhedrioni to intimidate or eliminate his opponents.[59] By the late 1990s, however, when he no longer required the services of paramilitaries, the president disbanded them and jailed Ioseliani.

In his battles with stronger informal actors, such as Ioseliani's paramilitaries, Shevardnadze relied on the support of weaker informal power brokers. This reliance led not only to the deformalization of state institutions but also to their criminalization. For example, throughout the 1990s, Georgian police widely engaged in blackmail, racketeering, and extortion.[60] As Shelley details, "Collusion between organized crime groups and government officials often blurred the distinction between the two groups," enabling *vory-v-zakone* to operate with impunity.[61] Not surprisingly, more than 60 percent of respondents to a poll conducted by the World Values Surveys in Georgia in the mid-1990s expressed their distrust of police.[62] Since pro-regime informal power brokers remained above the law, "impunity was the rule of the Shevardnadze administration."[63] According to Lincoln A. Mitchell, across Georgia, "notably [in] Samegrelo and Svaneti, criminal gangs represented the real political power for most of the 1990s and early twenty-first century."[64] In Shelley's view, criminality, particularly *vory-v-zakone* culture, "flourished in Georgian society" because "rule evasion [was] valued over legal compliance."[65]

In this context, informality thrived in Shevardnadze's Georgia, exceeding the spread of informal practices and institutions during the Soviet period. Informal networks (*natsnoboba*) and unofficial payments (*krtami*), which had been shadowy and frowned upon under Soviet rule, became part of the daily routine for the majority of Georgians.[66] With the state's retreat from many areas of service provision and welfare, informal institutions substituted for state agencies. According to the Transparency International's Corruption Perceptions Index, Georgia was one of the most corrupt countries in the world, ranking eighty-fourth among ninety-nine countries.[67] As Mitchell points out, "Corruption under Shevardnadze had become simply the way business was done, the rule rather than the exception."[68] Unlike Soviet times, when socialist morality and the watchful eye of Kremlin's apparatchiks kept illegality and informality at bay, Georgia in the 1990s possessed no checks and balances at all. Given Shevardnadze's open nepotism and favoritism, no limits existed on what and who could be bought and sold through bribes and informal channels. Positions in ministries and other public institutions were distributed almost entirely through bribes or contacts.[69] Admission to universities, particularly the Tbilisi Medical Institute and the Tbilisi State University, could be bought for between two thousand and twenty thousand U.S. dollars.[70] Officially free-of-charge medical services at state clinics and hospitals were provided mostly in exchange for out-of-pocket payments, gift-giving, or references from connections.[71]

Along with the ubiquitous petty corruption, embezzlement and expropriation were also common practices among government officials. For example, Christoph H. Stefes reports that the Ministry for Fuel and Energy embezzled more than $380 million—about half of an international aid package intended to rebuild Georgia's energy sector.[72] Although the Georgian economy recovered slowly in the mid-1990s, leading to an increase in the per capita GDP from $540 in 1992 to $743 in 1998, more than "70 percent of Georgia's economy was in the shadows."[73] The lack of economic development was accompanied by the deterioration of the infrastructure: the population lacked access to basic amenities such as sewage services, heating, and steady electricity.[74] Laurence Broers posits that this "wide-ranging atrophy" of formal institutions was "concurrent with the informalization of the state."[75]

Georgians, who had prided themselves on their status as citizens of one of the richest Soviet republics, became poorer than many other post-Soviet nations.[76] Under Soviet rule, Georgians had used corruption and informality to target the communist system, seeking opportunities for embezzlement and profiteering; in contrast, the postsocialist informal institutions "were destroying the Georgian state from within."[77] Since informal practices served not only as social safety nets but also as mechanisms for pilfering and misappropriating state resources, the extensive use of informal behaviors had ruinous effects on both the state and society. Despite the reliance on informal institutions, a significant percentage of the Georgian population continued to live in poverty.[78] Georgians' Soviet-era high living standards made postsocialist poverty and social inequality particularly unbearable.[79]

Along with many other ills of postcommunism, poverty was popularly associated with ubiquitous corruption, the omnipresence of which was blamed on Shevardnadze's government.[80] However, Shevardnadze's lack of centralized control meant that the Georgian system of governance remained both rather informal and fairly liberal. Mitchell explains that "Georgia was characterized by an unusual combination of democratic and undemocratic elements."[81] Valerie Bunce and Sharon Wolchik have labeled Shevardnadze's Georgia a "classic example of a mixed regime."[82] The absence of transparent and free elections and the presence of high levels of clientelism among state officials contrasted with the relatively free media and a vibrant civil society.[83] On the one hand, Shevardnadze's weak position in the legislative branch enabled a breathing space for dissent and antiregime coalition building within parliament; on the other hand, Tbilisi's limited resources for co-opting or coercing heads of regional administrations into compliance meant that "provincial authorities maintained a high degree of independence from Tbilisi and often ignored directives from the center."[84]

Shevardnadze's government was neither able nor willing to implement effective institutional reforms.[85] As Kupatadze observes, a range of anticorruption measures carried out in 1997 targeted only low-ranking public officials, "leaving corruption pyramids untouched."[86] Shevardnadze had extensive experience in using the fight against corruption to eliminate his political enemies and cleanse the system of petty corruption that depleted government coffers. For example, the 2001 establishment of the Anticorruption Policy Coordination Council, as Broers points out, "resulted in the dismissal—but neither arrest nor prosecution—of a number of high-ranking officials."[87] Shelley concurs, adding that efforts to implement institutional reforms "did more for the promotion of Shevardnadze's career than the elimination of this deep-seated phenomenon in Georgian society."[88] Only two low-ranking officials were convicted of corruption as a result of the 2001 anticorruption campaign, and each around fifty dollars.[89] The Shevardnadze era reforms not only were cosmetic and poorly executed but also faced fierce resistance from informal interest groups that opposed any change in the status quo. Notwithstanding the dominance of informal power elites, discontent was brewing both among broader circles of Georgian society and within parliament.[90]

Although the prevailing extensive informalization and criminalization of the Georgian state were among the main reasons for its collapse, a number of other causes contributed to the 2003 Rose Revolution. The economic crisis of the late 1990s and fraudulent presidential elections of 2000 became instrumental to the withdrawal of international support for Shevardnadze's regime. As a consequence, internal strife within the ruling party, the Citizens Union, expedited high-profile defections to the opposition.[91] Following the resignation of the minister of justice, Mikheil Saakashvili; the Speaker of parliament, Zurab Zhvania; and his immediate successor, Nino Burjanadze, Georgia's political crisis intensified. In that light, the fraudulent 2003 parliamentary elections did not in and of themselves prompt the regime change; rather, they provided a spark that caused smoldering dormant civic and political forces to catch fire.

THE ROSE REVOLUTION: INSTITUTIONAL REFORMS BEGIN

The Rose Revolution, a series of anti-Shevardnadze protests that led to the president's November 2003 resignation, not only comprised the first "color" revolution in the post-Soviet space but also culminated in the establishment of a prodemocratic and Western-oriented government. Since that time, a voluminous body of literature has been produced on various aspects of the revolution.[92] The postrevolutionary government led by Saakashvili and his newly minted United National Movement (UNM) took as its primary objectives formalizing state institutions, fighting corruption, and decriminalizing society. The existing institutional system was not simply dysfunctional and corrupt but also staffed by former communist apparatchiks and members of informal interest groups who promoted and prioritized their own interests over those of the state. Since Georgia lacked a functional institutional framework, Saakashvili's inherent goals of democratizing Georgian institutions required extensive institutional transformation. Formalizing, modernizing, and liberalizing state institutions required creating new institutions as well as countering, displacing, and layering existing ones. As early as 2004, Saakashvili realized that democratization would not be possible without complete institutional overhaul, which could be achieved only after informal actors and criminal networks were undermined.

The scope and scale of institutional reforms in Saakashvili's Georgia remain unmatched in the post-Soviet space. Unlike institutional reforms previously carried out in Georgia or in non-Baltic former Soviet states, Saakashvili's reforms deliberately sought to formalize and modernize state institutions. This characteristic distinguishes Georgia's institution-building from institutionalization in other post-Soviet republics, where institutional changes were implemented with the goal of cementing the incumbent's control over informal power bases and centralizing institutional framework around the executive's office rather than democratizing formal institutions.

Eradicating the systemic corruption that has eroded Georgian institutions since the country's independence represented the centerpiece of Saakashvili's campaign against Shevardnadze even before the success of the Rose Revolution. On the eve of Shevardnadze's resignation, Georgia ranked 124th of 133 countries on Transparency International's Corruption Perceptions Index.[93] In January 2004, after taking 96 percent of the vote in elections declared free and fair, Saakashvili launched an ambitious and comprehensive institutional reform program. Relying on his team of young and mostly Western-educated officials, the new president began cleansing the system of members of the communist-era *nomenklatura*, criminal elements, and Shevardnadze's power networks.[94]

The officials arrested in 2004 included several high-ranking ministers as well as eighty mid- and low-ranking public officials and entrepreneurs. That year alone, more than fifty million dollars' worth of property was confiscated. In addition, seventy million dollars embezzled by officials was returned to the state.[95] The Ministry of Justice reported that during the first two years of the anticorruption "crusade," some one thousand state officials, six former members of parliament, and fifteen deputy ministers were arrested on charges of corruption. The Saakashvili administration took a similar "shock therapy" approach to reforming other sectors.

According to 1998 World Bank surveys, traffic police, local courts, and customs services were the most corrupt state institutions. Of these three institutions, the traffic police most symbolized Georgian corruption. A 2000 survey by Georgian Opinion Research Business International demonstrated that seven out of ten motorists pulled over on the streets of Tbilisi by the traffic police were asked to pay a bribe even if they had not violated any traffic rules.[96] According to popular anecdote, the minister of interior had said that his "guys" at traffic police do not need salaries, they only need petrol for their cars and they will collect their own salaries.[97] Lili di Puppo has detailed how the Georgian police not only engaged in mass corruption but also worked alongside criminals and participated in criminal deals and racketeering.[98] The World Bank found that about 40 percent of police employees and 50 percent of customs officers had purchased their positions through bribes of between two thousand and twenty thousand dollars. Corruption pyramids flourished at every level of police hierarchy from patrol officers to top administrators and generals.[99]

The first phase of the reforms intended to decriminalize the police involved massive layoffs: sixteen thousand police employees were dismissed overnight as part of a reduction that ultimately shrank the number of police personnel from sixty-three thousand to twenty-seven thousand.[100] The entire traffic police agency was disbanded, and the Patrol Police was created to replace it. Modeled on the US police, the new Georgian police force was staffed by well-trained personnel, and salaries were increased to as much as four times the wages paid to the previous police force.[101]

The police reform took place in conjunction with the massive decriminalization campaign.[102] The fight against organized crime began in the first months after UNM's electoral victory, with hundreds of arrests of criminal authorities and confiscation of their property. A series of laws directed against organized crime, patterned on American and Italian antimafia legislation, was adopted in 2004–5 as a legal basis for the crackdown on *vory-v-zakone* and other criminal organizations. In fact, the 2005 Law on Organized Crime and Rackets targeted the *vory-v-zakone* by outlawing membership and criminalizing their conduct. According to minister of justice Zurab Adeishvili, approximately one billion dollars was confiscated from criminal authorities during first few years of the decriminalization campaign. Between 2004 and 2011, some 180 *vory-v-zakone* (including 37 in Tbilisi) were arrested and imprisoned. Some "cleaner" *vory-v-zakone* members were forced to pay hefty fines to avoid imprisonment, and many decided to leave Georgia.[103] This massive confiscation of property from both criminal bosses and former She-vardnadze officials allowed the Georgian state to increase spending on those sectors in the need of urgent reform.

Among those areas, the education sector was particularly paralyzed by informal institutions and required immediate and extensive reform.[104] The process of relieving institutions of secondary and higher education of informal payments and the culture of gift-giving started with the introduction of new accreditation system for universities.[105] Only 43 of the country's 237 universities received postreform accreditation and resumed their work.[106] In addition, all instructors were required to verify their professional credentials.

The comprehensive reform of the education sector sought to bring the Georgian system into accordance with European standards. Legal bases for the reform were the Law on Higher Education (2004) and the Law on General Education (2005), which abolished the communist-era system of university entrance examinations, which was infamous for its corruption and nepotism. Under the old system, entrance exams had been administered by a group of university professors, who admitted students based on their informal connections or by extorting bribes. After 2005, the Unified Admissions Exam, administered by the National Assessment and Examinations Centre, instituted computer-graded exams, removing the possibility that bribes or connections could play a role in admissions. Along with significantly increasing the budget for education, the government introduced school boards to decentralize the decision-making process.[107]

Between 2004 and 2007, the health care budget, too, was increased from 108 Georgian lari in 2004 to 250 million lari in 2008 (almost 130 percent).[108] To reduce corruption in the judicial sector, salaries of judicial staff were increased to reach an equivalent of $1,090 for judges in regional and district courts.[109] Although judges could not be dismissed en masse, as police officers had been, efforts were made to hire younger judges with no connections to the ancien régime.

The civil service reform involved massive institutional displacement.[110] The Law on Structure, Authority and Regulation, adopted in the early 2004, reduced the number of ministries from eighteen to thirteen. The notoriously corrupt public registry, which bore responsibility for issuing passports, land registers, and other official documents to citizens and businesses, was dissolved in 2004. It was replaced by the new Civil Registry Agency, a self-funded entity under the control of the Ministry of Justice. The new computerized registry is coordinated through a central office that does not directly interact with the members of the public. This new agency not only replaced more than seventy local civil registry offices but also brought together six public agencies, including the Notary Chamber and National Archives, that had previously played a role in providing or registering official documents. Unlike the old registry, which required bribes or waiting periods as long as several years before issuing documents, the new agency features a simplified and formalized process: for example, passports can be issued within twenty-four hours with payment of a standard fee or without charge in less than ten days. Whereas the plethora of pre-reform civil offices had issued 909 types of permits and licenses, that number fell to 160 after 2004. Late that year, twenty-two hundred employees of the old public registry were fired. By 2005, nearly half of the country's 120,000 public servants had either been fired from their positions or forced to reapply to confirm their credentials.[111]

The debureaucratization of the state resulted in either the abolition or merger of eighteen state departments. For example, the Chamber of Control, infamous for its corrupt practices, was converted to new purposes. In 2004–5 alone, the Customs Department was restructured at least six times, and some ministries were reorganized four or five times.[112] The administrative institutional transformation was accompanied by the extensive neoliberal economic reforms needed to rebuild the country's economy almost from scratch. Saakashvili's economic reform rested on three main pillars, each of which required massive transformation of both economic and political institutions.

First, tax reform was implemented to simplify existing taxes and expand the number of taxpayers.[113] By 2003, only eighty thousand taxpayers were registered, and the majority of entrepreneurs evaded taxes by bribing officials or via interpersonal networks.[114] As a result, taxes accounted for only 12 percent of Georgia's GDP under Shevardnadze's rule. The enactment of a new Tax Code in 2005 was followed by reductions in the number of taxes (from twenty-two to eight) and in tax rates. Improvements in tax collection policies increased the amount collected from 1.2 billion Georgian lari in 2003 to 2.6 billion lari in 2004. In 2010, the number of taxpayers increased to 252,000.[115]

Prior to the Rose Revolution, customs control was distributed among nine agencies, which had overlapping responsibilities. All of these agencies extorted bribes for customs services.[116] The reorganization reduced the number of customs agencies to two—passport control services and other customs services. Lowering and simplifying tariffs as well as replacing numerous corrupt staff members further increased the service's credibility.[117]

Second, a massive privatization campaign sought to attract investment and liberalize the economy. Between the start of privatization in 2004 and 2005, some four thousand state-owned entities were privatized, attracting more than $1.5 billion in income to the state.[118]

Third, both the tax reform and privatization campaigns were closely associated with trade liberalization. Reorganization and formalization of customs control enabled the creation of free trade regimes and attracted foreign direct investment. During Saakashvili's first term in office, the amount of foreign direct investment climbed from $499 million to $955 million.[119]

Institution-building during the Saakashvili era also encompassed many other sectors of the economy, society, and politics, including infrastructure rebuilding and environmental projects.[120] Nevertheless, the fight against corruption, the formalization of state institutions, and economic reform were the key aspects of the Georgian government's efforts to create efficient, transparent, and liberal institutions. As some scholars have argued, these efforts focused almost exclusively on state-building rather than on democratization.[121] Yet formalization and liberalization of state institutions enhanced their efficiency and transparency, thereby cementing the basis for democratic institutional transformation, indispensable for regimes embarking on democratization. The 2008 Russo-Georgian war over the breakaway enclave of South Ossetia and the 2007–8 global financial crisis marked the start of Saakashvili's second presidential term. Following a wave of televised corruption-related arrests conducted during Saakashvili's first years in office, the anticorruption campaign began to wane in the late 2000s, and many of those arrested in later years appeared to be Saakashvili's political rivals.[122] As a result of UNM's covert but continuous persecution of its political opponents, Georgia entered a political crisis that lasted throughout the remainder of Saakashvili's presidency.[123] In 2010, the adoption of amendments to the constitution designed to limit presidential powers and transform Georgia into a parliamentary republic did little to divert popular support from the UNM.

The 2012 parliamentary elections brought victory to Georgian Dream, a coalition of anti-Saakashvili parties brought together by billionaire Bidzina Ivanishvili, and resulted in the first democratic regime transition in Georgia's post-Soviet history. A new tide of anticorruption arrests followed, this time targeting former UNM officials, including Saakashvili.[124] After Georgian Dream's success in the 2013 presidential elections, the new government pursued a number of legislative and judicial reforms aimed at decentralizing the executive and transforming the judicial branch.[125] One of the most notable reforms implemented by the Georgian Dream government is the Local Self-Governance Code, which increases the autonomy of local administrations. The campaign of investigations and detentions of former UNM officials has continued.[126] The transfer to a semipresidential system occurred soon after the start of Georgian Dream's tenure and has resulted in an uneasy equilibrium between President Giorgi Margvelashvili and Prime Minister Irakli Garibashvili.[127] With the strengthening of prime minister's role, the legislature began to increase its independence from the executive. The presidential domination of the parliament practiced by Saakashvili has disappeared under Georgian Dream.[128] Two years after Georgian Dream replaced the UNM, most of institutional changes implemented since the Rose Revolution continue functioning.

ASSESSING THE IMPACT OF REFORMS

The impact of Saakashvili era's reforms on Georgian political and economic spheres has been assessed not only by a voluminous body of academic literature but also by countless reports drafted by international organizations and civil society.[129] It is well documented that although "anti-corruption strategy in Georgia appears to reflect more the demands of international organizations," in 2014, Georgia ranked fiftieth on the Corruption Perceptions Index.[130]

The effectiveness of the institutional transformation and the scope of the anticorruption campaign in post–Rose Revolution Georgia minimized petty corruption.[131] In most areas of public administration, petty corruption has become a thing of the past.[132] For example, 99 percent of respondents to a 2013 survey by the Caucasus Research Resource Centers (CRRC) indicated that they had not paid a single bribe during the past twelve months, up from 96 percent in 2008.[133] Although some observers have claimed that "high-level corruption continued" and remains a "persistent concern," the UNM's reforms of the bureaucracy, the business sector, taxes, and public administration have been praised as highly effective, leading the World Bank to proclaim Georgia the "best reformer in the world" in 2008.[134]

The major shortcomings of Saakashvili's reforms have appeared in the judicial and health care sectors, which continued to underperform during UNM's time in power and therefore figured prominently in Georgian Dream's anti-Saakashvili's campaign.[135] As Shelley argues, the judicial sector "has been largely untouched since the Rose Revolution," a situation that sparked scandals about prisoner abuse, excessive sentences, and biased judges.[136] The lack of transparency in economic privatization and the management of economic resources has hindered economic development and affected the growth of the gross domestic product.[137] Many mass media sources came under the Saakashvili government's control, dealing a significant blow to media independence.[138] Postrevolutionary civil society reforms resulted in tighter UNM control over the NGO sector, which some observers have termed the "decapitation" of civil society.[139] An informal "merger" of pro-UNM NGOs with the government in the immediate aftermath of the Rose Revolution provided scores of civil activists with jobs in the government.[140] These shortcomings were often criticized in conjunction with Saakashvili's "autocratic" control of the executive branch, which led some scholars to claim that the Rose Revolution replaced Shevardnadze's "super-presidentialism" with Saakashvili's "hyperpresidentialism."[141] H. Charles Fairbanks and Alexi Gugushvili assert that the regime change was not too notable, because the new regime forced the "old, corrupted one out, only to become another link in the chain."[142] John A. Gould and Carl Sickner add that despite the massive "elite cleansing" under Saakashvili, certain elements of Shevardnadze's elites have remained in power by pledging their loyalty to the UNM.[143] Other observers have claimed that loyalty to Saakashvili's regime enabled elites to engage in corrupt practices as they did under the previous regime.[144]

Post-Saakashvili Georgian democratization and institution-building are still overshadowed by behind-the-scenes politics within the ruling coalition and particularly by the influence exercised by Ivanishvili, the former prime minister and the founder of Georgian Dream, who handpicked both the president and the prime minister of the post-UNM government. The legitimacy of Georgia's democratic processes thus remains questionable. Although Ivanishvili holds no official government position, he remains at the center of Georgian political life, frequently appearing in media and making political statements. Though the extent of Ivanishvili's influence on the government is debatable, he undoubtedly retains control over various informal power brokers.[145]

Nevertheless, Georgia under Saakashvili evolved from a failing state eroded by corruption into a hybrid or transitional regime with functioning state institutions and formal commitment to democratization. Unlike regimes in most other non-Baltic post-Soviet states, the Georgian government continues to formalize state institutions and to tackle the culture of informality. The massive and rigorous post–Rose Revolution reform campaign has changed the long-standing prevalence of informal practice and institutions in Georgia. However, neither the existing scholarly literature nor the assessments and reports by international organizations offer a conclusive answer regarding what has happened to informality since the Rose Revolution.

Attitudes toward Institutional Reforms

Informal institutions, unlike their formal counterparts, come to life not as a result of deliberate institution-building processes but because they bear utilitarian value for agents. Consequently, the popular perception of institutional changes is crucial to the effectiveness and survival of informal institutions. Following the view that informal behaviors are born out of deficiencies of formal institutions, effective institutional reforms can be expected to undermine informality.[146] If institutional transformations underscore the importance of informal institutions, then actors relying on informal institutions may simply stop using them. One of the main explanations for why informality thrived in Georgia associates the reliance on informal institutions with the deep-seated distrust of public institutions.[147]

Since the literature has made few efforts to assess population's attitude toward reforms, closed-ended public surveys remain the only source of data regarding the popular perception of institutional reforms. Public surveys confirm scholars' assumptions regarding the lack of institutional trust in postcommunist Georgia. The only representative survey that measured levels of institutional trust in Shevardnadze's Georgia, the 1996 World Values Surveys, captured markedly high levels of distrust of the government, political parties, and state institutions (table 4.1). The data collected by the International Republican Institute on the eve of the Rose Revolution presents further decline in the levels of institutional trust. By contrast, a series of public surveys conducted during Saakashvili's first and second terms in office demonstrates an increase in trust of both the government and state institutions. While levels of distrust of the government and political system have fluctuated since the Rose Revolution, trust in police and other state agencies increased through 2014 before falling again in 2015.

The European Bank for Reconstruction and Development's 2011 "Life in Transition" survey recorded rather high levels of popular satisfaction with service delivery with consistent increases from the 2006 survey. For example, 75 percent of respondents (63 percent in 2006) expressed satisfaction with the performance of the health care system, 92 percent (59 percent) were satisfied with the process of issuing official documents, and 83 percent (72 percent) were satisfied with the education sector. However, the percentage of those satisfied with the courts fell from 43 percent in 2006 to 36 percent four years later. Moreover, these relatively high levels of satisfaction with institutional performance and increasing levels of institutional trust during Saakashvili's period did not necessarily correspond to the population's attitude toward reforms. Only 11 percent of respondents to CRRC's 2014 "attitudes towards the judicial system" survey agreed that courts had worked well during Saakashvili's presidency. Another 55 percent of survey participants noted that courts improved after Georgian Dream's 2012 parliamentary victory.

Despite the international community's broad acknowledgment of Saakashvili's success in wiping out petty corruption and dismantling criminal networks as well as in reforming many state institutions, ordinary Georgians did not have a particularly high opinion of the reforms. Respondents to the Georgian National Study (GNS) positively acknowledged improvements in the energy sector such as twenty-four-hour electricity and reconstruction of roads (table 4.2). A quarter of the participants in the 2012 GNS survey cited successful decriminalization, while three years later, the GNS survey confirmed the population's satisfaction with health care reforms implemented under Georgian Dream.

However, survey participants largely did not notice the highly praised anticorruption campaign. More than half of those who responded to the 2011 survey believed that corruption continued to thrive unabated among

TABLE 4.1. Levels of Institutional Distrust in Georgia (%)

	1996	2003	2006	2008	2012	2014	2015
Legal system	53	—	44	35	37	25	35
Police	61	—	21	22	11	10	24
President	—	72	18	23	36	23	39
National government	48	74	32	22	8	23	45
Parliament	58	74	35	32	10	25	44
Political parties	64	62	43	44	23	44	58
Education system	—	32	—	17	11	25	30
Health care system	—	—	—	14	18	—	—
Banks	—	38	45	22	24	32	—

Sources: World Values Survey; International Republican Institute (IRI) "Georgian National Study"; EBRD "Life in Transition" 2006; CRRC "Caucasus Barometer" 2012, 2013

high-ranking officials. And the 2013 Global Corruption Barometer found that 26 percent of Georgians believed that corruption still existed among public officials and police, 32 percent thought that the health system was corrupt, and 22 percent suspected corruption in education. However, the population saw the judicial branch as the most corrupt state institution, with more than half of respondents identifying corruption in courts as a serious problem.[148]

Since 2005, the economy, health care, and education have dominated the Georgian population's list of areas in need of reform. According to the 2015 GNS survey, Georgians see unemployment and the lack of economic development as the country's most urgent problems. While the recent health care reform addressed some of the population's health care concerns, the economic crisis, which prompted the devaluation of the national currency in late 2014–early 2015, continued to be associated with the government's failure to reform the economy. The same survey showed that the Georgian people expect their government to create jobs, provide economic stability, and improve infrastructure.

The government's success in ensuring twenty-four-hour electricity and reconstructing roads and communication services has received much more popular recognition than the fight against petty corruption, which remains a major government priority. Yet the provision of communal services remains far from satisfactory. For example, none of the respondents to the CRRC's 2013 survey had access to public central heating. Instead, 55 percent

TABLE 4.2. Major Achievements of the Georgian Government

% of Respondents Who Judged the Reforms Successful	2007	2010	2012	2015
Electricity supply	32	35	26	—
Roads	22	36	24	—
Health care	4	—	2	30
Police reform	6	12	16	—
Crime	4	16	23	—
Pensions/wages	6	10	5	2
Corruption	2	—	8	—
Agriculture	—	—	-	8
Nothing	5	3	4	18

Source: IRI, "Georgian National Study"

of survey participants heated their homes with wood-burning stoves, 24 percent used gas stoves, and 15 percent used electric heaters. These data show that state institutions remain unable to supply the population with basic services. Given that Georgians maintain rather lukewarm attitudes toward the post–Rose Revolution institutional reforms, the impact of those reforms on informality is even harder to assess.

Reliance on Informality

The population's use of informal structures is a clear indication of effectiveness or the lack thereof of institutional reforms designed to reduce informality. Because the formalization of state institutions and ongoing institution-building were among the key goals of Saakashvili's reforms, the size of informal sector and the spread and importance of informal practices are crucial indicators of the reforms' success. Unlike corruption and bribery, which fell significantly after the start of reforms, little is known about the use of informal networks, gift-giving, and other informal behaviors that previously dominated formal institutions.

In contrast to the fairly notable reduction in petty corruption, the informal economy decreased from more than 67 percent of total economic output in 2000 to 60 percent in 2008.[149] Survey findings suggest that a significant proportion of the Georgian population continues to earn income outside of formal employment. For example, less than half of the respondents in the 2013 CRRC survey declared that salaries were their main sources of income.[150] The existence of unregistered and undeclared sources of household income clearly indicates the presence of a sizable informal economic sector.

The comprehensive institution-building campaign conducted by Saakashvili's government and the creation and modernization of institutions were expected to expand the public sector job market. But only 30 percent of the CRRC's respondents worked for the state, with the rest employed in the private sector.[151] Georgia's National Statistics Office reported an official unemployment rate of 14.6 percent for 2013, down from 17 percent in 2009; however, the Caucasus Barometer survey found that more than 60 percent of Georgians did not have jobs.[152] The scarcity of jobs, in turn, encourages informal behavior in the job market.

As in the Shevardnadze period, informal contacts and connections remain crucial to obtaining a job in the private sector. In 2014, more than 33 percent of Georgians indicated that the most important factor in finding a job was connections, a figure that rose from 26 percent in 2010 and 30 percent in 2012.[153] Interpersonal networks also appear to be indispensable in obtaining state jobs. Shelley notes that despite the large-scale campaign to eradicate informal behavior from government institutions, "hiring for most vacancies, outside of the traffic police, [is] still not made on the basis of objective criteria. Corruption and nepotism all too often still determine who is hired for a position."[154]

For many Georgians, the definition of corruption remains limited to bribe taking among high-ranking officials and politicians.[155] Unofficial payments in return for preferential treatment by state institutions are still seen as reciprocal "signs of attention" rather than bribery. Erik R. Scott declares that "many practices common in Georgia that we might describe as clientelistic were not exposed as corrupt, such as helping relatives get jobs. Nor was paying bribes to 'get by,' avoiding paying traffic tickets, or securing admission into university considered corrupt."[156] For example, 45 percent of respondents to the CRRC's 2011 Volunteering and Civil Participation survey did not think that giving a gift to a doctor to receive preferential treatment was a corrupt activity. In addition, 40 percent did not see a situation when a state official recommends a relative for a job in a ministry as a case of corruption or nepotism.[157]

Nevertheless, the reforms in Georgia have reduced unofficial payments and the use of informal channels in dealings with state institutions to the lowest levels found in the former Soviet Union.[158] The UNM's institutional overhaul brought an end to many of the informal practices that were attributes of Georgian formal institutions after the collapse of communism.[159] In the European Bank for Reconstruction and Development's 2011 Life in Transition, only 7 percent of Georgians reported relying on informal channels when dealing with the public health system, 5 percent mentioned using informality in the education sector (primary and secondary), and 3 percent used informality in the civil courts. Only 1 percent of respondents relied on unofficial payments or gifts when approaching traffic police or obtaining official documents.[160] These data sharply contrast with Shevardnadze-era accounts of highly corrupt civil registry offices and criminalized traffic police.[161] The overall decline in informal institutions' role in the population's contact with state agencies suggests that institutional transformations delivered a heavy blow to the competing and substitutive informal institutions that previously thrived within Georgian formal institutions.

However, the disappearance or dramatic decline of some informal institutions did not necessarily undermine the ensemble of informal practices and networks traditionally embedded in Georgian society. Survey data reveal that Georgians continue to use informal networks in their daily lives. Thus, 90 percent of respondents to the 2014 Caucasus Barometer survey agreed that they had a great number of people on whom to rely in case of need. In light of the fact that more than 70 percent of survey participants expressed a distrust of strangers, informal "circles of trust" seem to be limited to close friends and relatives. Further evidence suggests that present-day Georgian informal networks consist primarily of close friends, whom the plurality of Georgians meet either once a week (34 percent) or every day (21 percent), and close relatives, with whom informants interact once a week (19 percent), once a month (30 percent), or only on special occasions (37 percent). Despite the decrease in kinship circles' importance as a consequence of moderniza-tion and urbanization, more than 80 percent of Georgians acquire new friends through their relatives, while 55 percent do so through other friends.[162] This suggests that referral by relatives remains an essential crite-rion for building networks.

Although informal networks in present-day Georgia are based more on friendships than on kinship, as was the case prior to urbanization and mod-ernization, their tightly knit structure remains virtually unchanged. Each network continues to resemble a closed circle of people connected by com-mon interests. New members can enter a "strong tie" network only through introduction by in-group members.[163] Networks continue to generate social capital and function as social safety nets. More than 90 percent of respon-dents to a CRRC 2010 survey declared that their first source of help in an emergency would be family members and friends.[164] A 2014 CRRC survey found that 81 percent of its participants confirmed that there were people who would look after them without compensation. [165]

Although informal networking as a form of social capital and as a coping mechanism seems to have survived the reforms unscathed, decriminaliza-tion efforts weakened semicriminal networks, such as urban tradition of "male bonding" networks (*birzha*).[166] According to Evgenia Zakharova, it is not so much the Saakashvili government's stringent anticriminal legislation but modernization and globalization that have impacted the importance of semicriminal networks, such as *birzha*, which are seen as a "backward heri-tage" of Soviet period and the turbulent 1990s.[167]

The surveys demonstrate that the reliance on informality has trans-formed since the start of the reforms in 2004. On the one hand, the use of

informal connections in dealings with formal institutions significantly declined. Following the transformation of state institutions, employing informal connections to obtain favors from institutions became either impossible
or impractical. The creation of electronic services and establishment of official service fees have eradicated the need to seek informal access to institutional actors, and the reduction in bureaucracy has eliminated the need to
avoid informal waiting lists. Favor exchanges and gift-giving, along with
bribery, became much less frequent in daily contacts with state institutions.
However, incomplete and ineffective economic reforms and unrelenting social insecurity among Georgians continue to encourage the use of informal
networks of friends and relatives.

Georgia's post-Soviet sociocultural transformation, massive urbanization, and modernization shifted the composition of networks. The large patriarchal kinship groups that were characteristic of Georgian rural areas were
replaced by smaller nuclear families more reliant on friendship circles than
on ties with relatives. This transformation, however, occurred side by side
with the continuous reliance on the network capital. Informal networks still
perform many of their traditional functions, such as providing community
welfare, family support, and economic assistance.

SUMMARY

Over the past twenty-five years, Georgia has undergone extensive institutional transformation. Following decades of informalization under Soviet
rule and during the immediate postsocialist period, Georgia's transformation into a hybrid regime has been accompanied by comprehensive institutional reforms. Many of these reforms were designed to target informal institutions, which paralyzed and incapacitated the Georgian state. Georgia's
institutional reforms were not always democratic and as in many other hybrid regimes often bore autocratic overtones. Georgia under Saakashvili and
during the Georgian Dream never transformed into a flawed democratic system, much less into a semiconsolidated democratic state. However, the regime's ability to hold free and fair elections, which ensured its succession in
2013, and its formal commitment to democratic institutional reforms, along
with its ability to implement some of these reforms, allows to classify the
Republic of Georgia as a consolidated hybrid regime. Like hybrid regimes in
Latin America and East Asia, Georgia continues to bounce back and forth

between democratization and authoritarianism. Rather than transiting toward democracy, it remains in between. As the literature notes, Georgian institutional transformations since the Rose Revolution resemble institution-building more than democratization. Indeed, along with extensive conversion, layering, and displacement of previous institutions, scores of new institutions were built to fill the institutional vacuum previously occupied by informal structures.

What distinguishes Georgian institutionalization from analogous transformations in neighboring post-Soviet republics is the purposeful attempt to replace informal structures with formal rules. Instead of converting some informal institutions to different purposes or layering formal institutions on their informal counterparts, as authoritarian regimes do, Georgia's institution makers sought to replace informal institutions with formal ones. Formal institutions could not always be completely cleared of informal practices. For example, political bargaining and coalition building required informal pacts and the use of power networks. This, in turn, fostered elite-level corruption and favoritism, which replaced the previously omnipresent low-level corruption and nepotism. A myriad of domestic and external challenges have prevented many of UNM's ambitious reform goals from reaching fruition. As a result, Georgia's democratic institutionalization remains fractured and incomplete, enabling the survival of informal institutions in various areas of socioeconomic and sociopolitical life.

Georgia demonstrates that post-Soviet informal institutions, regardless of their entrenchment and pervasiveness, can be reformed and formalized. Yet even such a comprehensive reform program as that implemented in Georgia cannot guarantee a complete dismantling of informal institutions. Many of Georgia's current informal practices and institutions continue to fill gaps in formal institutions and therefore are still needed by the population and elites. Informality thus has not completely disappeared.

CHAPTER 5

Moldova: Informal Reforms of Formal Institutions

THE EAST EUROPEAN republic of Moldova shares a great deal of similarities with the Republic of Georgia. Like Georgia, Moldova is a small nation (3.5 million people), with no access to fossil fuels and locked in an unresolved territorial conflict with Russian-supported separatists. Commonly labeled the "poorhouse of Europe," Moldova has remained one of the least developed Eastern European states throughout most of its recent history. Partly as a consequence of the lack of elite consensus and partly as a result of the inherent weakness of state institutions, authoritarianism has never firmly taken root in Moldova. However, both the country's political and economic spheres remained highly informal throughout the first postcommunist decade. The Communist Party's 2001 return to power marked further informalization of Moldova's political sphere. Until the end of communist rule in 2009, the reform process was slow and was often derailed by the informal relations that prevailed in state institutions. The lack of elite consensus after the end of Soviet rule inadvertently created a relatively liberal political scene, but deliberate efforts to implement continuous and comprehensive institutional reforms—including attempts to formalize state institutions—have occurred only since that time. In contrast to Georgia, Moldova remains an "informal state," and many of the reform projects planned by a series of prodemocratic governments remain in progress. Nonetheless, Moldova offers a suitable case study of the association between democratic institutional reforms and informality, not only because of the high levels of informalization of its state institutions but also because of the Moldovan regime's formal commitment to creating democratic and transparent state institutions.

SOVIET MOLDOVA: THE "FORSAKEN REPUBLIC"

Like most other states in the former Soviet Union (fSU), the informal practices and institutions that thrive in Moldova today have roots in the Soviet period. While little is known about informality in Soviet Moldova, the available evidence suggests that Moldova was much like other Soviet socialist republics (SSRs) in terms of its informal sector. The Moldovan SSR stood out, however, because of the scale of its socioeconomic underdevelopment and institutional stagnation under the Soviet communism. As a result of these factors as well as ethnic issues and political instability, post-Soviet Moldovan formal institutions remained dysfunctional, mismanaged, and deformalized for well over a decade. Therefore, the Soviet-era history of Moldova offers valuable insight into country's institutional framework and its informal structures.

The 1939 Molotov-Ribbentrop Pact carved the present-day republic of Moldova out of Romanian territory. In 1940, the Romanian-speaking lands of Bessarabia were merged with the existing Slavic-populated Moldovan Autonomous Soviet Socialist Republic to create the Moldovan SSR.[1] During the late 1940s, overwhelmingly rural Moldova experienced forced collectivization, followed by en masse deportations of *kulaks* (wealthy peasants).[2] Repression and cultural assimilation during the late Stalinist period sought both to increase the impact of sovietization and reduce ethnic Moldovans' sociocultural ties with Romania.[3]

In contrast to the Georgian SSR, known as one of richest and most prosperous Soviet republics, Moldova, which Charles King has dubbed "the forgotten Soviet republic," was among the poorest parts of the Soviet Union.[4] From the time of its incorporation into the Soviet state, the Moldovan SSR perpetually fell below Soviet standards in most areas of socioeconomic development and remained one of the nation's least developed economies.[5] According to William Crowther, as late as in the 1980s, Moldova "produced lower income per capita than any other non–Central Asian [Soviet] republic."[6] With more than 40 percent of Moldova's economy dependent on agriculture, deficiencies in Moldovan agricultural management were often a matter of concern for the Communist Party of the Soviet Union (CPSU), prompting the party officials to reevaluate the republic's agricultural development strategies.[7] Soviet sources report that Moscow made only limited investments in the Moldovan SSR.[8] In 1964, Moldova ranked seventh among the fifteen SSRs in terms of its economic growth; by 1990, it had fallen two places.[9] Because Soviet authorities made few efforts to urbanize Moldova, it and Central Asian SSRs had among the highest percentages of rural residents.[10] Heavily dependent on viticulture, the Moldovan economy received a heavy blow when Mikhail Gorbachev sought to eradicate chronic alcoholism in the USSR by reducing production of alcoholic beverages.

As in other Soviet republics, the informal economy was an inseparable attribute of Moldova's command economy. In the 1960s, private plot activity accounted for nearly half of all household income.[11] In Moldova (as in Ukraine and Georgia), more than 40 percent of housing in urban areas was privately owned.[12] However, in other respects, the scope of Moldova's informal economy was not remarkable by Soviet standards. Simon Johnson and his coauthors estimate that at the end of Soviet period, the informal economy accounted for only 18 percent of Moldova's total GDP.[13] In Moldova, only 17 percent of cattle were in private hands, compared to 60 percent in Georgia, 53 percent in Uzbekistan, and 50 percent in Turkmenistan. In 1975, only 22 percent of the Moldovan SSR's meat and 17 percent of milk products were produced privately.[14] In Armenia, almost 80 percent of vegetables were grown and sold privately; in Moldova, that figure was 11 percent. Given Moldova's heavy dependence on agriculture, these figures indicate a very low level of informal entrepreneurial activity.[15] The most obvious explanation for this rather limited informal economy lies not in the absence or weakness of informal institutions in the countryside but in the endemic impoverishment of Moldovan peasants.

Despite being portrayed by Soviet propaganda as a "flourishing orchard" and "the Soviet vineyard," the Moldovan SSR was also notorious for its fairly low living standards.[16] The republic had one of the USSR's lowest life expectancy rates (matched only by Central Asian republics) and the highest infant mortality rate in Eastern Europe.[17] By the end of 1970s, the Moldovan SSR had the Soviet Union's lowest average annual wages (seventy-six rubles). Gertrude S. Greenslade and Gregory Grossman have calculated that Moldovan households' consumption exceeded their personal incomes per capita.[18] In 1959, only 4.3 percent of Moldova's population had completed primary education and at least some higher education, and although this figure more than doubled by the 1970s, it remained at just over 10 percent. Moldovans thus ranked as the least educated ethnic group in the USSR, far below the next two groups, the Tadjiks (17 percent) and Turkmen (17.2 percent).[19] Though Georgia's population was about the same size as Moldova's,

Georgia had 157 specialists employed in Soviet economy in 1970, while Moldova had only 44.[20]

Outside perspectives on Soviet Moldova are scarce. As King comments, the republic "was rarely featured in foreign analyses of the Soviet Union."[21] Therefore, little is known about society in the Moldovan SSR beyond the Soviet sources. By the end of the 1950s, massive sovietization and the expansion of industrial complex, which took place mostly in Transnistrian region, were followed by large-scale migration of Russians and Ukrainians into Moldova's urban centers.[22] Slavic migrants resettling in Moldovan regions brought with them the Soviet-Russian *blat*, which easily adapted to local conditions.[23]

Although research on specifics of *blat* in Moldova is nonexistent, the use of *blat*-related practices not only by ethnic Russians and Ukrainians but also by Moldovans shows that the practices encapsulated under the concept of *blat* did not differ markedly from those in Russia or Ukraine.[24] The massive russification of Moldova's urban settlements meant that as in Russia, *blat* functioned as a classical "economy of favors," with reciprocal exchanges of services and favors.[25] In light of the fact that Soviet statistics show that only about 36 percent of ethnic (Romanian-speaking) Moldovans had knowledge of the Russian language, the spread of *blat* in rural areas—where ethnic Moldovans were concentrated until the 1980s—was likely limited.[26] Nonetheless the reliance on informal patronage networks and their use for the misappropriation of state resources was not confined to urban enclaves.

Moldova was one of the most corrupt Soviet republics, matched only by the Georgian and Azerbaijani SSRs. Informal power network connections between Moldovan communist elites and the Kremlin *nomenklatura* dated back to Leonid Brezhnev's tenure as first secretary of the Communist Party of Moldova from 1950 to 1952.[27] On becoming general secretary of the CPSU, Brezhnev entrusted the republic's leadership to his former colleague, Ivan Bodyul, who served as first secretary until 1980. Under Bodyul, the dynamics of Moldovan political corruption and nepotism differed from those in Georgia. Rather than accumulating private wealth and spending it lavishly, as their Georgian counterparts did, Moldovan apparatchiks channeled the lion's share of their "incomes" to their patrons in Moscow, who in turn ensured protection (*krysha*) and elite continuity.

Despite Moldova's status as a quiet backwater of the Soviet Union, the republic's communist *nomenklatura* had close links to the Kremlin.[28] Remarkably, the list of first secretaries of the CPSU who worked in Moldova includes not only Brezhnev but also Konstantin Chernenko as well as Nikita

Khrushchev. According to King, "Moldovan political elites were among the most loyal in the union."[29] Regardless of cordial relationships between Moldovan communist elites and their patrons in Moscow, Moldova had one of the lowest rates of membership in the CPSU.[30] Ellen Jones and Fred W. Grupp estimate that in 1970 only 38 percent of Moldovans were members of the CPSU. Only Ingush nationals in the North Caucasus had a lower rate of CPSU membership (34 percent).[31] Moldova's low level of CPSU membership also indicates a gap between predominantly ethnic Russian and Transnistrian communist elites and the Moldovan majority.

The evidence of large-scale corruption in state institutions is abundant in communist-era sources.[32] Crowther writes, "The republican Party apparatus was packed with Brezhnev cronies who misappropriated millions of rubles and relied on connections with Moscow to protect them from prosecution."[33] Almost no anticorruption campaigns took place in the republic, and between 1965 and 1990, only thirteen Moldovan officials were dismissed from their positions, and two were imprisoned for official crimes.[34] Over that period, fifty officials in Georgia were removed from their posts and twenty were convicted, while in Azerbaijan, twenty-four were dismissed and eighty-four were imprisoned.[35] Both ethnic divisions and a strict hierarchy within Moldovan communist elites ensured that the abuse of state institutions was limited to close circles of pro-Moscow elites and therefore never reached the scale embezzlement and profiteering that Soviet Georgia experienced. Economically impoverished and lacking networking access to state officials, the Moldovan population had limited opportunities to subvert formal institutions beyond already existing informal relations within *nomenklatura* networks.

Brezhnev's stasis ended with Bodyul's dismissal. However, his successor, Semion Grossu, "proved to be a tenacious opponent of reform," and the Moldovan Communist Party remained impervious to change.[36] Despite Grossu's resistance to the wave of reforms encouraged by perestroika, dissident movements reached Moldova unaffected. The relative liberalization of the Moldovan public scene during this era spurred the creation of numerous informal political and cultural groups.[37] As in other nonethnic Russian Soviet republics, Moldova's informal (*neformaly*) circles were dominated by nationalist and anti-Soviet elements, with pan-Romanian activists comprising the core of Moldova's dissident movement.[38] The emergence of the Popular Front and a number of other anti-Soviet opposition groups, some of which obtained legal status, precipitated Moldova's rupture with the crumbling Soviet state.

FROM INDEPENDENCE TO THE END OF COMMUNIST RULE

Moldova declared its independence from Soviet Union in 1991, following the August putsch in Moscow. As in many other former Soviet republics, the first government of independent Moldova was formed by former dissidents—in this case, members of the nationalist pan-Romanian Popular Front, led by Mircea Snegur. Given that many members of Moldovan nationalist government had switched to the Popular Front from the Communist Party of Moldova, former members of communist *nomenklatura* dominated postcommunist Moldovan political elites. As Crowther details, more than 87 percent of the members of the Moldovan parliament during the early 1990s were former party members.[39]

During the first years of Snegur's presidency, Moldova, like other post-Soviet republics, was affected by a severe economic crisis.[40] By 1994, economic production had decreased by more than 60 percent, and the country's GDP had plummeted, reducing purchasing power by almost 80 percent. With the loss of more than half of Moldova's industry to Transnistria, the republic's economy came to depend heavily on the agricultural sector, which required extensive reforms and decollectivization. The failure of agricultural reform and the glacial pace of decollectivization encouraged the mass emigration of Moldova's labor force to Russia or Romania. The exodus of nearly one million Moldovans created an enormous economy of remittances, which by 2007 accounted for more than 36 percent of the GDP.[41] With the majority of its active labor force abroad, a significant part of Moldova's population was living on less than two dollars a day. Nina Orlova and Per Ronnas observe that post-Soviet Moldova "holds the unenviable record of having suffered the most devastating peacetime decline in economic performance and living standards of any country in modern times."[42]

The economic crisis exacerbated existing tensions among pan-Romanian ultranationalists of the Popular Front, moderates, and pro-Russian forces.[43] Yet unlike the immediate post-Soviet governments in many other former Soviet republics, which were almost entirely composed of former dissidents, the Moldovan government consisted of former members of the communist *nomenklatura* who had turned to dissidence in the late 1980s and early 1990s. The Moldovan ruling elites' previous political experience and reliance on well-established informal networks enabled the first president to remain in office for a full term. The pace of reforms during the first postcommunist years was slow, and privatization was perhaps the only reform successfully implemented in the mid-1990s.[44]

Though Snegur never attempted to construct a democratic regime, his inability to consolidate the executive resulted in the dispersal of political power between the legislative branch—represented by the head of parliament—and the prime minister.[45] They fiercely challenged the president in all areas of governance, limiting his powers and reducing his chances of resorting to authoritarian means of governance.[46] In the closely contested 1996 presidential election, Snegur lost to Petru Lucinschi, a former communist apparatchik and the pro-Moscow leader of a left-wing party. Lucinschi's presidency was overshadowed by ongoing confrontations with parliament, which ultimately reduced the executive's powers by transforming Moldova into a parliamentary republic.

Despite the omnipresence of informal institutions in political and economic life during the immediate postcommunist decade, both Lucan A. Way and Theodor Tudoroiu insist that Moldova's informal institutions featured weak network ties.[47] This means that network members' allegiances, loyalties, and commitments were rather unstable. Unlike Georgia's informal institutions, which not only were cemented by members' kinship ties and common geographic origins but were also bound by notions of individual honor and patronal obligations, informal structures in Moldova were centered on personalities. As Way details, informal networks were almost always connected "with a particular leader rather than any broader corporate notion of 'fictive kin,' ethnicity, or even territory."[48] Such personalized informal relations affected the stability and continuity of informal institutions.

In Ecaterina McDonagh's observation, Moldova's elites during Lucinschi's presidency were relatively open to the democratization agenda and often eagerly embraced external democratization efforts advocated by the European Union (EU) and the Council of Europe.[49] Yet the absence of a single power base capable of asserting control over various interest groups and informal power networks prevented either further democratization of the Moldovan state or its transformation into an authoritarian regime.[50] Way dubs this weakness of institutional power brokers "pluralism by default" and describes it as a condition that "cannot be traced to leadership commitment to democratic values."[51] In other words, given that both Snegur and Lucinschi harbored latent autocratic ambitions, the weakness of their power bases and the lack of national unity "prevented any single group from consolidating authoritarian control."[52]

Following the 1998 economic crisis, Moldova plunged into a deep recession.[53] The already struggling Moldovan economy had limited resources with which to overcome the financial crisis. Infighting among communists, members of the Agrarian Democratic Party, and neoliberals meant that land reform and other modernizations of the agricultural sector such as decollectivization never succeeded.[54] The vast majority of farming collectives and individual agricultural producers refused to follow the government's reform plans, resulting in "a largely subsistence-based peasantry with some of the lowest incomes in Europe."[55]

Despite their initially ambitious reform plans, post-Soviet Moldovan institution-builders have done little to modernize and formalize state institutions or to strengthen the country's economy.[56] Reforms implemented in the aftermath of 1998 crisis, as Larisa Lubarova, Oleg Petrushin, and Artur Radziwill point out, were driven primarily by the International Monetary Fund and World Bank rather than initiated by the Moldovan government.[57]

Both the 1992 and 1998 economic crises contributed to the growth of informal economic activities. Johnson and his coauthors argue that Moldova's informal economy began booming after independence.[58] The informal economy's share of the republic's GDP increased from 18 percent in 1989–90 to more than 29 percent in 1991–93 and to almost 38 percent in 1994–95. Friedrich Schneider, Andreas Buehn, and Claudio E. Montenegro report that Moldova's informal economy accounted for more than 44 percent of the country's GDP by 2007.[59] The Center for Strategic Studies and Reforms estimates that by the late 1990s, Moldova's informal economy accounted for 60–65 percent of the total economic production and employed more than 40 percent of the labor force.[60] According to the Economic Survey Moldova in Transition, the informal economy's share of the Moldovan GDP grew from less than 20 percent in 1991 to more than 40 percent in 1997.[61] In 2004, the International Labour Organization calculated that almost 60 percent of Moldova's informal jobs were in rural areas.[62]

Corruption has grown rapidly as the informal economy has expanded. Transparency International reported that the number of economic crimes in Moldova grew from 1,867 in 1992 to 3,603 in 2000.[63] The number of registered bribes grew from 31 in 1992 to 130 in 2000, with thousands more unregistered cases of official corruption.[64] In Transparency International's 2000 Corruption Perceptions Index, Moldova occupied ranked seventy-fourth among ninety countries.[65] A report on state capture (private individuals' or firms' informal influence on state institutions through informal payments or connections and patronage networks) by the European Bank for Reconstruction and Development (EBRD) rated the impact of private firms and individuals on legislative decision-making and political party financing as the second worst in the fSU, behind only Azerbaijan.[66]

By the end of Lucinschi's presidency in 2000, the confrontation between the executive and legislative branches and the lack of agreement among prodemocratic parties had left Moldova's political elites in disarray.[67] In such a situation, the direct successor of the Moldovan Communist Party, the Party of Communists of the Republic of Moldova (PCRP), emerged as the country's most well-organized political party. In 2001 parliamentary elections described by observers as free and fair, the PCRP won just over 50 percent of the vote.[68] The party's longtime leader, Vladimir Voronin, thus assumed the presidency. The PCRP promised economic modernization and European integration, and its success at producing moderate economic growth, combined with the weakness of other political parties, led it to win reelection four years later.[69]

The PCRP tackled the ongoing problem of informal institutions' weakness by building up a strong grassroots party organization with both formal and informal support structures branching out into rural areas.[70] The PCRP's institutionalized system of networks not only was constructed around Voronin's personal image but also relied on Soviet-era nostalgia. The PCRP exploited widespread public regret about the dissolution of the Soviet Union.[71] The PCRP thus provided the population with a surrogate for the old Moldovan Communist Party, deploying former Soviet cadres and creating relative harmony between the executive and parliament.

Although the country officially transitioned in 2001 from a presidential to a parliamentary system, making Moldova the only non-Baltic parliamentary republic in the fSU, Moldova did not progress toward democratic governance during the PRCP's two terms in office. Rather, the communists' return constituted a setback for democratization.[72] During the PCRP's eight-year domination of the Moldovan political scene, the country vacillated between a semiconsolidated authoritarian state (sustained by Voronin's autocratic control over the parliament and government) and a hybrid regime. From 1997 to 2000, Freedom House labeled Moldova a semiconsolidated democracy.[73] Yet just a year after the start of the PCRP's first term, Moldova's democracy score was downgraded to that of a hybrid regime.[74] By the end of Voronin's second term in office in 2009, the Nations in Transit project ranked Moldova as a semiconsolidated authoritarian state.[75] However, in spite of the PCRP's reliance on autocratic forms of governance and its efforts to monopolize Moldova's political scene by distributing government positions to its loyalists, institutional weaknesses prevented the communists from creating a full-fledged authoritarian state. For example, as Henry E. Hale describes, the PCRP never managed to gain control of the post of Chişinău's mayor.[76]

Despite the fact that informal institutions had played a prominent role in Moldova's politics and economy even before the communist return, Moldova experienced its highest level of institutional deformalization during Voronin's tenure. On the one hand, the use of informal practices in the population's dealings with state institutions increased substantially. More than half of the respondents to the EBRD's 2011 Life in Transition survey indicated that they had used informal channels to access the public health system.[77] The reliance on informal practices undoubtedly increased during the · 2008–10 global financial crisis. According to the EBRD, only 20 percent of Moldovans relied on public safety nets, while more than half turned to informal social safety nets. That figure is higher than the reliance on informal safety nets in the Central Asian republics (35 percent) and in Russia (47 percent) but lower than in the South Caucasus (58 percent).[78] According to the EBRD's 2006 survey, more than 70 percent of Moldovans believed that corruption had increased between 1989 and 2006.[79]

On the other hand, Moldova experienced one of the world's highest increases in state capture, one of the most obvious outcomes of communists' attempts to monopolize the informal sphere.[80] The frequency with which individuals interfere in the work of state institutions has reached a colossal scale that the World Bank describes it as one of the worst in the fSU.[81]

Overall, reform stagnated under the communist government. The PCRP either reversed or abandoned some of liberal reforms adopted during the first post-Soviet decade, while new reform initiatives were scarce, underfunded, and poorly managed. Some scholars consequently have argued that the PCPR favored "re-sovietization and anti-reformism" over democratization and institutional change.[82] One of the PCRP's major reform projects was the reintroduction of the Soviet administrative division of the country into thirty-two districts, a reversal of the Lucinschi government's creation of thirteen larger districts, which had been criticized as an effort to restrict the independence of regional administrations.[83] Under pressure from the EU, particularly within the framework of the 2005 EU-Moldova Action Plan, Moldova implemented a series of judicial reforms aimed at addressing the issue of human rights.[84] In 2007, the Moldovan government attempted to adopt a national anticorruption reform strategy for 2007–9.[85] The increase in corruption levels captured by Transparency International demonstrated the failure of that reform.[86]

The PCRP failed to win a majority in the 2009 parliamentary elections for a variety of reasons, most notably the party's inability to follow through on any of its major promises, particularly in the areas of economic development, resolution of the Transnistrian conflict, and European integration.[87] Moldova's new government involved a coalition of four opposition parties, the Alliance for European Integration (Alianța pentru Integrare Europeană, or AIE), with Vladimir Filat as prime minister. Moldova's weak formal institutional framework and the communists' failure to undermine competing informal power bases contributed to the defeat. A series of popular protests against the electoral fraud by the PCRP, the "Twitter Revolution," has further weakened the communist party's popular base, reducing Voronin's chances of rallying support for reelection.[88]

Nonetheless the communist period has left an imprint on Moldova's institutional scene. By the time the PCPR lost its majority in parliament, the Moldovan state institutions had almost completely been overtaken by their informal counterparts.[89] Patronage networks, fostered through extensive state capture by private actors, have deeply permeated formal institutions, impairing their efficiency and obstructing reform efforts.

THE REFORMIST GOVERNMENT IN POWER

Moldova regained the status of a hybrid regime after a move toward democratization that began with the AIE's victory in the 2009 parliamentary elections. Drawing its legitimacy from a far-reaching agenda of European integration, the Alliance pledged sweeping institutional reforms as an essential part of a campaign to modernize and democratize the country in preparation for closer integration with the European Union. However, the AIE initially failed to gain a majority in parliament and thus could not elect a president and execute its reform agenda. After three rounds of parliamentary elections in less than three years, the AIE finally managed to obtain a majority in 2012 and elected Nicolae Timofti as president.

The AIE's agenda included an extensive anticorruption campaign and reforms of local governance and the judicial system as well as reforms of the public, health care, education, business, and energy sectors and of the electoral process.[90] All of these reforms sought not only to establish closer ties with the European Union, which required thorough institutional reforms, but also to building transparent and accountable state institutions. The Moldovan government has also reached agreement with the European Union on a more recent reform program, the Single Support Framework (2014–2017), which includes (1) administrative reform, (2) agriculture and rural development, and (3) police reform and border management.[91]

Excessive centralization of local governance remained one of the biggest challenges facing Moldovan reformers.[92] Though the PCRP never established absolute control over local administrations, its massive centralization program created the need for comprehensive reform of local governance. In 2012, the AIE promoted the National Decentralization Strategy that sought to allocate greater authority and funding to local administrations. However, the regions' tightly knit system of patronage networks connecting local administrators to their patrons among influential businessmen and politicians in Chișinău meant that the decentralization scheme encountered staunch resistance from both communists and business elites.

Nevertheless, parliament continued to promote local governance reforms through 2013–14. Amendments to the law on local government funding allocated 75 percent of locally collected income tax to remain in regional budgets. In line with the EU's requests for reform of the notoriously corrupt and ineffective judicial sector, a 2011 law increased the legal system's accountability and efficiency.[93] In 2012, the Ministry of Justice instituted further reforms that reduced the number of judges from forty-nine to thirty-three, increased judges' salaries, and required background tests for applicants.[94]

The AIE also oversaw the adoption of anticorruption legislation.[95] The Center for Combating Corruption and Economic Crime was reorganized into the National Anticorruption Center.[96] Though layered on top of the Center for Combating Corruption, the National Anticorruption Center was established as a new institution, with rigid selection procedures for staff that decreased the agency's size from 540 employees to 350. Along with the National Anticorruption Center, the Anticorruption Prosecutor's Office and the National Integrity Commission carried out an anticorruption campaign. Although these institutions have overlapping functions, these initial efforts led to a notable reduction in corruption, as evidenced by Transparency International's Corruption Perceptions Index.[97] Subsequently, however, Moldova's corruption scores again began to fall.[98] Both anticorruption and judicial reform (the latter funded by a sixty-million-euro assistance package from the EU) were implemented under the pressure from the European Union. EU pressure was also associated with visa liberalization program and with the preparation for the Moldova-EU association agreement that Moldova signed in 2014.

Following Georgia's example, Moldovan reformists launched a campaign to reorganize the police force. In early 2012, the Border Guard was reorganized into the Border Police, and a new system of evaluation exams for police staff was introduced. After only 10 percent of the police department's employees passed the professional evaluation test, almost seven hundred police employees were fired over the second half of 2012.[99] Parliament then ratified the new Law on Police to allow further institutional changes. The minister of the interior was replaced, and a number of televised arrests—modeled on Georgian anticorruption arrests—of corrupt police officers and officials took place. An increase of as much as 30 percent in police employees' salaries sought to curb corruption. However, institutional changes within the Ministry of Internal Affairs were limited to renaming existing institutions rather than converting them to different purposes or creating new structures, as was the case with the police reform in Georgia.

The pace of economic reform has been less impressive. Despite being ranked as one of the top ten successful reformers in Doing Business's 2014 rankings, Moldova has since 2009 lost about 25 percent of its foreign investment as a consequence of corruption of tax officials, corporate raiding, and bureaucratic complexity.[100] The recovery from the 2008–9 global financial crisis was rather slow, and Moldova's economy continued to underperform.[101] Since 2013, the Moldovan economy has picked up its growth, with the GDP increasing to $13.25 billion (up from $12.26 billion in 2011).[102] The scope of economic reforms, however, remained limited to an increased commitment to the privatization campaign and the attraction of foreign investment, both of which remained largely ineffective.[103]

Given that the AIE and its political successors derived their legitimacy and based their electoral campaign promises of integration with the European Union rather than specifically on combating corruption and thoroughly reforming state institutions, as the UNM did in Georgia, Moldova's reforms have been tailored to satisfy the EU's demands. State building and democratic institutional change remain secondary. The efforts to formalize informal relations within formal institutions have thus far been patchy and inconsistent. Furthermore, informal politics and the use of informal practices are inseparable parts of the institutional reforms currently being implemented.

The other caveat of Moldova's post-2009 politics is that since the prodemocratic coalition assumed power, the government's agenda has been dominated by oligarchic interests of its leaders. Both Vlad Filat, the longtime leader of Liberal Democratic Party, and Vlad Plahotniuc, the head of another major pro-European party, the Democratic Party, belong to a small group of billionaire oligarchs who amassed their wealth under dubious circumstances during the 1990s. Like their oligarchic opponents within the opposition camp, Filat and Plahotniuc promote their own business and investment interests. Although the oligarchization of Moldova's political scene had already started under Voronin, whose family owned massive financial assets, the arrival of pro-European coalition has elevated an elite club of Moldova's oligarchs into the higher echelons of power.

ASSESSING THE IMPACT OF REFORMS

The European Union and many international organizations positively acknowledged Moldova's post-PCRP reforms.[104] For example, the World Bank named Moldova "one of the world's top performers in terms of poverty reduction."[105] Nevertheless, both the EU and other members of the international community described Moldovan institutional reforms as incomplete and insufficient.[106] Seemingly endless political infighting among members of the coalition and between pro-reform and procommunist forces in parliament were accompanied by the rise of political and economic corruption. The government's failure to efficiently implement most of its reforms played a prominent role in the AIE's demise after a February 2013 no-confidence vote.

The coalition was succeeded by the Pro-European Coalition (Coaliția Pro-Europeană), formed in May 2013 from three prodemocratic parties. The Pro-European Coalition survived until February 2015, when it was replaced by the Alliance for European Moldova (Alianța Politică pentru Moldova Europeană), which formed a minority government with support from Voronin's PCRP. The Alliance for European Moldova thus forged an informal need-dictated alliance with the communists. The unwritten agreement between the two parties exemplifies the reformist pro-European coalition's informal politics.

Turbulent and chaotic, Moldovan party politics display characteristics of a hybrid democratic political system. Reformist agendas have often fallen victim to political instability and failed coalition-building. One of the major ob-

stacles for institutional reforms in Moldova remains the lack of political consensus among ruling elites, a phenomenon that has plagued Moldovan
politics since the end of Soviet rule. Prodemocratic coalition governments
have consistently proven incapable of achieving agreement on almost any
major reform program. The rifts within pro-European coalitions detailed by
Vladimir Socor have resulted in the fragmentation of the reform camp,
which, in turn, hinders the speed and the effectiveness of reforms.[107] In contrast to Georgian reformists, who had a majority in the government and
widely enjoyed popular support, especially during Mikheil Saakashvili's first
term in office, Moldova's pro-reform forces are dispersed among various ministries and political parties and lack legislative backing and popular approval.

Moreover, Moldovan institutional transformation has been hamstrung
by a lack of consistency on the political scene and the pro-reform coalition's
waning support base.[108] The weakness of the reformists' political base is com-
pounded by the overall vulnerability of prodemocratic forces. Moldova's
democrats face the prospect of being overpowered by the rapidly expanding
Socialist Party or by the return of communists.

Informality pervades the pro-reform coalition, which is cemented by
countless informal deals and shadowy agreements between politicians and
oligarchs, making formalization challenging and even lethal for the reformists. Formalization of the behind-the-scenes politics may further undermine
the reformist coalition's power bases and ultimately destroy it. The continuity and effectiveness of institutional reforms closely depend on the political
survival and success of pro-reform forces, and Moldova's democratic institutional transformation remains in its infancy, complicating any assessment
of the reform campaign.

Attitudes toward Institutional Reforms

The start of democratic institutional reforms in the aftermath of the AIE's
2009 electoral success has undoubtedly reshaped Moldova's political
scene, making the country a hybrid regime with an internationally recognized reformist government. Following almost two decades of institutional
stagnation and underdevelopment, the population would be expected to
notice institutional improvements. The EBRD's Life in Transition surveys,
conducted before (2006) and during (2010) the AIE's reforms, recorded notable increases in popular satisfaction with service delivery. The number of
people satisfied with the public health system rose from 43 percent in 2006

to 67 percent in 2010, while the percentage satisfied with the work of the civil courts rose from 43 percent to 65 percent and with traffic police service rose from 27 percent to 39 percent. The highest degree of institutional improvement occurred in the education sector, whose approval ratings increased from 44 percent in 2006 to 79 percent four years later, and in the issuing of official documents, where positive responses increased from 49 percent to 82 percent.[109]

Notwithstanding these positive developments, levels of institutional trust have fallen since the start of reforms (table 5.1). Although popular trust of the educational system and police have increased slightly since the 1990s, levels of trust in all other state institutions have declined markedly. For example, in 2015, popular trust in political institutions—including the office of the president office, parliament, and political parties—reached its lowest levels since independence.[110] By 2015, Moldovans expressed exceptionally high levels of distrust in most formal institutions.

While surveys recorded mixed satisfaction with governance during Voronin's first term as president, popular discontent with government's work began to grow after his reelection. By 2008, more than 80 percent of respondents to the Barometer of Public Opinion (BPO) survey expressed their discontent with living standards and with the government's efforts to improve economic and political governance. The change in government and the ensuing promises of reform and European integration improved popular attitudes toward the government, and by 2010, 55 percent of respondents were satisfied with the work of public servants, while slightly over half disapproved of the government's performance. Two years later, however, the pro-

TABLE 5.1. Levels of Institutional Distrust in Moldova (%)

Have no trust (confidence) in:	1996	2003	2006	2008	2012	2014	2015
Legal system (courts)	50	70	58	74	78	74	80
Police	65	70	60	74	71	67	66
President	—	43	52	57	75	73	86
National government	55	60	60	70	72	72	86
Parliament	57	54	58	69	80	76	88
Political parties	78	80	70	84	82	79	86
Education system	—	72	50	65	61	60	56
Health care system	—	85	68	72	74	73	78
Banks	—	67	55	72	63	61	72

Sources: World Values Survey; Institute for Public Policy (IPP) "Barometer of Public Opinion"

European coalition's failure to produce noticeable institutional improvements had alienated significant segments of Moldova's population: only 22 percent of respondents judged the AIE government as better than the communists, while 31 percent said it was the same and 25 percent saw it as worse (25 percent).[111]

The population judged that the government's efforts to deal with the problem of corruption not only had failed but were also counterproductive. More than 70 percent of the respondents to the 2013 Transparency International Corruption survey thought that the level of corruption in the country had increased, and the same number believed that government's actions in the fight against corruption were ineffective. Similarly, the 2012 BPO found that only 15 percent of respondents believed that the level of corruption had improved during Filat's tenure as prime minister, while more than 43 percent thought that it remained unchanged and 30 percent thought that it had worsened. And in the 2015 BPO survey, 72 percent of respondents declared that corruption remained a major problem, an increase from 2006–9, when that figure averaged 65 percent. People also have maintained their views regarding which institutions are particularly corrupt: in both 2006 and 2015, police and medical authorities were described as the most problematic institutions.[112]

According to a series of surveys conducted by the International Republican Institute, the Voronin government's most important 2008 accomplishments included increasing pensions (cited by 13 percent of respondents) and paying them on time (10 percent) as well as paying wages on time (4 percent). In contrast, respondents cited the government's largest failures as inflation (12 percent), the unresolved territorial conflict in Transnistria (6 percent), unemployment (5 percent), and corruption (3 percent). In 2010, the most important achievements of the AIE government were improving relations with the EU (10 percent), receiving grants from abroad (7 percent), and economic development (5 percent); 38 percent of respondents said that the government had no achievements. The biggest failures were increased prices for consumer goods and taxes (23 percent), higher utility fees (6 percent), and delays in the payment of pensions and wages (4 percent).[113]

According to the BPO surveys, government reforms have produced increases in the level of public satisfaction only in the health care and education sectors (table 5.2). In all other areas, including such high priorities as improving living standards, unemployment, and agricultural development, satisfaction has remained roughly the same or has declined.

The 2014 International Republican Institute survey found that the country's most important problems were unemployment (34 percent), corruption (32 percent), and low income (31 percent).[114] The pro-reform government seems to have failed in its efforts to address these problems. The process of restructuring old institutions and constructing new ones may have solidified Moldova's institutional scene and established the foundation for long-term institutional changes but has produced at best limited short-term effects. With the persistence of the most pressing problems (unemployment, corruption, and the quality of public services), the population has not looked kindly upon reforms. The reformist coalition's inability to achieve intraparty consensus and to consolidate its gains has caused a dramatic decline in institutional trust (see table 5.1), which presents a serious challenge to formalization efforts and raises speculation that the reforms would have almost no influence on the informal sector.

Reliance on Informality

Have Moldova's post-2009 reforms had any visible effect on informality? In the absence of academic attempts to assess the spread and importance of Moldova's informal sphere beyond the issue of corruption, the most obvious observation is that informality has not retreated either from formal institutions or from the country's everyday social and political life. The reliance on informal institutions has risen steadily since Moldova achieved independence from the USSR. And a 2000 poll found that the majority of respondents associated the growth of informality with the end of Soviet rule and the transition to a market economy.[115]

The end of Soviet period also brought a structural change in the nature of

TABLE 5.2. *Satisfaction with Moldovan Reforms (%)*

Satisfied with government policies on:	2002	2004	2006	2012	2014	2015
Health care	11	20	28	23	25	20
Fight against corruption	8	11	12	6	10	1
Education	24	29	40	30	32	34
Agriculture	17	18	22	14	16	16
Living standards	14	18	21	11	10	10
Employment	12	12	15	7	12	7

Source: IPP "Barometer of Public Opinion"

informal relations in Moldova. Unlike Soviet-era informal practices, which favored the use of contacts and networks over monetary gifts and bribes, the transition to capitalism increased the importance of cash transactions. Just as Russian *blat* has experienced a massive monetization in the postcommunist period, the Moldovan equivalent has been transformed from exchanges of favors to cash-centered services.[116] The predominant unofficial channels of access to formal institutions in present-day Moldova are bribery and other forms of material gift-giving.[117]

Alexandru Roman portrays the complex nature of Moldovan informality, emphasizing that monetary gifts are deeply embedded in the cultural context, in the problem of collective action, and in popular perceptions of corruption.[118] Indeed, the issue of collective action comes to the forefront of Moldovan social and political life as a consequence of the unavoidable need to do things informally.[119] Since much of the reform agenda projected by the pro-EU coalition required intracoalitional consensus and legislative approval, informal practices became embedded into institutional changes and therefore deformalized the reform process.[120]

Without a power center capable of planning and implementing institutional changes comparable to what existed in Saakashvili's Georgia, Moldovan reformists must coordinate their activities with other coalition members by engaging in informal brokering and pacts. In light of the fact that many of pro-reform coalition's cadres originated within the communist ranks, Moldova's political scene has experienced almost none of the revolutionary change among the ruling elites that is necessary to break the deeply rooted Soviet-era habit of using informal practices.[121] As a result, rather than weeding out informal practices, the reform process legitimized and formalized informal consensus-making mechanisms within formal institutions. As a morally acceptable social norm, the use of informal channels by public administrators, policymakers, and most of all reformers embedded the informal institutions into the newly built or "reformed" formal institutions.[122] One instance of such reverse formalization occurred when the pro-European coalition and the communists created an informal pact that enabled the Alliance for European Moldova to form a minority government in 2014.[123] By accepting communists' support, the Alliance agreed to avoid decentralizing local administrations in communist-dominated rural areas.[124]

While elites continued or expanded their reliance on informal institutions, the populace's use of informal institutions grew even further. Pamela Abbott has demonstrated that informal networks are omnipresent in Moldova as a form of private safety net.[125] Thus, 58 percent of Moldovans use their informal networks when they need help to pay "urgent bills," and 42 percent used contacts in search for jobs. In addition, 88 percent have "someone" to help them in crisis, while 73 percent have plenty of friends to "confide in."[126]

Informal relations also continue to pervade the population's dealings with state institutions. The 2013 Transparency International Corruption found that 52 percent of the public used informal channels to deal with the police, while 38 percent did so in medical and health care services.[127] According to the 2010 International Republican Institute survey, 36 percent of Moldovans used various informal channels to receive preferential treatment in formal institutions. Though the introduction of a health insurance system in 2005 supposedly reduced informal practices in health care, the World Health Organization estimates that Moldovan households' informal payments for health care increased from 43 percent of total health care expenditures in 2009 to 44 percent in 2010 and topped 45 percent in 2012. Similarly, the practice of informal payments in the education sector has continued unabated: more than 50 percent of teachers and 30 percent of parents confirmed the use of informal transactions in primary and secondary education.[128] Moreover, the size of informal economic sector is believed to be rising, with the percentage of labor force employed in informal sphere increasing from 12 percent in 2011 to 25 percent two years later.[129]

Moldova's institutional reforms have not only failed to reduce the population's reliance on informal ways of accessing formal institutions but also done little to shift popular perceptions of informal practices and bribery. As in many other parts of the fSU, Moldovans generally remain fairly accepting of informal behaviors. For example, 64 percent of respondents to one survey did not think that offering a material gift to a doctor in exchange for preferential treatment constituted corruption or bribery.[130]

Both members of the elite and the general population have been profoundly affected by the lack of focus on economic reform, job creation, social security, social welfare, and other areas identified as in need of improvement as well as by the political instability created by the shifting nature of coalition politics.[131] While economic instability—exacerbated by the 2015 devaluation of the national currency—increased the importance of informality in daily life, the need for continuous pact-making and coalition-building raised the value of informal networks for the ruling elites.[132] With an extensive history of state capture stretching back to the PCRP period, Moldova's political institutions are increasingly dominated by business elites, who further their financial interests via informal connections within political parties. The February 2015 appointment of an influential business-man, Chiril Gaburici, as the head of the minority government and the long-term control of the pro-reform Democratic Party by Moldova's wealthiest oligarch, Vlad Plahotniuc, are among the most prominent examples of the informal behind-the-scenes merger of political and financial elites in the re-formist government. In the wake of the June 2015 resignation of the Gabu-rici's government as a result of corruption scandals, Moldovan politics be-came even further bogged down in oligarchic takeover. That month's legislative elections saw the rise of Our Party, a pro-Kremlin group headed by oligarch Renato Usatyi, while another Russian-grown oligarch, Ilan Shor, won the governorship of Orhei.

The lack of political stability since 2009 has not only strengthened infor-mal relations among political parties within the ruling coalition but also led to the appearance of informal opposition forces. For example, an informal civic platform, Pride and Truth (Demnitate și Adevăr) emerged on the political scene in February 2015. It has organized a series of mass antigovernment pro-tests, including a September 2015 demonstration in Chișinău against oligar-chic government politics and the embezzlement of funds from the national bank.[133] Instead of registering as a political party or as a civil society organiza-tion, Pride and Truth has chosen to remain an informal civil movement.

SUMMARY

Moldova's path toward institutional reforms has thus far been closely inter-twined with informality. Remarkable among other East European fSU states due to its implacable elite fragmentation and weak agrarian economy, both of which are legacies of the Soviet past, Moldova plunged into massive defor-malization during the first years of its independence. Post-Soviet political actors' weakness and inability to monopolize power has prevented Moldova either from effectively democratizing or from becoming a full-fledged au-thoritarian regime like many of its fSU neighbors. Notwithstanding the ram-pant corruption and extensive deformalization of state institutions, by the end of the first post-Soviet decade, Moldova was neither more corrupt nor more informal than Georgia or any other former Soviet republic.

Moldova is distinguished from other post-Soviet republics, however, by the fact that the absence of a consensus among the ruling elite combined with the country's pressing economic ills to create an alarmingly rapid process of informalization. Regardless of the prodemocratic awakening and the rise of reformist elements among Moldova's political elites by the late 2000s, informal institutions were indispensable both in politics and in socioeconomic life. The comprehensive institutional reforms inaugurated in 2009 remain in their early stages, and their effects on the informal sphere are yet hard to observe. Moldova's transformation from a semiconsolidated authoritarian state during the PCRP period into a hybrid regime under the AIE demonstrates the existence of prodemocratic forces with a will to liberalize and reform the state. If the pro-reform coalition remains in power, institutional improvement may be expected to occur in a due course.

The reform agenda is obviously enmeshed in informal politics. In an environment dominated by the omnipresence of informality, the implementation and the effectiveness of reforms tend to be conditioned by reformers' ability to employ informal channels to secure intracoalitional consensus. As a result, the reform process has been repeatedly hijacked by antireform political actors such as the communist party and the financial elites, who seek to influence the institutional transformation for personal gain. While Moldova's inherent elite fragmentation prevented the consolidation of autocracy during the 1990s and thwarted communist efforts to monopolize power in the 2000s, the lack of unity within the pro-reform coalition remains a major handicap. On a positive note, an association agreement with the EU signed in 2014 has institutionalized the previously obscure process of European integration and created a blueprint for reform.

But Europeanization also has negative consequences for Moldova's institutional reforms. The scope and the scale of reforms continue to depend on the EU's push for compliance. Hence, the initiation of reforms continues to take precedence over their effective implementation. Rather than overseeing and carrying out reform objectives, Moldova's reformers focus on launching projects, many of which are subsequently neglected or abandoned. Because achieving political consensus in present-day Moldova often requires relying on informal institutions, reformists have no choice but to employ informal practices to speed up the reform process. The effects of reform have yet to trickle down to the public, limiting the impact of the reforms and forcing the population to continue to rely on informality. A great deal of current institutional change apparently is implemented through informal institutions, bogging Moldova's institutional transformation down in informality.

CHAPTER 6

Ukraine: Reversing Decades of Informalization

SINCE THE BREAKUP of the Soviet Union, Ukraine has undergone massive deformalization of its state institutions. Soviet institutional legacies cancerously persisted in Ukraine more than in many other post-Soviet republics, meaning that socioeconomic and sociopolitical relations have seen little change since the country achieved independence in 1991. Unlike much smaller Georgia and Moldova, Ukraine, which has a population of 44.49 million and tremendous regional, ethnic, and socioeconomic diversity, has encountered all sorts of obstacles on its journey toward democratic institutionalization. The consistent failure or absence of reform efforts that initially pervaded Ukraine's post-Soviet political and economic scene was coupled with growing oligarchization and systemic corruption in formal institutions. These factors have given rise to a complex and deeply rooted informal institutional framework that functioned above and instead of formal institutions. The vicious circle of failed reforms, oligarchic continuity, and omnipresent corruption have continued unabated well into the second decade of the twenty-first century. However, the success of Euromaidan, Russia's annexation of Crimea, and a violent armed conflict with Russian-backed separatists have brought dramatic changes to Ukraine. As the old equilibrium—sustained for decades by patronage networks and oligarchs—eventually began to collapse, a comprehensive and radical institutional reform became the only remaining option for Ukrainian elites to salvage the crumbling state institutions and, therefore, ensure their own political survival. Since early 2014, Ukraine's reformers have battled to implement one of the most ambitious reform agendas in the post-Soviet region, but they have encountered a seemingly unsolvable puzzle. On the one hand, dismantling the well-entrenched system of informal institutions is imperative for the long-term success of the reform program. On the other hand, forcing democratic reforms on a sociopolitical system rooted in informality appears impossible without relying on informal channels. The challenge of detaching the formal sphere from its informal counterpart lies at the heart of the contentious relationship between Ukraine's attempts at democratic institutional reforms and the informal sector.

INFORMALITY IN SOVIET UKRAINE

As in most other former socialist societies, Ukraine's informal traditions originated during the communist period, though informal social relations have flourished among Ukrainians for centuries.[1] Until their incorporation into the USSR, Ukrainians had limited experience with either formal institutions or the nation-state. The Bolshevik conquest of Ukraine, accompanied by two decades of persecution of private landowners (kulaks) and a human-caused 1932–33 Great Famine (Holodomor) that claimed millions of lives, was the early phase of Soviet state-building in Ukraine. Under Lenin, local cadres were appointed to leadership positions in the new Ukrainian Soviet Socialist Republic (SSR), but Stalin discarded the idea and purged most ethnic Ukrainians from the Communist Party of Ukraine (CPU) during the Great Terror of 1935.[2]

Throughout the 1920 and 1930s, Soviet communist institutions spread across the sprawling Ukrainian countryside, as state-run collective farms (kolkhozy and sovkhozy) replaced private farmsteads. The violent collectivization of Ukrainian peasants was combined with the communist-caused famine to force hundreds of thousands of rural dwellers into rapidly growing urban settlements. According to Orest Subtelny, the number of urban residents in Ukraine more than doubled between 1926 and 1939.[3] At the end of the World War II, the western Ukrainian-speaking territories of Galicia and Bukovina as well as the Ukrainian-populated territories of Hungary and Poland were incorporated into the Ukrainian SSR. This unification of Ukrainian-inhabited lands within Soviet borders heralded the start of nation-building and the institutionalization of Ukraine.

Until the end of Stalinist period, the Kremlin saw Ukraine as a rogue and unruly borderland requiring close monitoring by Moscow-appointed ethnic-Russian cadres from the Communist Party of the Soviet Union (CPSU). Unlike the eastern Russian-speaking region of Donbas, which experienced heavy industrialization and was lavishly "showered with resources," Stalin-era Soviet functionaries perceived the rest of the country as the "USSR's Wild West" and most of the region's population as unenlightened and hostile to "socialist values."[4]

As one of Stalin's confidantes overseeing the socialist development of Ukraine, Nikita Khrushchev, who had years of experience with sovietizing Ukraine, realized that fully incorporating the country into the USSR would require seeding the central government's informal power structures with ethnic Ukrainians.[5] After succeeding Stalin as the head of the CPSU in 1953, Khrushchev employed his extensive connections with Ukrainian elites to cement closer links between them and the Kremlin's *nomenklatura*. In 1953, Khrushchev replaced Stalin's ethnic Russian protégé, Leonid Melnykov, with an ethnic Ukrainian, Oleksii Kyrychenko, as the CPU's first secretary. This move represented the start of a new phase of Ukraine's institution-building, implemented to make the republic second in importance only to Russia in the USSR. This rapprochement between Ukrainian and Russian elites caused Ukrainian membership in the Communist Party to expand rapidly.[6] As Khrushchev and his officials vigorously pursued de-Stalinization, a new Ukrainian Soviet *nomenklatura* emerged. To further cement Moscow's ties with Ukraine, Khrushchev engineered the 1954 transfer of Crimea from the Russian SSR to the Ukrainian SSR.

During the 1950s, Ukraine experienced massive agricultural and industrial development, helping to raise Ukraine's annual increase in per capita consumption from 1 percent in the 1940s to more than 4 percent in the 1950s.[7] Ukraine soon became a laboratory for Khrushchev's numerous agricultural experiments, and the CPSU "funneled more state investment into [Ukraine's] agricultural sector" than into agriculture in other SSRs.[8] The republic's massive production of wheat and corn led to the nickname the "breadbasket of the USSR."[9] The process of agricultural development did little to halt massive urbanization, and by the end of the 1950s, more than 30 million of Ukraine's 49.7 million residents lived in cities.[10] In the late 1970s, Paul Kubicek declares, "most of the population of Ukraine lived in cities."[11] Unlike other Soviet republics, urbanization in Ukraine did not necessarily result in higher levels of education. For example, Ukrainian specialists with higher education accounted only for 15 percent of the total Soviet workforce, while Russians comprised almost 60 percent.[12] Most urban Ukrainians held low-paying blue-collar jobs, meaning that informal practices and institutions—in particular, the Soviet-Russian practice of *blat*—functioned as an essential private safety net.

Informal links between Ukrainian elites and the CPSU became even more pronounced with the 1957 appointment of Mykola Podhorny as the CPU's first secretary. Many party first secretaries in other Soviet republics had virtually no influence among the CPSU elites in Moscow, but Khrushchev's patronage made Podhorny one of the most influential figures in Kremlin. He was sometimes described as second only to Khrushchev in the CPSU, and he retained that position until Khrushchev's 1964 removal.[13] In John P. Willerton Jr.'s estimation, Podhorny was a member of at least thirteen informal patronage networks within the CPSU.[14] This overarching system of informal power networks tightly embedded Ukrainian elites in the Soviet governance machine, transforming the republic from a rogue borderland into the CPSU's crucial power base.

The next phase of informal institutionalization of Ukraine began with Khrushchev's dismissal in 1964 and appointment of Ukraine native Leonid Brezhnev to head the CPSU. Born and raised in Dnepropetrovsk, Ukraine's third-largest city, Brezhnev maintained close ties with Ukrainian elites throughout his career. In fact, Brezhnev's rise to the post of Soviet leader was largely attributed to his vast informal connections within the CPU. Paul Robert Magosci explains, "Brezhnev built a political machine consisting of former engineers, factory directors, and officials from his home region," and that network, combined with Khrushchev's favorable attitude toward Ukrainian elites, enabled Brezhnev to ascend the party ladder.[15] This "Dnepropetrovsk Mafia" produced generations of senior CPSU cadres. In the 1970s, for example, more than half of all CPU *nomenklatura* members in Kiev were originally from Dnepropetrovsk.[16] Dnepropetrovsk was thus an informal "launching ground for the political careers of many Soviet politicians in Moscow because of its close association with the Brezhnev clan."[17]

During the early years of Brezhnev's rule, Ukraine was one the most densely industrialized Soviet republics, a sharp contrast from heavily agrarian Soviet Moldova. The Ukrainian SSR constituted not only the Soviet Union's "major industrial power" but also the key CPSU power base outside Russia.[18] This status led ethnic Ukrainian elites to increase their assertiveness vis-à-vis the Kremlin. CPU first secretary Petro Shelest attempted to promote Ukrainian national identity within the heavily Russified Ukrainian *nomenklatura*, provoking indignation in Moscow.[19] Shelest was removed from his position "on charges of being 'soft' on Ukrainian nationalism and encouraging economic 'localism.'"[20]

The rise of Shelest, a prominent member of Brezhnev's informal network, and his fall after attempting to rebel against the Kremlin show that Ukrainian elites used informal networks within the CPSU not only to forge closer ties with Moscow but also to assert their independence. As in Soviet Georgia, where the removal of Khrushchev's crony Vasil Mzhavanadze became essential for the restoration of effective Soviet administration of the republic, the dismissal of pro-Ukrainian Shelest was crucial for the continuity of Brezhnevite orthodoxy in the Ukrainian SSR.

In 1972, Shelest was replaced by Vladimir Shcherbytsky, a close friend of Brezhnev and a fellow member of the Dnepropetrovsk Clan described as an "ultra-loyalist and pro-Moscow Brezhnevite."[21] According to Willerton, Shcherbytsky was associated with sixteen informal patronage networks, serving as both patron and client, while Shelest was associated with only five patronage networks. From 1964 to 1982, only Brezhnev, whose official title was general secretary of the CPSU, had connections with a larger number of patronage networks, forty-eight.[22] While Soviet Ukraine was no less corrupt than other republics, the close connections between the Kremlin *nomenklatura* and Ukrainian elites meant that anticorruption campaigns occurred only during interclan cleansings and the ensuing changes of leadership. For example, with Shelest's dismissal and the fall from grace of his Kharkiv Clan, thirty-seven thousand members of his network were expelled from the CPSU during 1973–74 on charges of political corruption and abuse of power.[23]

With the appointment of Shcherbytsky, who was "totally servile to the leaders in Moscow," as the CPU's first secretary, informal patron-client networks between the Kremlin and Kiev were absorbed into a power vertical (*vertikal` vlasti*) that was typical of the USSR.[24] This system provided protection for local communist elites, enabling them to embezzle state resources in return for their loyalty. During Shcherbytsky's 1972–89 tenure, "Ukraine's communist elites were among the most conservative of the Soviet Union."[25] The Ukrainian elites' loyalty to Kremlin, which was maintained through the numerous members of the Dnepropetrovsk Clan stationed at all levels of the CPSU policymaking apparatus, provided relative immunity from prosecution.[26] Ukrainian *nomenklatura* members, particularly from Russian-speaking Dnepropetrovsk and the Donetsk region, occupied the top tiers of the USSR's informal clientelist and patronage networks.

Informal practices were omnipresent in Ukraine's private sphere as well. Shcherbytsky's two decades of leadership were characterized by high levels of Russification.[27] As a result of mass migration from Russia and the diffusion of Soviet popular culture, *blat* practices were as widespread across Ukraine as they were in Russia. Thoroughly and extensively sovietized under Soviet rule, particularly during Khrushchev's and Brezhnev's periods, the Ukrainian population became conditioned to use Soviet ways of circumventing communist formal institutions and employing informal networks to obtain services and favors from the state. The emergence of *neformaly*—underground cultural, artistic, and literary clubs—in the late 1960s coincided with the appearance of the generation of the 1960s (*shestydesiatnyky*). Nonetheless, the Ukrainian national and anti-Soviet dissidence were rather slow to emerge.[28]

The start of Mikhail Gorbachev's perestroika and glasnost in the mid-1980s brought little change to Ukraine, as Shcherbytsky remained firmly in control and kept it one of the most conservative and reform-resistant Soviet republics.[29] However, Shcherbytsky's continued refusal to embrace perestroika led to his 1989 replacement by a Gorbachev associate, Vladimir Ivashko.[30] Yet Ivashko's appointment occurred too late to salvage perestroika reforms in Ukraine. Although the Soviet Union still maintained a strong hold on the republic, and its emerging nationalist movement, Rukh, was still too factionalized and immature to openly oppose the CPU, the demise of the Soviet state was already well under way. Ukrainian political elites' embeddedness in the Soviet system, cemented by the extensive informal patronage networks forged since the 1950s, posed a challenge not only for the dismantling of the Soviet state in Ukraine but also for postcommunist institutional reform and democratization.

KUCHMA'S "INFORMAL STATE"

Ukraine declared its independence from the USSR on August 24, 1991. In contrast to most other Eastern European and South Caucasian states of the former Soviet Union (fSU) but similar to many Central Asian republics, the reins of power in postcommunist Ukraine were inherited not by nationalists but by a former CPSU team led by an ex-*nomenklatura* functionary, Leonid Kravchuk. In independent Ukraine, the process of postcommunist transformation was among the slowest in the fSU. Kataryna Wolczuk posits that the dismantling of the CPU and formal disengagement with communism "did not entail a simultaneous rejection of the Soviet legacy," which persisted unabated in most areas of public and private spheres.[31] In Taras Kuzio's words, "The new state was often simply built on the old. Many institutions were simply renamed. For example, the KGB became the 'National Security Service of Ukraine.'"[32] Mychailo Wynnyckyj argues that "a key factor that differentiated Ukraine from other areas of the FSU, was that its Kyiv-based political-economic elite did not change after the collapse of the USSR."[33] The Soviet legacy persisted in Ukraine despite and beyond all of the Kravchuk government's efforts to convince the outside world that the communist order was a thing of the past.

Though the Communist Party was outlawed in 1991, former members of Ukraine's powerful *nomenklatura* created an informal power network instead of establishing a formal political party. That network became known as the Party of Power (Partia Vlady).[34] Established as an elite club, the Party of Power functioned as a consensus-bound coalition. The Party of Power not only possessed access to material assets previously controlled by the CPU but was also in charge of a complex system of power networks established during the decades of Soviet rule and employed to sustain and enlarge those assets.[35] During the late 1990s, the Party of Power was steadily formalized as its members began creating mostly centrist personality-oriented political parties.[36]

During the immediate post-Soviet years, the Party of Power functioned as a single, albeit highly factionalized, political force that opposed the nationalist Rukh and other center-right political movements. Lucan A. Way describes the group's key characteristic as "a total absence of organization or coordination."[37] Along with regional rivalries within the Party of Power, such as between influential Dnepropetrovsk and Donetsk Clans, informal networks were divided between sociopolitical elites (former communist political and ideological administrators) and socioeconomic elites (economic managers).[38] In 1992, the economic faction formed the Labor Party of Ukraine, which became known as the party of the Red Directors.[39]

In light of these divisions, Kravchuk focused not on democratization and institutional reform but on building compromises and making pacts that would preserve the status quo among various informal stakeholders. Kravchuk did little to change the institutional arrangement established under Soviet rule. In the economic sphere, the president immediately rejected the Russian-style "shock-therapy" liberalization and transition to market economy, instead seeking to salvage the remnants of Ukraine's Soviet-era command economy. Kravchuk's administration developed no formal economic strategy but instead attempted to keep the economy running through a variety of informal channels, an approach that produced disastrous results. Hyperinflation sent the economy into deep depression. By 1994, the GDP had fallen by 23 percent since 1991 and inflation surged to 900 percent over a four year period. Not only had Ukraine failed to introduce its own national currency to replace the Soviet ruble, but the state's capacity to pay pensions and wages became severely impaired. Moreover, economic output fell to about half of pre-1991 levels.[40]

The failure of this economic transition led to the rise of the informal economy, which Daniel Kaufmann and Aleksander Kaliberda estimate accounted for more than 45 percent of Ukraine's GDP by 1995, up from 12 percent in 1989.[41] According to Ulrich Thießen, the informal economy's share of Ukraine's GDP topped 50 percent by the mid-1990s, a level higher than that in most other fSU states.[42] Because the growth of informal economic activity was "correlated with a bureaucratically complex but inefficient government," the increase in corruption closely accompanied the deformalization of economic production.[43]

The dire economic situation of the early 1990s was one of the key reasons behind the rise of the Red Directors, and by the middle of the decade, they dominated the Party of Power, both formally (through representation in parliament) and via informal channels. Many of the Red Directors retained their jobs as managers of industrial enterprises, where they had access to financial resources inherited from the Soviet period that enabled them to prevent parliament from implementing the privatization of state enterprises.[44] As hyperinflation continued, in Anders Åslund's description, "neither plan nor market governed the Ukrainian economic system."[45] With the country in deep crisis, the Red Directors emerged as the only force with the expertise and willingness to reform the decaying economy.[46] The 1994 presidential elections brought to power Leonid Kuchma, one of the most influential Red Directors and a prominent member of the Dnepropetrovsk Clan.[47]

Following his victory, Kuchma, a typical representative of the Party of Power, was in no hurry to reform state institutions, which he considered inferior to and less efficient than informal channels. In a stark contrast to Kravchuk's approach to state-building, which favored preserving Soviet institutions and networks, Kuchma envisioned constructing a new type of state that would function on informal networks directly subservient to the president. Rosaria Puglisi estimates that more than two hundred members of the Dnepropetrovsk Clan moved to Kiev immediately after the start of Kuchma's presidency to assume leading positions in the new government.[48] By the mid-1990s, almost 80 percent of Ukrainian political elites came from that clan, giving it dominance over state institutions.[49] Throughout his two terms in office, Kuchma promoted his fellow clan members to top positions in the government, including prime ministers Pavlo Lazarenko and Viktor Pinchuk and the minister of fuel and energy Yulia Tymoshenko. The informal state built by Kuchma functioned through consensus-building among a coalition of informal political and business networks.[50] The president could informally advocate his economic and political agenda without having to share power with either the legislative or judicial branch.

In 1994, Kuchma announced a comprehensive state reform strategy that included massive privatization of state assets, a reduction in state subsidies to enterprises, and attracting foreign investment.[51] This attempt to transition to a market economy, however, favored incremental changes that Kuchma labeled the "Ukrainian model" over the shock-therapy approaches implemented in Russia.[52] The economy continued to decline over the rest of the decade, with the GDP falling to 60 percent of its pre-1991 level, and the failure of almost all of Kuchma's reform plans became obvious.[53] The introduction of post-Soviet currency (hryvnia) in 1996 had little effect on the economy's poor performance.[54]

A large-scale privatization campaign was the most informal and controversial of the reform efforts. The selective distribution of privatized assets enabled a small circle of individuals to amass enormous resources and resulted in the explosion of a class of oligarchs that included Ukraine's richest businessmen, Rinat Akhmetov, Viktor Pinchuk, and Ihor Kolomoiskyi.[55] Many of the oligarchs belonged to informal networks outside of Kuchma's immediate control—Akhmetov, for example, led the Donetsk Clan. The powerful and unruly oligarchs directly challenged the president's authority. According to Åslund, "The oligarchs, who were usually members of parliament, walked the corridors of the presidential administration and the parliament to extract formal decisions that granted them subsidies and regulatory privileges."[56] With enormous financial resources at their disposal and their patronal control over regional clans, oligarchs often functioned as influential power brokers.

Thus, despite his seemingly tight grip over the informal state, Kuchma faced continuous opposition not only from competing regional groups such as the rapidly expanding Donetsk Clan and the smaller Kharkiv network but also within his own Dnepropetrovsk "family." Tymoshenko and other high-profile clan members defected to the opposition.[57] Way argues that "informal elite networks in Ukraine have in fact been relatively weak. Cooperation has been almost entirely restricted to short term instrumental exchange involving relatively low levels of loyalty and group identity."[58] All of these factors prevented the president from monopolizing power and constructing an authoritarian state. Though the consolidation of presidency under Kuchma occurred at the expense of legislative and judicial independence, the executive's almost exclusive reliance on informal institutions, represented by a diversity of informal power brokers, thwarted the emergence of a single power base capable of enforcing formalization. Paul J. D'Anieri explains that Kuchma "used his de facto (informal, 'practical,' rather than theoretical) power to institute rules that gave him more formal powers. He was able to use those formal powers to gain informal power, and so on, in a self-reinforcing cycle."[59] This formal-informal symbiosis, which Way dubs "rapacious individualism," not only "hindered full-scale democratization but also undermined efforts to consolidate authoritarianism."[60] According to Åslund, the competition among oligarchs caused Ukraine's political sphere to remain rather liberal and prevented the country from following in Russia's footsteps and centralizing and monopolizing the reins of power.[61]

In Kuchma's Ukraine, informality trickled down to most other areas of public administration. D'Anieri observes that informal relations pervaded such state institutions as the army, hospitals, and prisons.[62] According to the Nations in Transit project, Ukraine was one of the most corrupt post-Soviet republics in 1999–2000.[63] In 1999, Transparency International's Corruption Perception Index gave Ukraine a score of 2.6 (with 10.0 for the least corrupt country and 1.0 for the most corrupt).[64] And a 1999 Socis-Gallup survey found that more than 60 percent of respondents believed that nepotism and corruption—which they considered a "part of everyday life"—were widespread among state officials.[65] The unequal distribution of informal power centers also contributed to variations in the depth and spread of informal practices. William L. Miller, Tatyana Koshechkina, and Åse Berit Grødeland found that 50 percent of residents of Kiev and 45 percent of those who lived in western Ukraine resorted to material bribes, while only 39 percent of individuals from eastern Ukraine did so. Residents of western Ukraine were also more than twice as likely to use contacts when dealing with officials than were people from other parts of the country.[66]

Kuchma's ability to accommodate various informal stakeholders and his skill at manipulating this plethora of informal actors to his advantage enabled him to win the 1999 presidential election. While some scholars insist that Kuchma won a second term as a consequence of "the threat of a communist *revanche*," it is more probable that Kuchma's victory was bolstered "by a largely informal set of institutions, inducements, and penalties used to discourage opposition and stimulate vote fraud during elections."[67] As in Kuchma's first presidential campaign, his reelection promises focused on economic growth, even though, as Åslund claims, Ukraine "was the only postcommunist country that had failed to achieve a single year of economic growth" since independence.[68] Because economic recovery was crucial not only for Kuchma's credibility but also for the stability and survival of the oligarchic political order, Ukrainian elites (except the communists) universally agreed on the need for comprehensive institutional reform.

In December 1999, Kuchma appointed the former head of the national bank, Viktor Yuschenko, as prime minister and tasked him with implementing a rigorous reform program.[69] Yuschenko announced an ambitious plan, "1,000 Days of Reform," and sought to thoroughly reconstruct most of Ukraine's stagnant economic and political institutions.[70] According to Åslund, 2000 witnessed the "greatest reform drive" since the end of 1994, heralding the start of Ukraine's transition to a market economy.[71] The pillars of Yuschenko's reform plan were financial and tax reforms as well as restructuring the energy sector and privatization.[72] While Yuschenko's reforms encouraged economic recovery and jump-started the transition to a market economy, they did little to weaken Ukraine's entrenched informal institutions.[73] Instead, as economic output increased to 12 percent by 2004, the oligarchic order continued to thrive as a result of economic growth and its political dominance. Rather than extracting their rents from the volatile energy (gas) sector, as they did during the 1990s, oligarchs began establishing themselves in the more stable and lucrative steel and mining industries.[74] However, Yuschenko's reforms threatened the rent-seeking interests of many informal power brokers and challenged Kuchma's informal state. Under mounting pressure from the oligarchs, Kuchma eagerly dismissed the prime minister.

Kuchma's ability and willingness to preserve the status quo among competing groups began to wane by the end of his second term. Kuzio explains, "Ukraine's oligarchs during Kuchma's second term preferred a fully authoritarian regime but they were also divided among themselves and faced a formidable opposition."[75] Numerous defections from the Dnepropetrovsk Clan weakened the president's power base, and the Donetsk Clan strengthened its position.[76] After the 2001 creation of the Party of Regions, the Donetsk Clan secured the position of prime minister for its candidate, former mayor Viktor Yanukovich. By the 2004 presidential elections, Kuchma was out of the equation and the informal equilibrium that he had designed and preserved

began to disintegrate. A head-to-head competition broke out between Yanu-
kovich and Akhmetov's oligarchic pro-Russian Donetsk Clan (the Party of
Regions) and Yuschenko and Tymoshenko's pro-Western opposition bloc
(Our Ukraine).

THE ORANGE REVOLUTION: INFORMALIZATION CONTINUES

The November 2004 presidential elections pitted Yuschenko against Yanukovich and were marked by electoral fraud and vote rigging in favor of Yanukovich. By strategically employing the Donetsk Clan's financial and human
resources, Yanukovich won the first round, but massive popular protests
known as the Orange Revolution brought Yuschenko victory during the second round made him the new president.

The Orange coalition's ambitious democratic reform plans were hijacked
by the incessant infighting that plagued the first years of Yuschenko's presidency. Members of the pro-Western coalition could not agree on either the
scope of or strategies for institutional reform.[77] The post–Orange Revolution
Ukraine received the status of a hybrid regime without even embarking on a
formal democratization process. Åslund points out that in the wake of the
Orange coalition's victory, "no broad, comprehensive reforms were
launched, and the orange coalition plunged into internecine strife."[78] A
highly contested reprivatization program promoted by Tymoshenko, who
became prime minister, was intended to undermine the influence of the oligarchs and was expected to release assets unlawfully acquired during the
Kuchma period but instead "became reminiscent of corporate raiding."[79]

The lack of consensus between the parliament and the president as well
as among various competing factions within the ruling coalition prevented
the implementation of most of the planned reforms, including those to the
judiciary and constitution.[80] Only the 2008 reform of the admissions process for the notoriously corrupt higher education system received praise.[81]
The replacement of the individual selection process by independently administered computer-based tests undermined the role of informal practices
in university admissions.[82]

Although anticorruption policies topped the Orange coalition's agenda,
Ukraine's corruption score remained static during the 2005–10 period.[83]
Grødeland's assessment that the anticorruption rhetoric "failed to translate
into firm action and tangible results" is confirmed by surveys conducted by

the Global Corruption Barometer, which reported a steady increase in corruption among the judiciary, registry services, and political parties.[84] A 2005 survey found that 80 percent of respondents believed that corruption was widespread among state officials, while more than 30 percent thought that justice could not be obtained in Ukrainian courts and 40 percent thought that justice could be obtained but required paying bribes that were too expensive. Almost 60 percent of participants declared that judicial verdicts (including acquittal and release from custody) could be bought for bribes, and 55 percent said that People's Deputy mandates were also for sale.[85]

The 2008 global financial crisis hit Ukraine's economy hard, causing a recession that lasted until the end of Yuschenko's term. The European Bank for Reconstruction and Development reports that 50 percent of Ukraine's population relied on private safety nets during the crisis and that less than 20 percent received support from the state.[86] Another survey revealed that in 2006–7, more than half of respondents relied on themselves in times of crisis, while 35 percent relied on their families and less than 25 percent received pensions from the state.[87] As reported by Friedrich Schneider and Dominik H. Enste, informal economic activity during the immediate post-Orange period increased from 53 percent of the total GDP in 2003 to more than 55 percent two years later.[88] As Abel Polese observes, "Informal economic transactions, whatever they are called [were] at the basis of the Ukrainian society and economy" after the Orange Revolution.[89] Colin C. Williams and John Round found that "some 40 percent of Ukraine households cite informal employment as either the principal or secondary contributor to their living standard."[90]

Round, Williams, and Peter Rodgers argue that informal practices in Ukraine during the second postcommunist decade "are concerned with far more than just the 'economic' as they rely on historical antecedents, cultural knowledge, non-monetized reciprocity and the ability to negotiate power relationships as well as formal exchange."[91] Polese agrees, adding that even those informal practices defined as corrupt "can be reinterpreted in terms of 'brift,' a phenomenon somewhere between gift exchange and bribe and a fundamental fact for surviving in the modern Ukrainian society."[92] The Soviet-Russian term *blat* and its Ukrainian equivalents (*viddyaka, podiaka, tormozka* [little brakes]) enjoyed widespread usage.[93]

In contrast to Russia's informal networks, which are dominated by relations centered on friends and acquaintances, the Ukrainian population relies on *kumovstvo,* "a close and valued triangular relationship between the Godfather (*khrestnyj tato*), the Godmother (*khrestna mama*) and the parents of a child."[94] Qualitatively different from Georgian kinship networks, *kumovstvo* enables individuals to amalgamate both kinship and friendship ties into a single informal structure that combines the intimacy and trust of blood ties with the broader extent of friendship connections. Unlike kinship networks, which promote members of extended (or nuclear) family, *kumovstvo* instead allocates priority in informal relations to individuals with whom godparents seek closer association. Numerous Ukrainians note that *kumovstvo* became particularly widespread during the presidency of Yuschenko, who was known to use this practice both in his private life and when choosing political allies and appointing public officials.[95]

The lack of political and economic stability that characterized Yuschenko's presidency increased reliance on informal practices and institutions.[96] Many top positions in the Yuschenko administration went to people of the "circle": individuals bound by *kumovstvo* (*kums*), immediate kin and trusted colleagues (*soratniki*) of the president.[97] Yuschenko's nephew, for example, was appointed as a deputy of the Kiev district administration. Online mass media and the blogging culture, unknown in Ukraine prior to the early 2000s, have exposed clandestine schemes involving politicians and oligarchs, revealing the depth and scope of informalization.[98]

Despite Yuschenko's efforts to follow in his predecessor's footsteps by consolidating governance in the hands of trusted individuals, the president had few options but to engage in informal deals with oligarchs. Insiders claim that Ukraine's oligarchs became stronger, richer, and more confident during Yuschenko's presidency.[99] The increase in oligarchic power resulted not only from the chaotic political system and the country's relative economic stabilization but also from the plural character of Ukraine's politics, which favored numerous power brokers. In contrast to Kuchma, Orange forces were neither willing nor able to engage in informal power balancing games, increasingly turning a blind eye as the oligarchs amassed wealth and expanded their political influence.

By the 2010 presidential election, the prodemocratic coalition not only was in complete disarray but also failed to follow through on most of the promises that had led to the founding of the Orange coalition.[100] The envisioned democratic institutional reform was never formally implemented. In addition to the president's informal networks, which were known by his favorite term, *lyubi druzi* (dear friends), all of the other major political actors continued to rely on informal networks inherited from Kuchma's years.[101] However, Kuchma's informal state, which functioned on the symbiotic relationship between formal and informal rules, had long since been transformed into a chaotic scene where power brokers no longer sought to disguise their preference for informal institutions. An incessant power struggle among various informal actors became an inseparable part of post–Orange Revolution Ukrainian "democratization."

Yanukovich's Party of Regions, which represented the interests of Donbas-based oligarchs, particularly Akhmetov, emerged from this power struggle as the best organized, best funded, most disciplined, and most united political force. Yanukovich's victory in the 2010 presidential election was most of all a victory for the Donetsk Clan, which surpassed all other informal groups as a semicriminal and highly oligarchic pro-Russian network, and influential clan member Mykola Azarov became prime minister.[102] As part of his formal commitment to democratization and integration with the European Union, Yanukovich, like the failed Orange coalition, pledged to implement extensive institutional reforms. However, the bulk of the reforms implemented during his term sought to reverse whatever democratic institution-building had occurred and solidify the president's control over all other branches of government. The 2010 judicial reform, for example, brought the Supreme Court under the informal control of the executive, effectively merging the two branches. Controlling the judiciary enabled Yanukovich to persecute his political opponents, and he jailed Tymoshenko and other critics of his regime. The anticorruption law adopted in 2010 essentially granted top public officials immunity from prosecution.

Unlike Kuchma, Yanukovich never envisioned compromising and accommodating various informal power bases but instead attempted to subordinate other informal actors to the Donetsk Clan. Relying on a combination of Donbas-based mafia networks and financial co-optation, Yanukovich subdued the Dnepropetrovsk and Kharkiv Clans. The Party of Regions, the facade for the Donetsk Clan, drew its resources not from the people but from the effective use of administrators (*adminresurs*). The Party of Regions used various informal channels to manipulate the state employees working at the Donbas industrial complex—most of which was owned by Akhmetov—to provide votes and thus give legitimacy to the party. Top-down informal patronal relations were thus just as essential for Yanukovich as they had been for Kuchma.[103] Yet the homogenous and hierarchical structure of the Donetsk Clan, with its Soviet-style loyalty and subservience of lower-tier network members, enabled Yanukovich to prioritize the informal network over the informal state.

Instead of co-opting informal power brokers outside the network, Yanu-kovich invested heavily in enriching and promoting his immediate circles, including family members.[104] In addition to Azarov, Donetsk Clan members appointed to top government posts included deputy prime minister Serhiy Ar-buzov, interior minister Vitalyi Zakharchenko, chief of the Tax Service Olek-sandr Klymenko, and minister of finances Yuryi Kolobov. These appointments generated strong public disapproval, which the president largely ignored. For example, a February–March 2012 poll found that 75 percent of the population disapproved of the practice of appointing officials from Donbas to serve in top government positions or as heads of local administrations outside Donbas.[105]

After securing control of the executive branch, the Party of Regions ad-opted an electoral law that replaced the proportional voting system with a proportional-majoritarian system that barred smaller parties from partici-pating in elections and all parties from forming coalitions. In the 2012 elec-tions, described by international observers as the least democratic and fair in Ukraine's post-Soviet history, Yanukovich's party then won a plurality in the next parliament—185 of the 450 seats.[106] The Party of Regions gained this control almost exclusively via the massive use of *adminresurs*.[107]

This strategy succeeded not only as a consequence of the Donetsk Clan's iron grip on Donbas and other eastern regions but also because the Party of Regions revived nostalgia for the Soviet past.[108] Indeed, positive memories of the Soviet period survived well outside the Russian-speaking eastern parts of Ukraine. In 2006–7, half the Ukrainian public described the seven decades of Soviet rule as a "period of stability, vital prospects and prosperity of the working people," while only 17 percent saw that era as a "period of totalitar-ian regime with disastrous consequences."[109] The Donetsk Clan coupled its reliance on *adminresurs* with the use of blackmail to provide control over po-litical elites outside the clan.[110] This style of governance not only exacerbated the long-standing east-west regional rivalries but also alienated from the president's camp oligarchic networks and power groups in eastern Russian-speaking regions of the country, such as Dnepropetrovsk and Odessa.

Despite his formal support for democratization and anticorruption re-forms, Yanukovich, in contrast to his Orange coalition predecessors, not only had no intention of tackling the systemic corruption but also deliber-ately appointed to government positions individuals interested in illegally enriching themselves. According to Grødeland, during Yanukovich's presi-dency, "to the extent corrupt officials are dismissed, they seem to simply be replaced by equally corrupt officials."[111]

Sixty percent of respondents to the 2013 Global Corruption Barometer survey believed that the level of corruption had increased during the two years that the Party of Regions had headed Ukraine. In addition, 84 percent of Ukrainians believed that the state was controlled by a narrow circle of elites acting in their own interests, and 82 percent believed that public officials were extremely corrupt, 84 percent thought that the road police were corrupt, 77 percent described health care officials as very corrupt, and 87 percent pointed out corruption in the judiciary.[112] In Grødeland's view, most of the anticorruption campaigns implemented in pre-Euromaidan Ukraine were imposed from outside the country and therefore were "been fairly insensitive to the cultural context into which they have been introduced."[113]

According to the European Bank for Reconstruction and Development, the Ukrainian state's capacity to deliver services to the population decreased as informal political institutions strengthened.[114] Olga Onoshchenko and Colin C. Williams confirmed that informal networks were "still commonly and widely used" in 2013.[115] More than 80 percent of the respondents to Onoshchenko and Williams's survey in the southern city of Mykolayiv indicated that they had relied on *blat* when seeking a jobs. Almost 90 percent of respondents viewed using *blat* connections to find jobs either positively or neutrally. *Blat* was used predominantly in the health care sector (56 percent), in the job market (34 percent), in dealings with traffic police (30 percent), in dealings with local authorities (23 percent), and in the education sector (22 percent).[116]

As in previous periods, the population perceived the health care sector and road police as the public institutions most pervaded by informal relations. Nearly 60 percent of respondents to a 2010 survey admitted to using informal channels when dealing with health care officials.[117] Almost 40 percent of respondents to another survey believed that in-kind gifts to medical staff did not constitute corruption, while 65 percent saw informal payments to health care staff as a sign of gratitude and more than 80 percent said that material gifts are an expression of gratitude for provided services. However, more than 90 percent of survey participants also believed that informal cash payments and gifts for medical services should be eliminated.[118]

The informalization of the health care sector prevented the state from raising the salaries of medical staff and from maintaining medical facilities, but resources collected through informal payments were often used to repair hospitals and clinics, purchase modern equipment, and improvement of staff qualifications.[119] In contrast to informal relations in other formal institutions, where the bulk of financial resources obtained through informal channels settled into the pockets of corrupt officials or was reinvested in other informal schemes, informal revenues in Ukraine's health care sector commonly went to develop and improve services and facilities.

Thus, the informalization of the Ukrainian state and society intensified after Yanukovich assumed the presidency. The president and his fellow clan members not only explicitly prioritized informal institutions over formal ones but made little effort to harmonize informal relations within the public sphere, as Kuchma had endeavored to do. Members of the Party of Regions also favored naked power grabs to consensus- and pact-building approaches when dealing with other informal power bases. However, this classical authoritarian tool set was hard to implement in a political and social system characterized by multiple heterogeneous regional and socioeconomic power centers. Regardless of the Donetsk Clan's resources and willingness to resort to violence to achieve its goals, Yanukovich and his team never subordinated all other informal power brokers. Instead, the informalization of Ukraine and the polarization of informal power centers severely weakened the regime's ability to control the state either through informal channels or especially formally.

In November 2013, the president refused to sign an association agreement with the European Union and instead chose to obtain a loan from Russia, opting for closer integration with Ukraine's eastern neighbor over strengthened relations with the West. The move sparked popular protests known as Euromaidan. Though often portrayed as a popular prodemocratic and anticorruption uprising, Euromaidan became primarily a battlefield for informal power actors marginalized by Yanukovich.[120] A plethora of informal interest groups, some represented by opposition parties ranging from the former Orange forces to radical ultra-right-wing and left-wing groups, united in the Maidan movement.[121] Euromaidan culminated in Yanukovich's February 2014 overthrow, the establishment of a pro-Western regime in Kiev, and Russia's annexation of Crimea and the start of pro-Russian insurgency in Donbas, beginning a new chapter in Ukraine's institution-building history.

REFORMS BEGIN

The victors of Euromaidan formed an interim government but soon realized that neither economic nor political recovery was feasible without thorough institutional reforms. However, such reforms would be impossible without uprooting the firmly established informal institutional framework. As economic crisis loomed, the adoption of reform agenda was hampered by the escalation of armed conflict with Russian-backed separatists in eastern Ukraine and the lack of consensus among Euromaidan forces. On May 25, 2014, Petro Poroshenko, a seasoned politician and a veteran member of Orange coalition, was elected president. The newly elected president found himself facing immense pro-reform pressure not only from the international community but also from factions of the Euromaidan camp.

Despite the pressing need, the process of drawing the reform plan was slow.[122] In contrast to post–Rose Revolution Georgia, which pushed through a reform agenda within a month after the regime change, Ukrainian reformists did not launch their program until November 2014, when the ruling and opposition parties signed a coalition agreement. This agreement—"an essential element of reform agenda"—enabling the major political actors to collaborate on a reform plan.[123]

In September 2014, a list of sixty-two reforms was presented as part of Strategy 2020, and the executive and legislative branches adopted the plan in January 2015.[124] A road map for a comprehensive institutional reform program, Strategy 2020 emphasized eight "priority" reforms: anticorruption, judiciary, decentralization, public administration, deregulation, law enforcement, national defense, and the health care sector. Other "reforms" on the list—for example, the development of a Ukrainian space program or a national film industry—constitute vaguely defined policy rather than actual reform plans. Strategy 2020 closely draws on the association agreement between the European Union and Ukraine, signed in June 2014 and ratified by both parties in March 2015, which outlines ten key reform goals for the Ukrainian government and prioritizes reforms of the judiciary, constitution, electoral system, and energy policy as well as anticorruption efforts and tax deregulation. Because the association agenda served as the legal basis for reform, that process became embedded in the process of European integration. In contrast, both Georgia and Moldova signed their association agreements with the European Union well after the start of the reform process.

The implementation of reforms is supervised by the National Council for Reforms, which includes the president, prime minister, and the cabinet. This agency is monitored by the Executive Committee for Reforms and advised by the Advisory Board and Project Office.[125] By late 2015, Ukraine's parliament, the Verkhovna Rada, had already adopted a significant number of legislative acts to implement the reform strategy, including the State Plan on Deregulation, the Law on Public Service Reform.[126]

At the top of the list of eight priorities are anticorruption reform and lustration, followed by the judicial reform and decentralization. In October 2014, parliament adopted a package of measures under the Law on Prevention of Corruption, which established an independent National Anticorruption Bureau (which came into existence in April 2015) and National Agency for Prevention of Corruption. The process of lustrating former regime officials has been high on the reformists' agenda, and the September 2014 Law on Purification of Government subjects more than one million public employees to checks over the following two years. By January 2015, 357 officials had already been registered for lustration.[127] Within three months, according to Prime Minister Arseniy Yatsenyuk, 2,000 former Yanukovich officials had been lustrated.[128] However, the vagueness of the law and its application to a large number of former officials not directly associated with Yanukovich's inner circle have made lustration highly controversial.[129]

Decentralization is expected to increase self-development and fiscal independence of local communities (*hromadas*), which the deputy head of the presidential administration, Dmytro Shymkiv, describes as "the basic item of local government."[130] In a nutshell, the decentralization reform proposes reducing the number of *hromadas* from fifteen thousand to twelve hundred and the number of local districts (*rayon*) from five hundred to one hundred. The most controversial aspect of decentralization, which led to violent August 2015 confrontations between radical protesters and police in front of the parliament, is the allocation of additional autonomy to separatist-held districts of the Donbas region.[131] As of December 2016, the decentralization bill had not yet received parliamentary approval. If passed, it will allow local governments significant independence in such areas as tax collection, obtaining loans, economic development, and administration.

One of the most publicized programs has been police reform, which culminated in the creation of a new patrol service. In July 2015, as part of the Poroshenko government's efforts to tackle corruption in public institutions and to regain public trust, thousands of new police officers started replacing the notoriously corrupt traffic police. At the same time, reforms of prosecutors' offices will replace all local prosecutors and their immediate deputies with more than seven hundred new prosecutors.

The reform of higher education, launched during Yuschenko's presidency and stalled under Yanukovich, was revived with the June 2015 creation of a national agency with responsibility in that area.[132] The current reforms seek to establish external control mechanisms and increased consideration for conflicts of interest, both of which are necessary to ensure that jobs are not distributed based on kinship ties and informal connections, as has been the case since the Soviet period.

Less notable reforms to reduce the importance of informal practices include the August 2015 creation of an online registration system for car owners.[133] The new system is specifically designed to target the institution of *reshaly*, "problem solvers" who offer preferential and expedited service to individuals who want to avoid dealing with state registry bureaucracy.

One of the key characteristics of Poroshenko's democratic reform strategy has been an effort to place control of reform in the hands of individuals who have experience outside of Ukraine's corrupt system and who may lack informal connections to their future employers. The appointment of the former head of Microsoft Ukraine, Dmytro Shymkiv, as the deputy head of the presidential administration, directly responsible for the implementation of reforms, is among the most well-known examples of Poroshenko's attempts to bring in fresh blood.

The scarcity of untainted individuals has been overcome by the addition of foreign-born reformers to Ukraine's government. Perhaps most notably, former Georgian president Mikheil Saakashvili was appointed to head the administration of the Odessa region.[134] Other foreign-born top executive officials in Ukrainian government include minister of finance Natalie Jaresko, economy minister Aivaras Abromavicius, health minister Alexander Kvitashvili, deputy prosecutor general David Sakvarelidze, deputy interior minister Eka Zguladze, and deputy justice minister Gia Getsadze.[135]

Along with Georgia's post–Rose Revolution program, Ukraine's agenda remains the most comprehensive effort at democratic institutional reform in the fSU. Though some of the reform measures in Strategy 2020 do not directly target informal relations, the ongoing reform clearly seeks to formalize state institutions and reduce their informal counterparts.[136] This approach represents a sharp reversal from the decades of informalization of state institutions deliberately pursued by various Ukrainian governments after the end of Soviet rule. Poroshenko's current efforts to reform state institutions parallel the botched post–Orange Revolution goals of institutional transformation. However, the Ukrainian reform process is a more recent phenomenon than its counterparts in Georgia and Moldova. Consequently, assessing the institutional reforms' impact on the informal sector in Ukraine becomes even more difficult.

ASSESSING THE IMPACT OF REFORMS

The International Monetary Fund, the European Bank for Reconstruction and Development, and individual European Union member states have praised the institutional reforms implemented in Ukraine since Euromaidan.[137] Nevertheless, the reforms are progressing at a painstakingly slow pace. An independent Ukrainian expert agency, Vox Ukraine, has declared that between January and August 2015, only anticorruption measures and reforms in public finance and monetary policy were progressing at an acceptable pace.[138]

The financial sector has experienced the highest inflow of reform-oriented specialists, which explains why banking sector and financial market reforms have been the most successful elements of the reform program to date.[139] Vox Ukraine measures "events" such as legal acts or other formally adopted measures, and finds that the anticorruption sphere has experienced up to fifty-five events, while the arenas of public and monetary policy have experienced forty-seven events per year. The energy sector experienced about fifteen events per year, while all other arenas had fewer than ten events per year.[140]

The relatively high number of anticorruption measures does not mean that they have been effective. The anticorruption campaign has progressed slowly, and Transparency International–Ukraine declared in 2015 that "both petty and grand corruption are still flourishing."[141] The anticorruption program has also been criticized as lacking instruments for measuring progress.[142] The government still lacks a "single strategy for combating corruption," and since exchanges of informal payments are still perceived as part of everyday life, "Ukrainian business practices (like other parts of Ukrainian society) have not [yet] embraced the fight against corruption."[143]

The law on lustration has proved one of the most ineffective and inadequate reforms in terms of either tackling political corruption or cleansing the system of elites from the former regime. While some subjects of lustration have been offered an opportunity to "redeem" themselves through military service in the antiterrorist operation in eastern Ukraine, others have been demoted but allowed to remain in their institutions.[144] Criticized by the Council of Europe's Venice Commission, the lustration law continues to be debated both in Ukraine's constitutional court and in the parliament. Though the current government has appointed numerous public functionaries with limited or no previous involvement in Ukrainian politics, many current members of parliament are former members of the ruling regimes.

The decentralization reform also remains plagued by controversy. Apart from inherent disagreements surrounding the legal status of the separatist-occupied Donetsk and Lugansk regions, the scope and scale of the decentralization bill mean that the reform process is envisioned as lengthy and complex. On the ground, resistance to decentralization has occurred not so much because *hromada* administrators are unwilling to relinquish authority and more because they fear that a failed reform will undermine their position in their community.[145] Experts also fear that a mismanaged decentralization will create additional opportunities for power abuse and tax evasion. At this stage of decentralization reform planning, some six hundred administrative services centers are spread across one thousand *hromadas*.[146]

Ukraine retains multiple avenues for bribery and the use of informal practices to speed up the process of acquiring formal documents. Yet the simplification of administrative services has become bogged down in ongoing scuffles among various camps of reformists. The deputy minister of the interior, Eka Zguladze, has insisted on creating a system of register service centers that is responsible for a handful of services, such as the issuing passports and criminal certificates. In theory, these centers could be launched faster than service centers in *hromadas* (which would have to await the completion of decentralization) and would be independent of *hromada* authorities. In practice, however, the system duplicates other services and therefore may encourage citizens to rely on informal channels to circumvent the complex bureaucracy.[137]

The executive's efforts to retain control over other branches continues to hamper reform of the judiciary and legislature. Poroshenko maintains control over the parliamentary process through his representative in the Verkhovnaia Rada, Ruslan Kniazevich. Nevertheless, significant progress has occurred in reducing informal practices in the legislative process. A series of laws has increased transparency regarding the personal income and employment of members of parliament, reducing the closed "informal club" nature of Ukrainian politics.[148] Parliamentary committee meetings are now recorded, preventing participants from making informal backstage deals. However, observers believe that the parties continue to make under-the-table deals regarding the distribution of seats in parliament.[149]

On the positive side, the informal system of parliamentary gatekeeping established at the time of independence was eliminated in 2014. Whereas seats in the Verkhovnaia Rada had to previously been purchased for informal payments of up to five million dollars, giving wealthy businessmen and their political representatives a stranglehold on the parliament, legislative elections are now open to the broader public, and representatives of civil society and the mass media as well as human rights activists (for example, Mustafa Nayyem, Serhiy Leshtchenko, and Svitlana Zalishchyk) have subsequently won seats.

The post-Euromaidan political transformation has also led to the decline of the clans. With Yanukovich's Donetsk Clan dislodged, a multitude of political forces—many of them aligned ideologically rather than regionally—have repopulated the political sphere.[150] This shift dealt a strong blow to the clan-based informal power networks and prevented them from continuing their long-standing practice of forcing state institutions to conform to clan interests.

Other aspects of reform implementation remain out of sight of observers. The most obvious challenge is the omnipresence of informal institutions, which for decades substituted for rather than supplemented formal structures. In that light, transforming formal institutions will require either co-opting or eroding informal structures. Not only veterans of the Euromaidan movement, who are well acquainted with relying on informal channels but also non-Ukrainian officials holding top government positions have had difficulty avoiding informal constraints. Saakashvili, for example, has been frustrated by the prevalence of informal networks among Kiev officials and has claimed that Ukraine's institutions are "controlled by oligarchic groups" and that consequently, "decisions about reforms are not being made."[151]

Particularly in such highly informalized areas of Ukraine's governance as the energy sector, reformers have no choice but to make pacts with informal interest groups.[152] According to energy sector insiders, many energy enterprises simply cannot be managed without the participation of experienced (informal) bureaucratic teams, which have enormous practical experience and insider knowledge.[153] As a result, informal power brokers wield extra influence and power that enables them to hijack the reform process toward their own ends.

Despite this disadvantage, pro-reform actors realize that breaking the vicious circle of informalization in state institutions requires them to cooperate with informal actors. For many reformists, informal channels are necessary to make formal relations work.[154] Reformers do not gain personally from these informal connections but must employ them to achieve work objectives. The quid pro quo character of Ukrainian political life makes informal exchanges of services unavoidable.[155] Not surprisingly, therefore, employing informal connections to advocate reform goals has become a well-established practice among Ukraine's reformers.

Positive signs are nevertheless plentiful. The May 2014 presidential elections were described as free and fair.[156] The new anticorruption legislature is being strengthened by the creation of new and independent anticorruption bodies charged with implementing reforms. The road map for reforms is not only enshrined in constitutional amendments but also part of Ukraine's commitments to the European Union. The importance of European integration for Kiev and the crucial role of European economic assistance, particularly in light of Russia's military aggression, means that the European Union may have substantial leverage to promote reform. The key difference between the current reform program and earlier efforts is that the present program is being adopted in close coordination with and under pressure from the public and civil society. In sharp contrast to Yanukovich's top-down governance and Yuschenko's chaotic lack of public transparency, the post-Euromaidan government is characterized by higher levels of horizontal accountability and commitment.

Attitudes toward Institutional Reforms

After decades of rampant corruption, oligarchization, and informalization of state institutions, the post-Euromaidan regime change was accompanied by expectations of sweeping structural transformations. Capitalizing on the post-Euromaidan public mood, Poroshenko's government came to power not on pledges of European integration—which seems a distant dream for the majority of Ukrainians—but on promises of all-encompassing institutional reforms. Widespread expectations regarding sociopolitical reform were soon upset by the start of armed conflict in the east and deep economic crisis, and the Ukrainian public has shifted its attentions away from reform and toward the more pressing issue of territorial integrity.[157]

Because implementation of crucial reform plans has become bogged down in bureaucracy and informal politics and some of the less visible reforms (for example, monetary policy, taxation, and market deregulation) remain unnoticed by the public, the popular support for post-Euromaidan institutional transformation has decreased markedly. A July 2015 poll by the Democratic Initiative Foundation and the Razumkov Center reports that only about 30 percent of Ukrainians believed in the effectiveness of reforms, while more than 60 percent of respondents expressed a lack of trust in the ongoing reform process. Nearly half of survey participants (48.4 percent) thought that the reforms had made no progress whatsoever, while a quarter believed that less than 10 percent of what should have been done had been accomplished.[158]

A 2015 International Republican Institute found similar results: 40 percent of participants saw no changes, and 32 percent said that changes were too slow. Eighty-eight percent of respondents lamented that the overall economic situation had worsened over the preceding year. Whereas 54 percent of the Ukrainian public thought that their household's economic situation had worsened in November 2011 and 47 percent did so in March 2014, that figure had risen to 84 percent by July 2015.[159]

Reform of the health care sector, which more than a third of the population had initially seen as a priority (table 6.1), seemed to have a negative effect on performance. By July 2015, 55 percent of respondents to a Rating Pro survey believed that health care quality had deteriorated since the start of reform, 38 percent thought that nothing had changed, and only 4 percent had seen improvement.[160] Outside of the capital, Kiev, where the most visible reforms such as police reform, were implemented, the only observable reform was a tripling of gas prices as a result of the government's efforts to achieve energy independence from Russia.[161]

The July 2015 survey by the Democratic Initiative Foundation and the Razumkov Center found that 50.4 percent cited the government itself as a major obstacle to reform, while 44.5 percent noted political parties in parliament, 51.5 percent named oligarchs, and 44 percent selected the bureaucracy. Only a quarter of respondents thought that the country's ongoing economic crisis resulted from the armed conflict in Donbas, whereas more than 70 percent argued that the crisis had resulted from political corruption, embezzlement by high-ranking officials, or the oligarchization of the economy and money laundering by oligarchs.[162]

TABLE 6.1. Popular Attitudes toward Ukrainian Reforms (%)

Which reforms should be a priority?	April 2014	June 2015
Anticorruption	65	63
Courts, prosecutor general's office, police	58	32
Social security system (pensions)	40	30
Health care	35	35
Army	30	42
Lustration	28	—
Tax reform	21	5
Decentralization	18	12

Source: Democratic Initiative Foundation (DIF), International Republican Institute, Razumkov Center

Although Euromaidan had focused on anticorruption, the public's attention shifted to price inflation and military conflict in the east. A February 2015 survey conducted by the Gorshenin Institute showed that respondents identified war in the east and state security (89.5 percent) as one of the most pressing issues for the government; only 33 percent cited the economy and state budget, and a scant 13.2 percent cited corruption.[163] Since 2014, popular support for many reform priorities had subsided (see table 6.1), and only the army is seen as urgently in need of reform.

By the fall of 2015, the Poroshenko government's most visible institutional reform was the creation of new patrol police in Kiev and other major cities. A July 2015 survey of residents of Kiev showed that 82 percent supported the new police service, and 42 percent its creation as a step forward in fight against corruption.[164]

Although the population never prioritized decentralization, the issue retains substantial popular support. The June 2015 found that 67 percent of respondents favored of allowing the *hromada* to have more authority and more than half believed that their local authorities and communities could handle a new system. Nonetheless, 80 percent of those polled thought that the country's almost four thousand state-run companies should maintain their status, and only 12 percent supported privatizing those enterprises.

Nevertheless, Ukrainians continue to possess fairly high levels of institutional distrust (table 6.2). All three branches of government in post-Euromaidan Ukraine are nearly as mistrusted as they were under Yanukovich.

The population had a mixed attitude toward foreign-born officials (par-

TABLE 6.2. Levels of Institutional Distrust in Ukraine (%)

State Institutions	2011	2014	2015
President	—	45	62
Local government	—	39	56
Executive	75	52	74
Education	35	44	—
Police	70	71	75
Prosecutor's office	—	73	80
Parliament	80	81	78
Banks	67	73	76
Political parties	78	75	—
Courts	75	77	80

Source: World Values Surveys, International Foundation for Electoral Systems (IFES), DIF

ticularly Georgians) in charge of the reform process: while 42 percent of the public viewed these reformers positively, 40 percent had a negative attitude.[165] In September 2015, almost half of Kiev residents attributed the establishment of the new police service to the deputy minister of the interior, Zguladze, a Georgian, while only 8 percent gave the credit to the minister of the interior, Arsen Avakov, a Ukrainian citizen. Among residents of the Odessa region, 41 percent approved of Saakashvili's work as Odessa's governor, while 37 percent disapproved. But Saakashvili was considerably more popular than Poroshenko (79 percent disapproval), Yatsenyuk (86 percent), or parliament (87 percent).[166] The gap in public trust of foreign-born reformers in the executive—all of whom Poroshenko personally hired—and elected Ukrainian officials seems to be both a legacy of decades of distrust of corrupt elected officials and a reflection of their performance relative to foreign reformists. Despite some civil society actors' complaints about Georgian reformists' disregard for the opinions of members of civil society and the threat of the "Saakashvilization" of Ukraine, the foreign-born reformists are generally regarded as more trustworthy than Ukrainian politicians.[167] For both foreigners and Ukrainian reformists from the private sector—the so-called self-made businessmen—the risk of losing their reputations in bribery scandals is higher than the possible gains from corruption.[168]

Low levels of public trust in the reform process and limited satisfaction with its effectiveness are coupled with the slow practical application of reforms and their relatively low efficiency. Though the Ukrainian reform process remains in its early stages, its numerous setbacks and the military conflict in the east seem to have weakened public backing for the much-anticipated institutional transformation. Consequently, Ukraine's ongoing institutionalization program is expected to have only limited impact on the informal sphere.

Reliance on Informality

Since the implementation of reforms began so recently, their effect on the informal sphere is not easy to observe, and by the end of 2015, no academic studies had been published on the role of informal practices and institutions in post-Euromaidan Ukraine. To fill in this gap, I conducted a series of in-depth interviews with members of the elite in Kiev in July 2015.

External observers believe that informal relations continue to flourish among the higher echelons of Ukrainian politicians, particularly in areas related to the private business interests of political and economic administrators.[169] Since top-level corruption is less tolerated in post-Euromaidan Ukraine, informal payments between high-ranking officials and representatives of the big business started assuming a different shape. Following the dismantling of many vertical patronage networks, informal relations among Ukrainian elites assumed more of a horizontal structure.[170] Civil activists who monitor corruption believe that both politicians and business elites perceive political corruption as a long-term investment.[171] Bound by mutual interests, representatives of political and economic elites perceive informal schemes as a way to purchase loyalty that will pay off in the future. Hence, the post-Euromaidan informal distribution of favors functions as an indirect form of reciprocal exchanges. Although money and material gifts no longer directly change hands, less obvious and notable schemes have taken their place. For example, businessmen pay for the foreign education of children of officials or give politicians' relatives top positions in private companies.[172] The long-standing custom under which Ukrainian business owners pay a share (*vidkat*) of their incomes to public officials as protection money and to develop the business persists despite the progress of financial and business reforms.

With the collapse of the hierarchical order established under Kuchma, both informal power brokers and oligarchs have encountered difficulty navigating a new political and economic order defined by the absence of hierarchy and the chaotic distribution of power.[173] Instead of being subordinated to a single power center, as during Yanukovich's time, oligarchic elites now operate in an environment dominated by public opinion and multiparty politics, free of control by regional clans. Even the decline of Donetsk Clan, with its industrial and mining magnates, did little to enable oligarchs from other networks to take the lead. Banking sector magnate Ihor Kolomoiskiy, whom Poroshenko appointed to serve as governor of Dnepropetrovsk in 2014, soon fell out of favor and was dismissed. Though both the regime change and the war in Donbas have weakened the oligarchs' economic and political power, some of Ukraine's powerful business elites continue to influence politics through informal channels. One avenues by which the oligarchs interfere in political processes is informal control of the mass media, which is facilitated by the absence of public information on the ownership of independent media channels.[174]

The process of political deoligarchization and formalization has not yet been launched. The persistence of informal channels is evident in a 2014 series of top appointments Poroshenko made from among his close friends and family members. The president's longtime friend, Boris Lozhkin, became head of presidential administration, and Poroshenko's son was elected to parliament. Since Ukraine's political parties generally remain personality-based, informal connections are fundamental for building alliances.[175] These "leadership parties" not only depend on their powerful founders for political guidance and leadership but also are fully funded by their leaders. The lack of transparent financing of political parties—most of which still receive money via private donations—hampers civil society's efforts to ensure accountability regarding sources of party funding and to formalize political financing.[176] Oligarchs' lavish "investments" in political parties remain among the most common sources of party financing.

As long as official salaries of Ukrainian members of parliament are as low as three hundred dollars per month, informal financial incentives remain a serious obstacle for impartial decision-making in legislature. Observers estimate that a member of the Ukrainian parliament needs about five million dollars per year to fund political activities.[177] Legislators thus have a strong incentive to engage in informal schemes with businessmen, who in exchange receive political protection (*krysha*) for their business interests from corrupt customs officials, the prosecutor's office, and business competitors.

The absence of open competition for jobs in the executive branch offers yet another venue for the reliance on informal networks. In July 2015, for example, Saakashvili called for applications for positions as heads of district administration in Odessa although he lacked a legal basis for such competition.[178] The absence of open competition for executive jobs has led to the appearance of freelance advisers and outside stakeholders, other types of informal actors.[179] The expertise and independence of these advisers and stakeholders are necessary to promote the reform agenda, yet low salaries in the executive make government jobs unattractive. Many private advisers prefer to remain informal rather than taking permanent jobs, creating an entire class of informal policymakers who function outside and beyond the formal institutional framework.

To a great extent, patron-client relations in state institutions remain omnipresent as a consequence of the unchanged Soviet-style system of wage distribution among appointed officials. Under this system, 70 percent of public officials' salaries consist of various bonuses awarded by superiors based on performance.[180] Public officials thus focus not on policy implementation but on satisfying their superiors, a task that commonly includes engaging in informal relations with and on behalf of administrators.

One of the key challenges to the reform of state institutions in Ukraine is the critical lack of trained professionals who can take over for the old cohort of Soviet-trained civil servants. Despite changes among senior officials, the bureaucratic framework—staffed by thousands of Soviet-era bureaucrats—remains unchanged. Newly appointed reformist ministers and their deputies thus must work against hundreds of entrenched civil servants, some of whom have been in place since the Soviet period.[181] This problem is particularly acute for foreign-born reformists, who lack the ability to replace their employees en masse.[182] As long as the old institutional culture and traditions persist, formalization will face an uphill battle.

The deeply rooted custom of informal financial exchanges has shown particular tenacity. Because most anticorruption legislation was not adopted until the second half of 2015, the post-Euromaidan reforms have not yet had time to affect informal payments and corruption. The February 2015 survey showed that more than 60 percent of the public believed that the level of government corruption had not decreased over the preceding year. Almost a quarter of respondents claimed that corruption had increased, while just over 8 percent thought that it had decreased.[183] According to the results of a January 2015 poll by the Kiev International Institute of Sociology, 80 percent of the respondents believed that corruption had remained unchanged or had increased after the change in government.[184]

Members of civil society see reforms as having done little to alleviate the complex bureaucracy that has resulted in the need for informal connections.[185] As a consequence of the persistence of what some Ukrainians labeled as "stable uncertainty" (*stabilnaia neopredelionnost`*), the population still uses informal networks to disseminate knowledge, assist in finding employment, and to access goods in short supply. The 2014–15 economic crisis exacerbated the importance of informal institutions to ordinary Ukrainians. Experts have observed an extremely high tolerance regarding informal relations, and even people who criticize informality may rely on it when they encounter bureaucratic barriers in formal institutions.[186] The recent economic crisis has reduced use of informal kinship connections in the private job market, as straitened finances have forced owners of small and medium-size businesses to hire trained professionals who are more qualified and competent than family members.[187]

Reshaly—well-connected individuals who charge a fee to help citizens and businesses circumvent bureaucratic procedures—have experienced some setbacks as a consequence of the introduction of e-governance but have also begun to offer services that speed up online waiting lists. In addition, some of the more successful *reshaly* have begun formalizing their services through public notary offices.[188] An energy sector official reports that *reshaly*, who in the business sector present themselves as agreement-builders (*soglasovateli*), remain omnipresent in high-level corporate deals.[189]

As in previous periods, the existence of networks keeps open venues for corrupt and nepotistic practices, which are more abundant among acquaintances.[190] Rating Pro's June 2015 survey revealed that almost 30 percent of respondents were required to make informal payments for medical services, and 17 percent of informants claimed that medical personnel had requested informal "signs of gratitude." A quarter of respondents described offering informal material gifts to health care employees as a "voluntary" sign of appreciation, 30 percent saw nothing wrong with offering informal gifts to doctors.[191] These findings correlate with the results of a late 2014 survey conducted by the International Foundation for Electoral Systems in which more than 40 percent of informants admitted to making informal payments for health care services. More than half of respondents considered informal payments part of daily life, while about a quarter believed that offering informal forms of gratitude to public officials was justified.

Ukrainian institutional reforms thus far appear to have had very limited impact on the informal sphere. In spite of positive achievements in the economic sphere, the economic crisis has ensured the continuity of informal practices. Many previously used forms of informal practices, such as *vidkat*, *krysha*, and *kumovstvo*, are still widely employed. Transformations of political institutions as a result of reforms to date have been too limited to introduce notable changes in formal-informal equilibrium. Moreover, reformists cannot ignore the prevailing informal relations within formal institutions and often must rely on informal channels to advance reform.

SUMMARY

Since their creation by Soviet authorities, Ukraine's formal institutions have been permeated by informal practices. Under Soviet rule, Ukrainian communist elites invested heavily in expanding and maintaining complex informal patronage networks that connected those elites with the Kremlin's *nomenklatura*. The demise of the Soviet state did little to transform the formal-informal balance in state institutions, and in fact, the independent

Ukrainian government deliberately sought to promote a massive deformalization of formal institutions. Kuchma's government implemented only a limited set of reforms necessary for the transition to market economy while preserving the existing system, which both the regime and the oligarchic elites found favorable.

The 2005 Orange Revolution created chaos as the informal clans competed for influence. The Orange coalition had the ability neither to restore the informal balance of power nor to push through institutional reforms, and the strongest informal clique, the Donetsk Clan, seized the reins of power. Yanukovich's presidency was characterized by further deformalization of state institutions and relentless efforts by the president to subdue all other informal power bases. His 2014 overthrow ended the Donetsk Clan's rapacious and autocratic dominance, but the informal system that allowed the clan to rise to prominence has remained in place.

To construct a modern welfare state, the post-Euromaidan government has prioritized extensive transformation of Ukraine's dysfunctional institutional system. Unlike all of postcommunist Ukraine's previous reform efforts, the ongoing reform plans are important for the new regime: the informal institutional order could not sustain a modern political system or ensure Ukraine's economic development. For the first time, neither political nor business elites found the "informal state," which for decades had accommodated rent-seeking state officials and opaque oligarchs, acceptable. However, the ambitious reform process, Strategy 2020, has continued to be hampered by the conflict in the east, economic crisis, and the inherent challenges of deoligarchization. In contrast to Moldova, where reformists are not only outnumbered by their opponents but also losing public support, Ukraine's government has full public backing and an overwhelming political consensus in favor of democratic reforms. And although reforms in areas of statebuilding and democratization have made steady progress, attempts to formalize state institutions have thus far remained rare and of dubious effectiveness. Once again, informal institutions have proved their tenacity and resistance to change. Regardless of the disappearance of informal state, various informal practices and institutions continue functioning in Ukraine's public and private spheres, demonstrating the intrinsic difficulty of reversing decades of informalization.

CHAPTER 7

Conclusion: Reforms and Informality in a Comparative Perspective

THIS BOOK EXAMINES how and under what conditions institutional changes aimed at designing democratic institutions affect the informal sphere. Since little is known about the impact of institutional transformation on informal institutions and practices of post-Soviet regimes, this book offers a perspective on the formalization of state institutions and the role of informal constraints in that process. The lack of democratic institution-building in the former Soviet Union (fSU) means that the question of how democratic institutional reforms impact informality in the post-Soviet region has remained open for nearly three decades since the dissolution of the USSR. Only after the emergence of hybrid regimes that pursue not only economic growth but also liberalization of political institutions did the process of formalizing the public sphere begin in earnest. This book does not offer a statistically tested causal explanation of the impact of institutional reforms on informality. What it does offer is a theoretically supported and empirically rich account of the effect of institutional change on the informal scene in the context of fSU.

The empirical analysis of three hybrid post-Soviet regimes points to the observation that successful institutional changes affect the functioning and proliferation of informal institutions. When challenged with formal constraints and implemented with elite and popular consensus through legal channels, informal institutions retreat from the public sphere. After formal rules are introduced and enforced, informal constraints vacate the niches they occupied in formal institutions. This observation supports the argument that the *strengthening of formal institutions leads to the weakening of their informal counterparts.* Informal institutions and informal practices indeed withdraw in the face of radical institutional transformation, as was the case with Georgian society's deeply rooted culture of circumventing formal institutions. The evidence from successful reforms from all three case studies illustrates that as in Central Europe, Latin America, and East Asia, consistent and robust reform efforts can eliminate informal constraints from public institutions in post-Soviet states. The former Soviet Union is not an exception to the formal-informal equilibrium, and despite their historical entrenchment, informal traditions in the fSU are as susceptible to the changes of formal rules as such traditions in other regions. This book demonstrates that the onset of formalization does not entail immediate transformation of formal-informal relations. Rather, institutional change has a complex impact on informality that is dictated by various factors.

When and Why Reforms Affect Informality

Despite country-specific divergences, a number of commonalities can be observed from an empirical comparison of institutional changes in Georgia, Moldova, and Ukraine. First, the relationship between institutional change and informality on the ground is far more complex than the formal-informal dichotomy theorizes. Embarking on institutional change and strengthening formal institutions will not, by itself, affect the informal sphere. In other words, the reform of an institution is not likely to affect an informal practice that thrives within the institution unless the reform occurs in political, economic, and social settings favorable to formal rules and conducive toward their prevalence over informal constraints. The continuity of an informal state and the absence of a reform climate make reforming the institution pointless because its chances of surviving in the informal state are limited. Informal states such as those that emerged in Georgia, Moldova, and Ukraine after the breakup of the Soviet Union depended on informal institutions to survive and therefore fiercely resented formalization and democratization. The preservation and expansion of informal structures inherited from the Soviet regime and enhanced by its successors were fundamental for elite continuity and prosperity. The informal state, however, is as (or more) vulnerable to both external and domestic crises as are states with solid formal institutional frameworks. Informal states are also vulnerable to the shifts in the balance among the informal power brokers who maintain the informal equilibrium.

The dire economic situation in Georgia and Moldova as well as authoritarian consolidation in Moldova and Ukraine prior to the start of the reform process have severely curbed popular and in some instances elite tolerance for the informal state and increased opposition to the informal system. In all three countries, the transition to hybrid regimes occurred as a result of incumbents' weaknesses and inability to consolidate sufficient levels of either informal control or authoritarian leverage. Georgia's Eduard Shevardnadze, Moldova's Vladimir Voronin, and Ukraine's Viktor Yanukovich harbored inherent authoritarian ambitions, and all employed informal institutions both to ascend to power and while in office. Yet all also failed to control and balance informal power centers.

This combination of internal structural failure and external cataclysms such as economic crises or international pressure (table 7.1.) cripples the informal state and creates settings that may be favorable for reforms—that is, a reform climate. The existence of a reform climate establishes underlying conditions under which the reform of an institution could theoretically affect an embedded informal practice. In reality, however, the reform climate provides nothing more than a basic environment conducive to implementing reforms. The effectiveness of reforms vis-à-vis informality is conditioned by several factors. Assuming that reforms in hybrid regimes seek to create institutions that abide by formal constraints, facilitate societal access, and therefore can be described as democratic, the following factors might be identified as determining these institutions' impact on the informal sector:

(a) *The longevity and continuity of reforms are crucial for their consistent and comprehensive impact on informal institutions.* The reform process was initiated in Georgia in 2004 and remains ongoing. In Moldova, the reform climate appeared in 2009, though the actual reform process did not begin until after 2012. In Ukraine, the reform climate emerged briefly in 2005 but then subsided again for almost a decade until 2014, and the reform process itself began in 2015. Georgia, with its uninterrupted decade of reform, has thus had the most success not only with the regard to institution-building but also in terms of relieving formal institutions of many negative characteristics of informal constraints. Since 2009, the reform agenda in Moldova has repeatedly been interrupted by intra-coalition disagreements and dissolutions of governments. In Ukraine, the first democratic reform efforts began after the Orange Revolution but were almost immediately halted by infighting among the Orange forces and remained on hiatus under Yanukovich's presidency.

(b) *The scope and scale of both political and economic reforms, as well as their enforcement and coordination among all three branches of the government are fundamental for the reforms to be effective.* None of the three post-Soviet hybrid regimes examined in this volume achieved such an all-encompassing reform agenda. While the Georgian reform program spotlighted both political and economic reforms, both the legislature and judiciary were subordinated to the executive until the transition from the United National Movement to the Georgian Dream in 2012. By contrast, the legislative branches in Moldova and Ukraine remained relatively liberal throughout the reform period. However, parliamentary support for reforms did not prevent the executive and judiciary branches from resisting institutional changes. In Moldova, economic reform has thus far persistently lagged behind political change, and the relative liberation and modernization of political institutions did little to relieve economic grievances of the population, which continued to favor informal institutions. Despite the notable progress of Ukraine's economic reforms, political reform has proceeded at a glacial pace and with dubious effectiveness. As a consequence, informal political institutions persist in all three countries.

(c) *Elite consensus and popular support for reforms are essential not only for the effectiveness of the reform strategy but also to ensure that both the elites*

TABLE 7.1. Post-Soviet Regimes before and during Institutional Changes

Countries	Georgia		Moldova		Ukraine	
	Before	During	Before	During	Before	During
Informal institutions' strength	▲	◇	▲	▲	▲	◇
Incumbent's strength	▼	▲	▼	▼	▼	◇
Incumbent's control over informal structures	▼	▲	▼	▼	▼	▼
Authoritarian consolidation	▼	◇	▼	▼	◇	▼
Economic development	▼	◇	▼	▼	▼	▼

▼ Low   ▲ High   ◇ Medium

and the people are willing and ready to replace the informal state with a formal institutional framework. In Georgia, both of these conditions were met only temporarily. The growing distance between reformists and the population soon led to a decline in popular support for the reform agenda. The number of elites disaffected with Mikheil Saakashvili's autocratic reform push also grew. Without a popular mandate, the United National Movement government was eventually replaced by the Georgian Dream, a coalition of political parties composed of numerous (semiformal and informal) elite groups alienated by Saakashvili. Moldova's reformers have lacked both an elite consensus and popular backing for their reform plans. The absence of agreement and coordination among Moldovan elites was accompanied by incessant infighting among pro-reform forces, resulting in constant coalitional transformation and the complete absence of a common reform strategy. Popular discontent with the government has simmered since the start of reform process. Despite initially securing both an elite mandate and popular support for institutional changes, Ukraine's reformists have been losing that backing at an alarming speed. The broad popular demand for sweeping institutional transformation encouraged by Euromaidan was overshadowed by military conflict and financial crisis. As the willingness of Petro Poroshenko's government to tackle oligarchs has increasingly come into question from both the public and prodemocratic elites, the levels of discontent among moderate elite groups has grown.

These three sets of reform criteria (table 7.2), along with the existence of a reform climate, provide a hint as to when and under what conditions institutional change can affect the informal sphere. Employing these three covariant sets of factors as criteria for measuring the reforms' effectiveness (or the lack thereof) enables a tentative prediction about whether the reforms might have affected informality.

Is There an Impact on Informal Institutions?

Because none of the post-Soviet hybrid regimes explored in this volume has achieved all of these reform criteria at the same time (see table 7.2.), a logical assumption would be that democratic institutional reforms in these countries have had limited effect on informality. A summary of the empirical findings of this study tentatively supports this idea. However, the observation is tautological because the relationship between institutional reform and informality has not been comparatively assessed. The key measurement indicators were presented in the introduction and discussed in each empirical chapter.

(a) *Levels of institutional distrust before and after the start of reforms indicate changes (if any) in the public perception of state institutions.* This indicator enables us to assess the impact of reforms on public institutions as seen through the eyes of the population. Levels of distrust of public institutions do not directly indicate the population's reliance on informality but nonetheless illustrate whether democratic reforms restored popular confidence in state institutions. Such support for formal institutions increases their legitimacy and enables them to replace informal constraints. Since one of the main objectives of institutional reforms is to construct transparent public institutions that provide services to the population on an all-inclusive basis, the popular perception of these institutions is likely to determine whether citizens would choose to continue relying on informal constraints or prefer dealing with formal institutions. Assessments of institutional distrust in the three hybrid regimes demonstrate relatively low levels of distrust of formal institutions in Georgia and markedly high levels of institutional distrust in both Moldova and Ukraine (see figure 7.1).

Popular distrust of state institutions grew in post-2009 Moldova rather than decreasing, as occurred in Georgia after the 2004 Rose Revolution. Although Moldova's collapse of institutional credibility seems to be associated

TABLE 7.2. Reform Criteria

Determinants of Reform Effectiveness	Georgia	Moldova	Ukraine
Number of reform years	11	4	1
Interruptions	No	Yes	Yes
Priority given to political reforms	Yes	Yes	No
Priority given to economic reforms	Yes	No	Yes
Reforms of executive, legislative, and judiciary	No	No	No
Elite consensus	Yes	No	Yes
Popular support through the entire reform	No	No	No

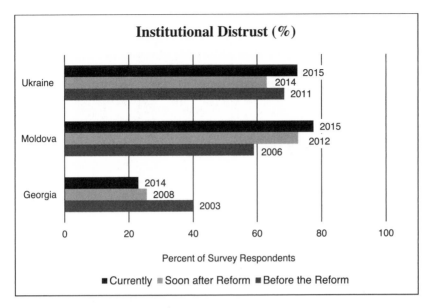

Fig. 7.1. Levels of Institutional Distrust (mean of total%)

with ongoing political instability and economic crisis, it also reflects insufficient reform progress in nearly all areas of institutional transformation. The popular attitude toward state institutions in Ukraine appears to have improved only slightly following Euromaidan's victory in 2014. However, the slow progress of reforms is evident from the decline of institutional trust in 2015 to pre-Euromaidan levels.

(b) *Analysis of popular satisfaction with reforms offers a more precise assessment of the population's attitude toward the reform than do levels of institutional distrust.* It also indicates the population's support for the reform process, which may not necessarily be reflected in levels of institutional (dis)trust. As with the previous indicator, popular satisfaction with reforms is an indirect method of measuring the population's preference for informal institutions. Even people who are satisfied with the reform progress may rely on informal channels to achieve their goals simply because progress does not necessarily mean that the reforms are effective in tackling informal institutions. The assessment of survey data on popular attitudes toward reforms shows little correlation with levels of institutional (dis)trust (figure 7.2.).

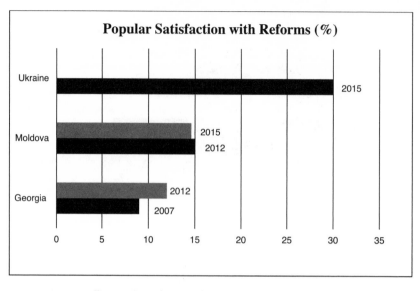

Fig. 7.2. Popular Satisfaction with Reforms (%)

The high level of institutional trust in Georgia is accompanied by relatively low popular acknowledgment of reform progress. At the end of the United National Movement's first and second terms in office, the public's assessment of institutional reforms was rather reserved. Slightly higher were levels of satisfaction with reforms in Moldova, where 15 percent of the public had a positive view of the reforms in 2012 and nearly as many citizens maintained their support three years later. Ukraine's public satisfaction with reforms remains the highest among three countries, with more than a quarter of the population supporting progress during the first year of reform implementation.

(c) *Elites' and the population's reliance on informal institutions is a primary indicator of institutional reforms' impact on informality.* The opinions of elite informants—the only available data and consequently the one on which this study relies—offer some information regarding institutional reforms' effects on the informal sphere. Despite possible bias in elite opinions, the views of experts from various fields who were asked to comment specifically on those fields provide qualitative perspective on the issue. Elites and experts in Georgia offered the highest assessments of reforms' effectiveness in affecting informality (table 7.3.).

Moldovan elites and experts judged institutional reform to have had only a small impact on the informal sphere in the public sector and almost no impact on either the political or private spheres. In Ukraine, reforms had the most impact on informal relations in politics, where many experts believed that the old system of the informal state had been shattered. Ukrainian reformers placed a much higher emphasis on economic reforms than on efforts to transform the political sphere, so this observed effectiveness might be explained by post-Euromaidan political changes, which occurred before or alongside the reform process rather than as a result of it.

These three indicators demonstrate that the relationship between institutional reforms and informality has been the weakest in Moldova and strongest in Georgia. The chaotic nature of Moldova's postcommunist institutional reforms offers an explanation for the limited effectiveness of reforms and their even more conspicuous effect on the informal sphere. In Moldova, less than a quarter of the population is satisfied with the reforms' achievement, and the country recorded the highest level of distrust of formal institutions in the study, two factors that contribute to the persistence of informal relations. Georgia represents the complete opposite: although popular satisfaction with the reform process is low as a consequence of high public expectations that outstrip reformists' abilities, reforms improved public attitudes to state institutions and reduced the role of informal channels. Partly as a result of the recency of reforms and partly as a consequence of the lingering effects of Euromaidan, Ukraine shows contradictory signs— popular alienation from state institutions and popular appreciation for reforms. These indicators translate into a combination of continued reliance on informal institutions and increasing preparedness to abandon them in favor of formal constraints.

TABLE 7.3. Elites' Opinions about Reforms' Effect on Informality

Reforms affected informal relations in:	Georgia	Moldova	Ukraine
Politics	76%	0%	96%
	(16)	(0)	(26)
Public sector	90%	25%	30%
	(19)	(2)	(8)
Private sphere	71%	0%	11%
	(15)	(0)	(3)
Total number of elites	21	8	27

Blurring the Boundaries

This study began with the expectation that the implementation of democratic institutional reforms in hybrid regimes irrevocably leads to the merger of informal institutions with their formal counterparts, as often occurs during nondemocratic reforms in authoritarian regimes.[1] Symbiosis between formal and informal institutions might be expected as a consequence of the unstable and inconsistent character of institutional reforms in hybrid regimes. In contrast to ongoing reform processes in established democracies, democratic reforms are a novelty for hybrid states, and the process of institutional change—involving either layering or displacement and conversion—inevitably requires dealing with informal structures. The role of informal constraints is greater when institutional change occurs as a process of transition from an informal state to a hybrid regime. Whereas the institutional frameworks of consolidated authoritarian regimes function on rigid autocratic rules coordinated by tightly controlled state institutions subordinated to a single power center, informal states are characterized by the existence of multiple power centers and heavily deformalized state institutions.[2] Unlike postauthoritarian institutional transformation, which requires reforming illiberal formal institutions into democratic ones, formal institutions in informal states are no more than a facade for ubiquitous informal constraints. Reform actors in postinformal states have few options other than employing the existing (informal) institutional framework to proceed with reforms. Whereas displacement might prove the best strategy to rid new institutions of old habits, reformists do not always have the opportunity to create institutions from scratch. More commonly, old institutions must be converted to new purposes, and formal rules must be layered on informal constraints. Since many postauthoritarian states already have fully functional formal institutions, the process of institutional change occurs by decentralizing and democratizing this existing institutional system. In postinformal states, the process of institutional transformation requires formalizing existing institutions and instilling formal rules into informal structures posing as state institutions.

Even when brand-new institutions are created to displace old structures, they often must coexist with their predecessors, increasing the chance of institutional contagion or the transfer of informal practices from old institutions to new ones. One example of a displaced institution coexisting with its successor has occurred in Ukraine, where since mid-2015, the new patrol police force has existed alongside members of the old police, who cannot be removed from their jobs en masse as a consequence of the lack of trained replacements. The new patrol police and the old, corrupt police force work under the same roof, sharing facilities and performing similar tasks. The practice of displacement employed in Georgia during the first two years of reforms showed that old institutions fail to contaminate their replacements as long as the process of displacement is implemented without procrastination. Institutional displacement occurred on the greatest scale in Georgia; in contrast, reformists in Moldova and Ukraine have sought to introduce formal constraints into deformalized state institutions. When the new institutions of hybrid regimes are layered on old institutions or when new institutions are created by converting their predecessors, informal actors become embedded into the reform process. The extensive use of informal channels, such as the reliance on informal networks and cooperation with informal stakeholders, is common in Moldova and Ukraine. In both cases, informal tools of reform are the only available means of implementing institutional change.

The process of institutional blurring assumes a variety of forms that depend on the specifics of the reformed institutions and the impact of reforms on informal practices within these institutions. Although hierarchical patronage and clientelist networks were replaced by reform-minded administrators, and the reform climate was instilled, informal institutions remain in place simply because no other alternatives exist. Lacking any other means, reformists in Moldova and Ukraine must use their personal power networks to implement institutional changes. Since informal networks employed by reformists differ qualitatively from the corrupt clientelist structures used by state officials prior to reform, reliance on these informal channels is recognized as a lesser evil. Georgia demonstrates that reformers' habit of doing things informally does not disappear after the challenges of the early reform period have been overcome. Once embedded in the process of reform implementation, informal institutions become ingrained into formal institutions. The subsequent fate of these informal institutions depends on the trajectory of reforms. In Georgia, informal relations within formal institutions did not disappear but instead acquired more positive and benign characteristics than their predecessors. In other words, informal institutions persist in areas of political coalition-building, elite pact-making, policy implementation, and other forms of political interactions. Many of these informal relations do not differ from informal politics in developed democracies.[3]

In hybrid regimes, however, informal relations within state institutions are not fully free of corruption and nepotism. Not only in Moldova and

Ukraine but also in Georgia, political corruption remains present. The difference between informal states and hybrid regimes lies not only in the spread of informal relations but also in elites' perception of informality, which affects the degree to which informal relations persist. Unlike informal states, where informal practices are favored over formal constraints, hybrid regimes shun and eschew informal institutions (particularly corrupt and clientelist ones). Officials of informal states commonly face prosecution for corruption only when they fall out of favor. In hybrid regimes, exposure in corruption scandals may be sufficient for an official to be removed from the job as a result of pressure from civil society.

In contrast to informal states, informal practices in hybrid regimes are not purposefully instilled into formal institutions; rather they are vestiges of the ancien regime that continue haunting new institutions because of incomplete institutional change. Unless the reform process is halted or reversed, as happened during the second half of Viktor Yuschenko's term in Ukraine, informal relations will remain in the shadows of formal institutions. Informal constraints do not dominate their formal counterparts but instead are used by institutional actors only in the absence (or weakness) of formal problem-solving mechanisms. As long as the reform process continues, institutional blurring—which occurs as a result of institutional change and leads to a formal-informal symbiosis—takes place at the expense of the negative functions of informal institutions, such as corrupt practices.

Informal Institutions Are Not Always Bad

This study expected to find that informal institutions in post-Soviet hybrid regimes are not entirely and exclusively negative. In the context of developing countries, detrimental functions of informal institutions, such as cover for corruption and patronage, overlap with their positive role as institution-building mechanisms—for example, by serving as advisory bodies for reform ministers or as coping mechanisms for the population. None of these three hybrid regimes has established a democratic institutional framework, and therefore none has replaced its vast informal institutional foundation with fully functional formal equivalents. Since little institutional improvement occurred in areas of social welfare, the role of informal institutions as safety nets and mutual assistance mechanisms remained virtually untouched by the reforms. Regardless of attempts to alleviate economic inequality, all of the post-Soviet hybrid regimes achieved little in terms of tackling unemployment, poverty, and low living standards. Given that the economic functions of informal institutions are closely interwoven with their political and social roles, the lack of institutional change in either of these spheres ensures the continuity of informality in the other two areas.

One of the key explanations for why informal practices persist in the political life of hybrid regimes is political actors' pursuit of financial gain via access to resources. Post-Soviet state officials and individuals interested in engaging in political activity have long used their jobs to extract as many rents as possible. Having obtained their jobs through informal payments or contacts, many politicians and officials in informal and authoritarian states took as their primary goal reimbursing their investment or to paying back their patrons. In hybrid regimes, the introduction of open competition for state jobs and some other antinepotism mechanisms has decreased the perception of government jobs as sources of bribe extraction. Yet low salaries for elected and appointed officials, particularly in Moldova and Ukraine, along with a close association between state officials and business elites in both countries do little to alleviate the political sphere of monetary exchanges of favors. Although political corruption, red tape, and nepotism have retreated, they have not disappeared from the political spheres of these hybrid regimes.

Much less progress has been achieved in terms of improving the people's economic situation. The reliance on informal institutions as private safety nets and coping mechanisms may only decline if these functions are "delegated" to formal institutions that can provide the population with public services. Thus far, however, the state remains absent from many areas of public administration and service provision. Informal networks fill the institutional vacuum, providing people with services that neither the state nor civil society can deliver. The bulk of informal relations in the socioeconomic sphere of hybrid regimes focus precisely on the provision of social safety nets for the population. Fragile economies in these post-Soviet transitional regimes, which lack the fossil fuel wealth of their authoritarian neighbors, are vulnerable to crises and other external shocks. As a result, regardless of the reforms' progress in areas of economic development, private safety nets provided by informal institutions remain just as important for the population as was the case prior to the start of reforms.

This finding confirms the assumption suggested by many scholars of postcommunism that informality is neither positive nor negative and that the withdrawal of the state left people with no better options than to rely on informal institutions in their daily lives.[4] Only when informal institutions are replaced by their formal equivalents does the population begin to shift from informal ways of doing things toward following formal rules. This change, however, would be improbable without the strengthening of formal institutional frameworks to make reliance on informal structures less efficient, less attractive, and more costly. Consequently, withering of informal relations is possible only following a radical institutional change that would not only rearrange the existing institutional order but also ensure that the new institutional framework is functional and sustainable in the long term.

Because the complete eradication of informal institutions is impossible even in countries with fully consolidated democratic institutions, mitigating the negative functions of informal institutions might prove more pragmatic than seeking to wipe them out. The experience of post-Soviet reforms shows that attempts to completely weed out all informal relations from formal institutions rarely succeed. Informality may withdraw or may cease dominating formal institutions, but the chances are low that informal institutions will completely disappear. With the creation of transparent state institutions, the influence of informal power brokers becomes irrelevant because the presence of robust formal constraints forces them to follow the formal rules of the game. Yet this situation is unlikely to occur in fresh institutional settings in the context of hybrid regimes, where a sufficient formal institutional system does not exist to replace informal relations and elites and the public are not prepared to abandon the old customs. Therefore, dismantling an informal state does not have to be accompanied by efforts to eliminate informal relations. Moreover, when formal actors use informal channels for institutional reform, as occurs in hybrid regimes, the results are far less detrimental than informal manipulations of formal rules by informal actors in informal states.

The process of employing positive aspects of informal relations for the benefit of reforms has unfolded in all three hybrid regimes since the start of reforms. Reformers did not deliberately choose to preserve informality and to employ informal relations for the needs of institutional transformation; rather, this process occurs spontaneously and remains beyond reformers' control. Lustration, decommunization, and other systematic efforts to uproot old habits and dislodge representatives of the old system have not yet proven effective in detaching the informal sphere from its formal counterpart. In all three post-Soviet hybrid regimes, the reliance on informal institutions is still perceived as rational not only by the population and the elites but also by the reformists.

Implications for Policy and Research

Democratic institutional reforms in post-Soviet hybrid regimes offer a trea-
sure trove of lessons not only for the postcommunist region but also for
other developing regions of the world. Reformers in hybrid regimes face the
daunting challenge of transforming an entire institutional framework and
reconstructing political and economic orders that have been in place for decades. This process often must occur in the midst of an armed conflict or
during an economic crisis. Dismantling the old system and creating a new
one is always enshrouded in risk. Failed reforms, as occurred in post-Orange
Ukraine, might empower and legitimize informal actors. Since successful democratization and institutional change are hard to duplicate, reformists often look cautiously on lessons from other regions and particularly from developed states. Examples of other reform efforts within the same region,
therefore, are invaluable. Georgia's post–Rose Revolution reforms continue
to serve reformers in other countries as a blueprint for how an entrenched
informal state can be reformed into a functional hybrid regime. Georgian
reformers are sought after in Ukraine, and Moldova's pro-reform ministers
attempt to replicate Georgia's success while avoiding Saakashvili's mistakes,
suggesting that experience and knowledge pertaining to institutional transformation are much in demand.

This study has a number of implications for policy and further research.
First, continuity and comprehensiveness of reforms are one of the most important factors in ensuring that institutional change decreases informality.
Continuity of reforms is commonly conditioned by external shocks or by
radical transformations within the reform camp such as political regime
changes, meaning that this factor often remains beyond reformists' control.
Conversely, the comprehensiveness of reforms depends on pro-reform actors' willingness and ability to challenge and change established norms. Unless reformers seek to change the entire institutional framework, transformation from an informal state to a hybrid regime is unlikely to occur, and the
transformation to a full-fledged democracy is even less likely. Partial reforms
that change only one or a few formal institutions and leave the remainder
undisturbed plagued early reformists in both Orange-period Ukraine and
post-2009 Moldova. The experience of incomplete institutional change illustrates that reforming one or two institutions fails to change the prevailing
institutional order. The failure of reforms that inevitably follows incomplete
institutional transformation might be expected to reverse the few changes

that were implemented. Hence, the combination of a reform climate and reformists' willingness to reshape the old institutional system are crucial prerequisites of a reform agenda that seeks to transform the informal state. The experience of post-Soviet reformers also shows that in hybrid regimes, reforms lacking both elites and popular support have only limited prospects for success. Unlike authoritarian states, which can push through their (undemocratic) reform agenda even in the absence of a popular mandate, hybrid regimes draw their credibility and legitimacy from elite consensus and popular opinion. While some reform efforts might succeed based solely on elite agreement or on public popularity, others require both.

Post-Soviet reforms might also teach future reformers that institutional change in an informal state cannot be attained without relying on informal institutions. In the absence of functional formal institutional framework, reform actors are compelled to use informal channels to implement their goals. Attempts to exclude the bulk of informal power brokers may not only alienate elites from the reform process, as was the case in Saakashvili's Georgia, but may also endanger the continuity of institutional changes. If the elites' informal power bases were unshaken by the regime change, they can be expected to resist the transformation of the existing order and unless offered participation in the reform process may well oppose it. The existing oligarchic order and informal power relations survived Ukraine's Orange Revolution unscathed, allowing oligarchs to hijack the reform process and to restore the informal state by exploiting weaknesses in the Orange coalition. The situation changed after Euromaidan, since neither the oligarchic order nor the informal power balance survived the regime change unaffected. This alteration in the balance of power enabled reformists to include the more accommodating elements of the oligarchic class in the reform process and to crack down on the less cooperative oligarchs.

In all of the three case studies, reformers did not deliberately incorporate informal practices and actors in the reform process, yet it systematically occurred. Interviews with members of the reform teams reveal that employing informal practices during the reform implementation was never part of the reform plan but rather was dictated by circumstances on the ground. This experience suggests that harnessing the positive effects of informality for the benefit of reform success may need to be institutionalized through its inclusion in reform policies and employed to boost the reform process. In light of the symbiotic character of formal-informal relations in the former Soviet Union and the fact that informal institutions cannot be thoroughly rooted out from the formal sphere, co-opting informal institutions so that they are part of the reforms may not be a bad idea. Reformers may benefit from taking a more harmonious approach toward the informal sphere, as in recent Ukrainian efforts to cautiously balance formal and informal constraints, rather than by following Saakashvili's radical crusade against informality.

The relationship between institutional change and informality in post-Soviet countries has inherent similarities to such processes elsewhere as well as notable differences. One of the most obvious of these disparities is the all-encompassing impact of informal institutions on institutional change in the former Soviet states, a phenomenon that makes the reform process and informality interdependent. Not only do reforms affect the informal sphere, but informality also leaves its imprint on the reform process. Further, the dismantling of an informal state does not require eradicating all forms of informal relations. Excessive efforts to wipe out all informal power centers competing with a ruling regime can bring reformists perilously close to authoritarianism. As in the case of Georgia's United National Movement, which was accused of monopolizing power and employing authoritarian tools to suppress opposition, particularly during its second term in office, reform agents who seek complete subordination of all political and economic forces to the center may fail to democratize their institutions.

These findings suggest that more research is needed into the relationship between institutional change and informality in the post-Soviet region. The causal connections between the implementation of particular reform goals and their immediate (or long-term) effect upon informal institutions remain unclear. The impact of such intervening variables as economic development, proximity to the European Union, and external pressures for institutional change fell beyond this book's scope. We do not know whether institutional changes may have a greater effect if a state is in the process of transitioning from an authoritarian regime rather than from an informal state. The answers to these and other questions may shed more light on the underexplored relationship between institutional change and informality in regimes transitioning to democracy and may thus enable reformers to avoid making errors in formulating policies.

Appendix: Research Methodology

This book is based on several types of data from a variety of primary and secondary sources. For primary data, this book employs elite (expert) in-depth interviews conducted between July 2013 and September 2015 to learn about opinions on the relationship between institutional changes and informality. The sample includes twenty-one informants from Georgia, eight from Moldova, and twenty-seven from Ukraine. The interviewees fall into two categories: thirty-one experts, academics, representatives of civil society, and analysts who were selected based on their expertise and/or relevant work and research experience in areas of institutional reform and the informal sphere; while twenty-five policymakers, government officials, and other members of the political elite were chosen both for their reliance on informal networks and for their role in implementing institutional changes.

I began by identifying the key informants by occupation and role in a particular organization or institution. These key informants were then asked for suggestions regarding colleagues or other potential informants to be interviewed. The interviews were conducted in the form of semistructured discussions based on open-ended questions, allowing informants to engage in a dialogue with the interviewer and to freely express their opinions and views. To address the common problem that elites in post-Soviet states are predisposed to provide biased or incorrect information, most informants were interviewed in informal settings and promised anonymity. As a consequence of the high probability of obtaining distorted or false information, interview data were cross-checked against local mass media sources and reports by international organizations. The data obtained from these open-ended interviews were supplemented by data from close-ended surveys.

Most of the survey data are taken from representative cross-national surveys. In particular, successive waves of such cross-national surveys as the

World Values Survey, polls conducted by the International Republican Institute, and polls conducted by the European Bank for Reconstruction and Development enable the observation of transitions and causality over an extended period. Cross-national survey data are combined with national-level surveys. For Georgia, these sources included surveys by the Caucasus Research Resource Centers—for example, the Caucasus Barometer—as well as the Georgia National Survey,. In Moldova, the Barometer of Public Opinion by the Institute for Public Policy was used alongside cross-national surveys. For Ukraine, public polls by the Kiev International Institute for Sociology, Gorshenin Institute, Rating Pro Center, Razumkov Center, Democratic Initiative Foundation, and International Foundation for Electoral Systems were used.

Notes

Introduction

1. Hart, "Informal Income Opportunities."

2. de Soto, *Mystery of Capital*; North, *Institutions*; Loayza, "Economics of the Informal Sector"; Helmke and Levitsky, "Informal Institutions and Comparative Politics."

3. While this book examines informality through the prism of informal practices, institutions, and networks, the formal sphere is analyzed through the framework of (formal) social institutions of state and society. According to Knight's definition, "an institution is a set of rules that structure social interactions in particular ways" (*Institutions and Social Conflict*, 2–3).

4. See Gel'man, "Unrule of Law"; Chong and Gradstein, "Inequality and Informality"; Kim and Koh, "Informal Economy and Bribery"; Rose, "Russia as an Hour-Glass Society"; Sik, "Network Capital."

5. Gel'man, "Post-Soviet Transitions"; Schneider and Enste, "Shadow Economies."

6. Helmke and Levitsky, *Informal Institutions and Democracy*, 284.

7. Williams, Round, and Rodgers, *Role of Informal Economies*; Morris, "Socially Embedded Workers"; Rodgers and Williams, "Informal Economy."

8. Ledeneva, *Russia's Economy of Favours*; Ledeneva, *Can Russia Modernise?*

9. D'Anieri, *Understanding Ukrainian Politics*; Gel'man, "Unrule of Law."

10. Hale, *Patronal Politics*.

11. Bunce, "Rethinking Recent Democratization"; Gel'man, "Post-Soviet Transitions."

12. Gel'man, "Post-Soviet Transitions," 87.

13. Ledeneva, *Can Russia Modernise?*

14. See Rasanayagam, "Informal Economy, Informal State"; Luong, *Institutional Change.*

15. Morris and Polese, *Informal Post-Socialist Economy.*

16. See, for example, Börzel and Pamuk, "Pathologies of Europeanisation"; Closson, "Networks of Profit"; Polese, "'If I Receive It'"; Round and Williams, "Coping with the Social Costs"; Williams, Round, and Rodgers, *Role of Informal Economies.*

17. Helmke and Levitsky, *Informal Institutions and Democracy,* 284.

18. Bunce, "Comparative Democratization," 713.

19. See Castells and Portes, "World Underneath"; Loayza, "Economics of the Informal Sector"; North, *Institutions*; Schneider and Enste, "Shadow Economies."

20. See, for example, de Soto, *Mystery of Capital*; Chong and Gradstein, "Inequality and Informality"; Loayza, Oviedo, and Servén, *Impact of Regulation.*

21. See Misztal, *Informality*; Gel'man, "Unrule of Law"; Ledeneva, *Can Russia Modernise?*; Rose, "Russia as an Hour-Glass Society"; Rose, "Getting Things Done"; James L. Gibson, "Social Networks"; Aliyev, "Post-Communist Informal Networking."

22. For "conversion" of postcommunist institutions toward communist-era forms of organization and purposes, see Magner, "Civil Society."

23. Ledeneva, *Can Russia Modernise?*

24. For example, studies on informal practices among elites in the Central European postcommunist countries demonstrate that the reliance on informality does not significantly affect the quality and performance of democratic institutions. See, for example, Aasland, Grødeland, and Pleines, "Trust and Informal Practice."

25. North, *Institutions*; Putnam, *Making Democracy Work.*

26. Morris and Polese, *Informal Post-Socialist Economy*; Ledeneva, *Russia's Economy of Favours*; Onoshchenko and Williams, "Paying for Favours"; Williams, "Surviving Post-Socialism."

27. See, for example, Morris and Polese, *Informal Post-Socialist Economy.*

28. See Rose, "Getting by without Government"; Ledeneva, *Russia's Economy of Favours*; Dershem and Gzirishvili, "Informal Social Support Networks"; Williams, "Surviving Post-Socialism."

29. Morris, "Unruly Entrepreneurs"; Morris and Polese, *Informal Post-Socialist Economy.*

30. Sik, "Network Capital."

31. O'Donnell, "Illusions about Consolidation"; Saavedra and Chong, "Structural Reform."

32. See, for example, Dimitrova-Grajzl and Simon, "Political Trust and Historical Legacy"; Kitschelt, "Formation of Party Cleavages."

33. Beissinger and Young, *Beyond State Crisis?*

34. Round, Williams, and Rodgers, "Everyday Tactics."

35. Karakoç, "Economic Inequality."

36. Morris and Polese, *Informal Post-Socialist Economy.*

37. Diamond, "Thinking about Hybrid Regimes"; Levitsky and Way, *Competitive Authoritarianism.*

38. Bunce, McFaul, and Stoner-Weiss, *Democracy and Authoritarianism*, 9–15.

39. Levitsky and Way, *Competitive Authoritarianism.*

40. Bunce and Wolchik, *Defeating Authoritarian Leaders*, 9.

41. See Freedom House, *Nations in Transit.*

42. Carothers, "End of the Transition Paradigm"; Mitchell, *Uncertain Democracy.*

43. Bunce and Wolchik, *Defeating Authoritarian Leaders*; Bunce and Wolchik, "Favorable Conditions."

44. Levitsky and Way, *Competitive Authoritarianism.*

45. O'Donnell, "Delegative Democracy."

46. See Freedom House, *Nations in Transit.*

47. Rose, "Getting by without Government"; James L. Gibson, "Social Networks"; Adrian Smith and Stenning, "Beyond Household Economies."

48. Slater, "Institutional Complexity," 135.

49. Levitsky and Way, "Rise of Competitive Authoritarianism," 54.

50. See, for example, O'Donnell, "Illusions about Consolidation"; Helmke and Levitsky, *Informal Institutions and Democracy*; Lauth, "Informal Institutions"; Luong, *Institutional Change.*

51. North, *Institutions*, 4.

52. See, for example, Luong, *Institutional Change*; Hale, *Patronal Politics*; Misztal, *Informality*; Aasland, Grødeland, and Pleines, "Trust and Informal Practice."

53. See Ledeneva, *Can Russia Modernise?*

54. Aasland, Grødeland, and Pleines, "Trust and Informal Practice."

Chapter One

1. Hart, "Informal Income Opportunities."

2. A study by the International Labour Organization on the socioeconomic situation in Kenya may have introduced the term *informal sector* to economics. See International Labour Organization, *Incomes, Employment, and Equality*.

3. W. Arthur Lewis, "Economic Development."

4. Harris and Todaro, "Migration, Unemployment and Development."

5. See Maloney, "Informality Revisited."

6. Bromley and Gerry, *Casual Work*.

7. Gaughan and Ferman, "Toward an Understanding," 18.

8. Gërxhani, "Informal Sector," 267.

9. Castells and Portes, "World Underneath," 33.

10. Maloney, "Informality Revisited."

11. de Soto, *Other Path*.

12. Godfrey, "Toward a Theory," 248.

13. North, *Institutions*, 4.

14. Helmke and Levitsky, "Informal Institutions and Comparative Politics," 726–27.

15. Ibid.

16. Lomnitz, "Informal Exchange Networks."

17. Boeke, *Economics and Economic Policy*.

18. Homans, *Sentiments and Activities*; Alberti and Sabatini, *Exchange Networks and Local Transformation*; Parry and Bloch, *Money and the Morality of Exchange*; Graeber, *Debt*.

19. Giordano, "Social Organization of Informality," 29.

20. Misztal, *Informality*, 17.

21. Homans, *Sentiments and Activities*; Mead, *Mind, Self, and Society*; Blunter, "Society as Symbolic Interaction"; Goffman, *Behavior in Public Places*; Garfinkel, *Studies in Ethnomethodology*.

22. Letki and Mieriņa, "Getting Support"; Thye, Lovaglia, and Markovsky, "Responses"; Siegel, "Social Networks."

23. Adler and Sheinbaum, "Trust, Social Networks, and the Informal Economy"; Passy and Giugni, "Social Networks."

24. Morris and Polese, *Informal Post-Socialist Economy*; Ledeneva, *Russia's Economy of Favours*.

25. Adrian Smith and Stenning, "Beyond Household Economies."

26. Loayza, "Economics of the Informal Sector."

27. Oviedo, Thomas, and Karakurum-Özdemir, *Economic Informality*, 4.

28. International Labour Organization, *Measuring Informality*, 5

29. Misztal, *Informality*, 8.

30. Ibid., 18.

31. Brie and Stölting, "Formal Institutions," 20.

32. Ledeneva, "Informality and Informal Politics," 375.

33. Böröcz, "Informality Rules," 351.

34. Ibid.

35. Brie and Stölting, "Formal Institutions," 19.

36. Knight, *Institutions and Social Conflict*, 172.

37. Ledeneva, *Can Russia Modernise?*, 246.

38. Gel'man, "Post-Soviet Transitions," 92.

39. Burns and Flam, *Shaping of Social Organization*, 223.

40. Helmke and Levitsky, "Informal Institutions and Comparative Politics," 729.

41. Misztal, *Informality*, 88.

42. Ibid., 43.

43. Gërxhani, "Informal Sector."

44. Granovetter, "Strength of Weak Ties."

45. Sindzingre, "Relevance," 64.

46. Lauth, "Informal Institutions"; Böröcz, "Informality Rules."

47. Homans, *Social Behavior*.

48. Misztal, *Informality*.

49. Uslaner, *Moral Foundations*.

50. Rose, *Understanding Post-Communist Transformation*, 60.

51. Ledeneva, *Russia's Economy of Favours*, 84.

52. Ibid., 39–40.

53. Helmke and Levitsky define informality as "socially shared rules, usually unwritten, that are created, communicated, and enforced outside of officially sanctioned channels" ("Informal Institutions and Comparative Politics," 727).

54. For example, some informal activities are illegal (corruption), while others are fully legal and even approved, depending on the context (connections).

55. Sindzingre, "Relevance," 5.

56. Williams and Lansky, "Informal Employment."

57. International Labour Organization, *Measuring Informality*, 61.

58. Schneider and Enste, *Shadow Economies*.

59. Pop-Eleches and Tucker, "Associated with the Past?"

60. Morris and Polese, *Informal Post-Socialist Economy*; Morris and Polese, "Informal Health and Education Sector Payments."

61. Helmke and Levitsky, *Informal Institutions and Democracy*, 25.

62. Ibid., 26.

63. Rupnik and Zielonka, "Introduction," 13.

64. Ibid.

65. Ledeneva, *Can Russia Modernise?*; Ledeneva, "Informality and Informal Politics," 377.

66. North, *Institutions*, 6.

67. Eggertsson, *Imperfect Institutions*.

68. O'Donnell, "Illusions about Consolidation."

69. Helmke and Levitsky, "Informal Institutions and Comparative Politics."

70. Ibid., 727.

71. Christiansen and Neuhold, *International Handbook*; Giordano and Hayoz, *Informality*.

72. Ostrom, *Understanding Institutional Diversity*, 3.

73. Grødeland, "'Red Mobs,'" 220.

74. Lomnitz, "Informal Exchange Networks."

75. Ibid., 42.

76. Granovetter, "Strength of Weak Ties," 1360.

77. Freeman, "Centrality in Social Networks"; Putnam, *Making Democracy Work*.

78. See Laumann and Pappi, *Networks of Collective Action*; Harrison White, Boorman, and Brieger, "Social Structure."

79. Ledeneva, *Can Russia Modernise?*; Mishler and Rose, "Trust, Distrust, and Skepticism"; Sik, "Network Capital in Capitalist"; James L. Gibson, "Social Networks"; Lonkila, "The social meaning of work."

80. Weatherford, "Interpersonal Networks"; Crenson, "Social Networks"; Folodare, "Effect of Neighborhood"; Sheingold, "Social Networks and Voting."

81. Malinowski, *Argonauts*.

82. Malkin, "Networks."

83. See Ledeneva, *Russia's Economy of Favours*.

84. Aasland, Grødeland, and Pleines define "informal practice' as behavior not in line with formal procedures stipulated for dealing with a given

problem or behavior aimed at solving problems for which there are no (clear) formal procedures' ("Trust and Informal Practice," 116).

85. Ledeneva, "Informality and Informal Politics," 378.

86. See, for example, Ledeneva, *Russia's Economy of Favours*; Mohamed and Mohamad, "Effect of *Wasta*."

Chapter Two

1. Yang, *Gifts, Favors, and Banquets*, 1.

2. See, for example, Yeung and Tung, "Achieving Business Success"; Chen, Chen, and Huang, "Chinese *Guanxi*."

3. Thomas Gold, Guthrie, and Wank, *Social Connections*, 3.

4. Yang, *Gifts, Favors, and Banquets*, 2.

5. Thomas Gold, Guthrie, and Wank, *Social Connections*, 9.

6. See ibid.; Qian, Razzaque, and Keng, "Chinese Cultural Values"; Hsiung, "*Guanxi*."

7. Thomas Gold, Guthrie, and Wank, *Social Connections*, 8.

8. Hwang et al., "Guanxi and Business Ethics."

9. Chow and Ng, "Characteristics."

10. Hutchings and Murray, "Australian Expatriates' Experiences."

11. For Japanese *amakudari* practices, see Colignon and Usui, *Amakudari*. For Korean "parachute appointments," see Lee and Rhyu, "Political Dynamics."

12. Barnett, Yandle, and Naufal, "Regulation, Trust, and Cronyism," 41.

13. Tlaiss and Kauser, "Importance of *Wasta*," 470.

14. Barnett, Yandle, and Naufal, "Regulation, Trust, and Cronyism," 42.

15. Ibid.

16. Gary D. Gold and Naufal, "Wasta"; Bailey, "Women and Wasta," 65.

17. Hutchings and Weir, "Guanxi and Wasta."

18. Izraeli, "Business Ethics," 1556; Danet, *Pulling Strings*.

19. Amado and Brasil, "Organizational Behaviors and Cultural Context."

20. Ibid.

21. Ferreira et al., "Unraveling the Mystery."

22. Daymon and Hodges, "Researching the Occupational Culture."

23. Lomnitz, "Informal Exchange Networks."

24. Fox, *Watching the English*.

25. Peter B. Smith et al., "Are Indigenous Approaches," 337.

26. Anne Gibson, "Old-Boys Network."

27. Vinten, "Participant Observation," 34.

28. de Sousa, "'I Don't Bribe'"; Putnam, *Making Democracy Work.*

29. Scheuch and Scheuch, *Cliquen, Klüngel, und Karrieren,* 71–108

30. Böröcz, "Informality Rules," 352.

31. Peter B. Smith et al., "Are Indigenous Approaches," 345.

32. This section is primarily interested with the analysis of postcommunist informality in non-Soviet societies of Central and Eastern European countries and the Balkan states. Although the only postcommunist states in Asia—Mongolia and Afghanistan—were, like the Central and Eastern European Countries, governed by Soviet-style communist regimes, communist rule in Afghanistan was too short-lived and too closely embroiled with the 1979–89 Soviet military occupation. According to the few available analyses, socialism had an extensive impact on informality in Mongolia that closely resembled its impact in Soviet Central Asia, which is discussed later in the chapter. For informality in Mongolia, see Sneath, "Transacting and Enacting."

33. Böröcz, "Informality Rules"; Sik, "Network Capital"; Rose, *Understanding Post-Communist Transformation*; Grødeland, "'Red Mobs.'"

34. Misztal, *Informality,* 210.

35. Ledeneva, *Can Russia Modernise?*

36. Chavdarova, "Institutionalization"; Begg and Pickles, "Institutions, Social Networks, and Ethnicity."

37. Adrian Smith and Stenning, "Beyond Household Economies," 197.

38. Böröcz, "Informality Rules."

39. Sik, "Network Capital," 17.

40. Böröcz, "Informality Rules," 348.

41. Bunce, "Rethinking Recent Democratization."

42. Grødeland, "'Red Mobs,'" 132.

43. Mishler and Rose, "Trust, Distrust, and Skepticism" 94; Dobovšek and Meško, "Informal Networks"; Vian and Burak, "Beliefs"; World Bank (www.worldbank.org) and the European Bank for Research and Development (www.ebrd.com).

44. Morawska, "Malleable Homo Sovieticus"; Williams, "Beyond the Formal/Informal Jobs Divide"; Ekiert and Hanson, *Capitalism and Democracy,* 28.

45. Karl and Schmitter, "From an Iron Curtain"; Schmitter and Karl, "Conceptual Travels."

46. Morris and Polese, *Informal Post-Socialist Economy,* 1.

47. Ibid., 6.

48. European Bank for Reconstruction and Development, *Life in Transition: After the Crisis*, 10.

49. Karanikolos et al., "Financial Crisis."

50. Adrian Smith, "Culture/Economy," 238.

51. Kim and Koh, "Informal Economy and Bribery."

52. Ledeneva, *Russia's Economy of Favours*, 1.

53. Ibid., 34.

54. Fitzpatrick, *Everyday Stalinism*, 63.

55. Michailova and Worm, "Personal Networking."

56. Keenan, "Muscovite Political Folkways."

57. Aliyev, *Post-Communist Civil Society*.

58. Vasmer, *Etymologicheskii Slovar' Russkogo Yazika*.

59. Ledeneva, *Russia's Economy of Favours*, 16.

60. Ashwin, "Endless Patience," 194.

61. Ledeneva, *Russia's Economy of Favours*, 104.

62. Morton, "Who Gets What," 250.

63. Ledeneva, *Can Russia Modernise?*, 8.

64. Rose, "Postcommunism and the Problem of Trust."

65. Ledeneva, *Can Russia Modernise?*, 13.

66. Kononenko and Moshes, *Russia as a Network State*; Marsh, "Social Capital and Democracy."

67. Ledeneva, *Russia's Economy of Favours*; Peter B. Smith et al., "Are Indigenous Approaches"; Rehn and Taalas, "'Znakomstva I Svyazi'"

68. Miller, Koshechkina, and Grødeland, "How Citizens Cope"; Onoshchenko and Williams, "Paying for Favours"; Tymczuk, "Public Duties"; Lennhag, *Informal Economy*.

69. Rose, "Getting Things Done," 164.

70. Ledeneva, *Can Russia Modernise?*

71. Onoshchenko and Williams, "Paying for Favours."

72. Wanner, "Money, Morality, and New Forms of Exchange"; Tymczuk, "Public Duties," 62.

73. Knudsen, "Story of Šarūnas," 35–51.

74. Aidukaite, "Welfare Reforms."

75. Knudsen, "Story of Šarūnas."

76. Williams and Padmore, "'Envelope Wages.'"

77. Habicht et al., "Social Inequalities"; Balabanova et al., "Health Service Utilization."

78. Aliyev, "Post-Communist Informal Networking."

79. Babajanian, "Social Capital."

80. Yalcin-Heckmann, "Informal Economy," 165–87.

81. See Aliyev, "Civil Society"; Aliyev, "Informal Networks."

82. Aliyev, "Post-Communist Informal Networking."

83. Ishkanian, *Democracy Building*; Safiyev, "Azerbaijan."

84. O'Hearn, "Consumer Second Economy"; Ofer and Vinokur, *Private Sources of Income*; Mars and Altman, "Cultural Bases"; Feldbrugge, "Government and Shadow Economy."

85. Altman, *Reconstruction*.

86. Aliyev, "Effects."

87. Ibid.

88. Rasanayagam, "Informal Economy, Informal State."

89. Koroteyeva and Makarova, "Money and Social Connections"; Mars and Altman, "Case of a Factory," 103.

90. Urinboyev, "Law, Social Norms, and Welfare," 36; Ruziev and Midmore, "Informal Credit Institutions."

91. Schatz, *Modern Clan Politics*.

92. Collins, "Clans, Pacts, and Politics," 142.

93. Rasanayagam, "Informal Economy, Informal State," 681.

94. Isaacs, "Nur Otan," 1060.

95. Roberts, "Doing the Democracy Dance."

96. Werner, "Gifts, Bribes, and Development."

97. Ledeneva, *Can Russia Modernise?*, 7.

98. Schatz, *Modern Clan Politics*, 68.

99. Collins, "Clans, Pacts, and Politics," 144.

100. Sik, "Network Capital"; Williams and Padmore, "'Envelope Wages.'" For example, the British practice of pulling strings is used primarily in dealings with high-ranking officials. Peter B. Smith et al. describe *wasta* as centered on tribal and clannish "loyalty and solidarity" ("Are Indigenous Approaches," 335). Similarly, Thomas Gold, Guthrie, and Wank demonstrate that *guanxi* derives from centuries of Confucianism and has "enduring significance in traditional Chinese philosophy" (*Social Connections*, 10).

101. Miller, Koshechkina, and Grødeland, "How Citizens Cope"; Mishler and Rose, "Trust, Distrust, and Skepticism"; Raiser et al., "Social Capital in Transition."

102. European Bank for Reconstruction and Development, *Life in Transition: After the Crisis*.

103. Round and Williams, "Coping with the Social Costs," 189.

104. Rose, "Getting Things Done," 164.

105. Ibid.

106. Ibid.

107. Jowitt, *New World Disorder*; Magner, "Civil Society"; Bernhard and Karakoç, "Civil Society"; Dimitrova-Grajzl and Simon, "Political Trust and Historical Legacy"; Pop-Eleches and Tucker, "Associated with the Past?"; Thelen, "Shortage, Fuzzy Property, and Other Dead Ends"; Crawford and Lijphart, *Liberalization and Leninist Legacies*.

108. For scholars of path-dependency, see Karl and Schmitter, "From an Iron Curtain"; Linz and Valenzuela, *Failure of Presidential Democracy*.

109. Rose, *Understanding Post-Communist Transformation*, 9.

110. Jowitt, *New World Disorder*.

111. Ekiert and Hanson, *Capitalism and Democracy*, 19–20.

112. Crawford and Lijphart, *Liberalization and Leninist Legacies*.

113. Mieriņa and Cers, "Is Communism to Blame," 1032.

114. Kopstein and Reilly, "Geographic Diffusion."

115. Ekiert and Hanson, *Capitalism and Democracy*, 30.

116. Kopstein and Reilly, "Geographic Diffusion"; Pop-Eleches, "Historical Legacies."

117. Pop-Eleches, "Historical Legacies," 910.

118. Kitschelt, "Accounting for Postcommunist Regime Diversity," 50.

119. Kitschelt, "Formation of Party Cleavages," 453–55.

120. Kitschelt suggested treating Baltic republics as "borderline cases" that managed to preserve democratic institutional traditions, largely as a consequence of their later incorporation into the Soviet Union (after 1939). In addition, the Baltic republics began contesting Soviet patrimonial communism well before perestroika and the collapse of state communism in Central and Eastern Europe (ibid., 455).

121. Ibid., 453.

122. Ibid., 455.

123. Bernhard and Karakoç, "Civil Society"; Dimitrova-Grajzl and Simon, "Political Trust and Historical Legacy"; Kopecký and Spirova, "'Jobs for the Boys'?"; Pop-Eleches and Tucker, "Associated with the Past?"; Thelen, "Shortage, Fuzzy Property, and Other Dead Ends"; Aliyev, "Post-Soviet Informality."

124. Kopecký and Spirova, "'Jobs for the Boys'?," 900.

125. Thelen, "Shortage, Fuzzy Property, and Other Dead Ends," 45.

126. Dimitrova-Grajzl and Simon, "Political Trust and Historical Legacy," 209.

127. Even in Baltic republics, thought to be success stories among fSU countries, "transition . . . in many cases is determined by the Soviet empire legacies" (Aidukaite, "Welfare Reforms," 212).

128. Rose, "Getting Things Done," 165.

129. Gel'man, "Post-Soviet Transitions," 97.

130. Williams, Round, and Rodgers, *Role of Informal Economies*, 16.

131. Zdravomyslova and Voronkov, "Informal Public," 50.

132. Rasanayagam, "Informal Economy, Informal State," 682.

133. Ledeneva, "Practices of Exchange and Networking," 154.

134. Alexeev and Pyle, "Note on Measuring," 153.

135. Ledeneva, *Russia's Economy of Favours*; Fitzpatrick, *Everyday Stalinism*; Ofer and Vinokur, *Private Sources of Income*.

136. Adrian Smith and Stenning, "Beyond Household Economies," 197.

137. According to Rose, in an "hour-glass" society, "the family sought to insulate itself from the state" ("Uses of Social Capital," 38).

138. Williams, Round, and Rodgers, *Role of Informal Economies*, 16.

139. Rose, *Understanding Post-Communist Transformation*, 22.

140. Miller, Koshechkina, and Grødeland, "How Citizens Cope," 625.

141. Rose, "Getting Things Done," 166.

142. Williams, Round, and Rodgers, *Role of Informal Economies*, 21.

143. For key studies on transitology, see Di Palma, *To Craft Democracies*; Huntington, *Third Wave*; O'Donnell, Schmitter, and Whitehead, *Transitions from Authoritarian Rule*; Przeworski, *Democracy and the Market*. According to Gans-Morse, "transitology as a *method* of studying transition [is] characterized by an actor-centric, elite bargaining approach" ("Searching for Transitologists," 326). Chapter 3 presents a more detailed discussion of the transition paradigm, exploring the relationship between transitology and institutional change in postcommunist contexts.

144. Williams, Round, and Rodgers, *Role of Informal Economies*, 19.

145. Round and Williams, "Coping with the Social Costs," 191, 189.

146. Rose, "Uses of Social Capital."

147. Uslaner, *Moral Foundations*.

148. Polese, "'If I Receive It,'" 48.

149. Giordano, "Social Organization of Informality," 29.

150. Adrian Smith and Stenning, "Beyond Household Economies," 208.

151. Round, Williams, and Rodgers, "Corruption in the Post-Soviet Workplace," 162.

152. Habdank-Kołaczkowska, *Eurasia's Rupture*, 1.

153. European Bank for Reconstruction and Development, *Life in Transition: After the Crisis.*

154. Karakoç, "Economic Inequality," 197.

155. Milanovic, *Income, Inequality, and Poverty.* Williamson coined the term *Washington Consensus* to refer to a set of policy prescriptions prepared by U.S. financial and economic officials as well as by Washington-based international financial institutions (the International Monetary Fund and World Bank) and proposed to Russia and other fSU countries in the aftermath of the collapse of Soviet Union ("Short History," 7). The name became firmly embedded in studies on post-Soviet political economy.

156. Karakoç, "Economic Inequality," 204.

157. Morris and Polese, "Informal Health and Education Sector Payments," 12.

158. European Bank for Reconstruction and Development, *Life in Transition: A Survey,* 25.

159. Giordano and Hayoz, *Informality in Eastern Europe,* 11; Ledeneva, *Can Russia Modernise?,* 108.

160. Misztal, *Informality*; Round, Williams, and Rodgers, "Corruption in the Post-Soviet Workplace."

161. Napal, "Is Bribery a Culturally Acceptable Practice?"; de Sousa, "'I Don't Bribe'"; Heidenheimer, "Perspectives"; Segal, "Dealing with the Devil," 2.

162. Napal, "Is Bribery a Culturally Acceptable Practice?," 231.

163. Besstremyannaya, "Out-of-Pocket Health Care Expenditures"; Morris and Polese, "Informal Health and Education Sector Payments." For the World Bank's definition of corruption, see http://www1.worldbank.org

164. Round, Williams, and Rodgers, "Corruption in the Post-Soviet Workplace"; Round and Rodgers, "Problems of Corruption." For example, Kotkin and Sajo anticipated that "in systems where the economy is functioning in a transition to a free and open market there are, simply speaking, incomparably more opportunities for corruption" (*Political Corruption,* 10).

165. Patico, "Chocolate and Cognac."

166. Haller and Shore, *Corruption*; Aasland, Grødeland, and Pleines, "Trust and Informal Practice"; Ledeneva, *Russia's Economy of Favours*; Tymczuk, "Public Duties."

167. Polese, "'If I Receive It,'" 51.

168. Ibid., 52.

169. Ibid., 48.

170. Wanner, "Money, Morality, and New Forms of Exchange."

171. Heinzen, "Art of the Bribe"; Kramer, "Political Corruption."

172. Misztal, *Informality*, 215.

173. Morris and Polese, "Informal Health and Education Sector Payments," 6.

174. Ibid., 12.

175. See European Bank for Reconstruction and Development, *Life in Transition:2011*; Transparency International (www.transparency.org).

176. Ledeneva, *Russia's Economy of Favours*, 39.

177. Ibid., 47.

178. Polese, "'If I Receive It,'" 47.

179. Portes, Castells, and Benton, *Informal Economy*.

180. Sindzingre, "Relevance," 66.

181. Ledeneva, *Russia's Economy of Favours*, 47.

182. Adrian Smith and Stenning, "Beyond Household Economies," 192.

183. Wedel, "Clans, Cliques, and Captured States," 432.

184. Adrian Smith and Stenning, "Beyond Household Economies," 192.

185. Round, Williams, and Rodgers, "Corruption in the Post-Soviet Workplace," 182.

186. Ibid., 183.

187. Ledeneva, *Russia's Economy of Favours*.

188. Adrian Smith, "Culture/Economy."

189. Morris and Polese, *Informal Post-Socialist Economy*, 8.

190. Sampson, "Second Economy"; O'Hearn, "Consumer Second Economy"; Ofer and Vinokur, *Private Sources of Income*; Feldbrugge, "Government and Shadow Economy."

191. Mars and Altman, "Cultural Bases"; Altman, *Reconstruction*.

192. Williams, Round, and Rodgers, *Role of Informal Economies*; Morris and Polese, *Informal Post-Socialist Economy*.

Chapter Three

1. Knight, *Institutions and Social Conflict*.

2. Brie and Stölting, "Formal Institutions," 30.

3. Ibid., 31.

4. Grzymala-Busse, "Best Laid Plans," 311.

5. Lauth, "Informal Institutions."

6. Knight, *Institutions and Social Conflict*, 171.

7. de Soysa and Jütting, *Informal Institutions and Development*, 12.

8. Chong and Gradstein, "Inequality and Informality"; Chowdhury, *Everyday Economic Practices*; Loayza, "Economics of the Informal Sector"; Oviedo, Thomas, and Karakurum-Özdemir, *Economic Informality*.

9. Wedel, "Clans, Cliques, and Captured States," 429.

10. Knight, *Institutions and Social Conflict*, 172.

11. Helmke and Levitsky, "Informal Institutions and Comparative Politics," 732.

12. Ibid.

13. Ibid.

14. Lauth, "Informal Institutions," 26.

15. Way, "Dilemmas of Reform," 581.

16. Helmke and Levitsky, "Informal Institutions and Comparative Politics," 732.

17. Dimitrova-Grajzl and Simon, "Political Trust and Historical Legacy," 209.

18. Pejovich, "Effects of the Interaction," 172.

19. Chavance, "Formal and Informal Institutional Change," 65.

20. North, *Institutions*, 88.

21. Ibid.

22. Ibid., 86–87.

23. Knight, *Institutions and Social Conflict*, 177.

24. Wedel, "Clans, Cliques, and Captured States," 431.

25. de Soysa and Jütting, *Informal Institutions and Development*, 12.

26. Knight, *Institutions and Social Conflict*, 172.

27. Way, "Dilemmas of Reform," 588.

28. North, *Institutions*, 91.

29. Pejovich, "Effects of the Interaction," 170.

30. Knight, *Institutions and Social Conflict*, 188.

31. Ledeneva, *Russia's Economy of Favours*, 68.

32. Pierson, "Increasing Returns," 478.

33. Ibid., 479.

34. Börzel and Pamuk, *Europeanization Subverted?*

35. Lauth, "Informal Institutions."

36. Wedel, "Clans, Cliques, and Captured States," 428.

37. Helmke and Levitsky, "Informal Institutions and Comparative Politics," 728.

38. Grzymala-Busse, "Best Laid Plans," 311.

39. Hale, "Formal Constitutions."

40. Ledeneva, *Can Russia Modernise?*; Gel'man, "Post-Soviet Transitions."

41. Ledeneva, *Can Russia Modernise?*, 25.

42. Knight, *Institutions and Social Conflict*, 190.

43. Ibid., 189.

44. Wedel, "Clans, Cliques, and Captured States," 428.

45. Ibid.

46. de Soto, *Other Path*.

47. See, for example, Chowdhury, *Everyday Economic Practices*; Hart, "Informal Income Opportunities"; Castells and Portes, "World Underneath"; Maloney, "Informality Revisited."

48. Way, "Dilemmas of Reform," 594.

49. Grødeland, "'Red Mobs,'" 218.

50. See, for example, Liaropoulos et al., "Informal Payments"; Balabanova and McKee, "Understanding Informal Payments"; Grødeland, "'Red Mobs'"; Morris and Polese, *Informal Post-Socialist Economy*.

51. O'Donnell, "Delegative Democracy," 57.

52. Ibid.

53. Ibid.

54. Lijphart, *Patterns of Democracy*.

55. O'Donnell, "Illusions about Consolidation," 44.

56. Beissinger, "Structure and Example."

57. Huntington, "Democracy for the Long Haul."

58. Democratization should not be confused with democracy, which is the final product of democratization.

59. Fish, "Hazards of Half-Measures," 248.

60. Gans-Morse, "Searching for Transitologists," 321.

61. Lipset, "Some Social Requisites"; Przeworski, *Democracy and the Market*; Cutright, "National Political Development"; Przeworski et al., "What Makes Democracies Endure?"; Przeworski and Limongi, "Modernization."

62. Inglehart and Welzel, "How Development Leads to Democracy," 34.

63. Bunce, "Comparative Democratization," 706.

64. Lipset, "Social Requisites of Democracy Revisited," 1.

65. Przeworski and Limongi, "Modernization"; Bunce, "Comparative Democratization," 706.

66. Kitschelt, "Accounting for Postcommunist Regime Diversity," 50.

67. Stephen White, "Is There a Pattern?"

68. Chavance, "Formal and Informal Institutional Change," 66.

69. Rustow, "Transitions to Democracy"; O'Donnell and Schmitter, *Transitions from Authoritarian Rule*; Higley and Burton, "Elite Variable"; Karl, "Dilemmas of Democratization"; Przeworski, *Democracy and the Market*; Colomer, *Strategic Transitions*; Linz and Stepan, *Breakdown of Democratic Regimes*; McFaul, "Fourth Wave."

70. McFaul, "Fourth Wave," 215.

71. On Latin America, see Karl, "Dilemmas of Democratization." On Southern Europe, see O'Donnell and Schmitter, *Transitions from Authoritarian Rule*.

72. Carothers, "End of the Transition Paradigm."

73. Rustow, "Transitions to Democracy."

74. Ibid., 350.

75. Bunce, "Comparative Democratization," 707.

76. Huntington, *Third Wave*; McFaul, "Fourth Wave"; Diamond, "Is the Third Wave Over?"

77. Huntington, "Democracy's Third Wave."

78. McFaul, "Missing Variable," 4, 9.

79. Carothers, "End of the Transition Paradigm"; Bunce, "Comparative Democratization"; Gans-Morse, "Searching for Transitologists"; Zhang, "Corporatism, Totalitarianism, and Transitions."

80. Gel'man, "Post-Soviet Transitions," 87.

81. Jović, "Problems."

82. O'Donnell, "Illusions about Consolidation."

83. Karl, "Dilemmas of Democratization"; Karl and Schmitter, "Modes of Transition"; Schmitter and Karl, "Conceptual Travels."

84. Przeworski, *Democracy and the Market*; Linz, "Transitions to Democracy."

85. O'Donnell, "Illusions about Consolidation," 40.

86. Ibid.

87. Gans-Morse, "Searching for Transitologists"; Bunce, "Should Transitologists Be Grounded?"

88. Bunce, "Comparative Democratization," 716.

89. Bunce and Wolchik, *Defeating Authoritarian Leaders*, 31.

90. McFaul, "Fourth Wave"; Schmitz, "Domestic and Transnational Perspectives"; Ambrosio, "Insulating Russia."

91. Linz, *Totalitarian and Authoritarian Regimes*; Way and Levitsky, "Linkage, Leverage, and the Post-Communist Divide."

92. Way and Levitsky, "Linkage, Leverage, and the Post-Communist Divide," 50.

93. Ekiert, "Patterns of Postcommunist Transformation," 105.

94. On institutional design theory, see Bunce, "Comparative Democratization," 711. On political cultural theory, see Zhang, "Corporatism, Totalitarianism, and Transitions."

95. Almond and Verba, *Civic Culture*.

96. Levitsky and Way, *Competitive Authoritarianism*, 3.

97. Kitschelt, "Accounting for Postcommunist Regime Diversity," 49.

98. Ekiert, Kubik, and Vachudova, "Democracy in Central and Eastern Europe," 107.

99. Diamond, "Thinking about Hybrid Regimes," 25.

100. Jowitt, *New World Disorder*, 300.

101. Bunce, McFaul, and Stoner-Weiss, *Democracy and Authoritarianism*, viii.

102. Linz, *Totalitarian and Authoritarian Regimes*.

103. Zakaria, "Rise of Illiberal Democracy"; O'Donnell, "Illusions about Consolidation"; Diamond, "Is the Third Wave Over?"; Levitsky and Way, *Competitive Authoritarianism*; Bunce and Wolchik, *Defeating Authoritarian Leaders*.

104. O'Donnell, "Delegative Democracy," 59.

105. Levitsky and Way, *Competitive Authoritarianism*, 3.

106. Ibid.

107. Ibid., 7.

108. Ibid., 183.

109. Ibid., 27–28.

110. However, other scholars continue to use more basic regime delineations. For example, McFaul simply divides all postcommunist regimes into democracies, partial democracies, and dictatorships, including Armenia, Azerbaijan, and Russia in the category of partial (semiconsolidated) democracies ("Fourth Wave").

111. Robertson, *Politics of Protest*, 6.

112. Carothers, "End of the Transition Paradigm," 6.

113. Gilbert and Mohseni, "Beyond Authoritarianism," 281.

114. Ottaway, *Democracy Challenged*, 19; Karl, "Dilemmas of Democratization."

115. Hale, "Regime Cycles," 134, 135; Hale, *Patronal Politics*.

116. Hale, "Regime Cycles," 134–35.

117. Hale, *Patronal Politics*, 9–10.

118. O'Donnell, "Illusions about Consolidation," 38.

119. Ibid., 40.

120. Gel'man, "Post-Soviet Transitions."

121. Huntington, "Democracy for the Long Haul."

122. Rose and Shin, "Democratization Backwards," 331.

123. Helmke and Levitsky, "Informal Institutions and Comparative Politics," 281.

124. See Böröcz, "Informality Rules"; Collins, "Political Role"; Gobel, "Towards a Consolidated Democracy?"; Hartlyn, *Struggle for Democratic Politics*; Lindberg, "It's Our Time to Chop"; Lauth, "Informal Institutions."

125. Diamond, "Thinking about Hybrid Regimes," 33.

126. Levitsky and Way, *Competitive Authoritarianism*, 27.

127. Grzymala-Busse and Luong, "Reconceptualizing the State," 540.

128. Levitsky and Way, *Competitive Authoritarianism*.

129. Di Palma, "Why Democracy Can Work," 27.

130. Rupnik and Zielonka, "Introduction," 13.

131. Helmke and Levitsky, *Informal Institutions and Democracy*; O'Donnell, "Illusions about Consolidation."

132. Langston, "Birth and Transformation."

133. Colignon and Usui, *Amakudari*; Lee and Rhyu, "Political Dynamics."

134. Rupnik and Zielonka, "Introduction," 5.

135. Grzymala-Busse, *Rebuilding Leviathan*.

136. Rupnik and Zielonka, "Introduction," 7.

137. Ibid., 12.

138. Grzymala-Busse and Luong, "Reconceptualizing the State," 541.

139. Ibid.

140. Rupnik and Zielonka, "Introduction," 13.

141. O'Donnell, "Illusions about Consolidation," 40.

142. Lauth, "Informal Institutions," 25.

143. Helmke and Levitsky, *Informal Institutions and Democracy*, 8.

144. Ibid., 2.

145. Ibid., 8.

146. Hale, *Patronal Politics*; Levitsky and Way, *Competitive Authoritarianism*.

147. Wedel, "Clans, Cliques, and Captured States," 429.

148. Luong, *Institutional Change*, 130.

149. Collins, *Clan Politics*, 206.

150. Ibid., 276; Transparency International, *Corruption Perceptions Index*.

151. Luong, *Institutional Change*, 122-23.

152. Collins, *Clan Politics*, 47.

153. Luong, *Institutional Change*, 136.

154. Werner, "Gifts, Bribes, and Development."

155. Collins, "Economic and Security Regionalism," 262.

156. See Freedom House, *Nations in Transit*; Fish, "Postcommunist Subversion."

157. Collins, *Clan Politics*, 60.

158. Luong, *Institutional Change*, 275.

159. Dynko, "Europe's Last Dictatorship."

160. Way, "Authoritarian State Building"; Marples, "Outpost of Tyranny?"

161. *Nasha Niiva*, accessible at http://nn.by/?c=ar&i=118728&lang=ru (in Russian).

162. Aliyev, "Institutional Transformation."

163. Bunce and Wolchik, *Defeating Authoritarian Leaders*, 182.

164. Franke, Gawrich, and Alakbarov, "Kazakhstan and Azerbaijan," 159.

165. Börzel and Pamuk, *Europeanization Subverted?*, 15.

166. Bunce and Wolchik, *Defeating Authoritarian Leaders*, 180; Börzel and Pamuk, *Europeanization Subverted?*, 15.

167. Börzel and Pamuk, *Europeanization Subverted?*, 9.

168. Bunce and Wolchik, *Defeating Authoritarian Leaders*, 180.

169. Hale, *Patronal Politics*.

170. See, for example, Freedom House, *Nations in Transit*; and *Economist Democracy Index*.

171. Levitsky and Way, *Competitive Authoritarianism*, 209-10.

172. Babajanian, "Local Governance."

173. Babajanian, "Social Welfare," 397.

174. Ibid., 398.

175. Ibid., 391.

176. Börzel and Pamuk, *Europeanization Subverted?*, 16.

177. See Organisation for Security and Co-Operation in Europe, *OSCE/ODIHR Final Report*.

178. Krastev and Holmes, "Autopsy of Managed Democracy"; Okara, "Sovereign Democracy"; Smyth, Lowry, and Wilkening, "Engineering Victory"; Cameron and Orenstein, "Post-Soviet Authoritarianism."

179. See, for example, Uhlin, *Post-Soviet Civil Society*; Ross, *Federalism and Democratization*; Lukin, "Transitional Period."

180. Stoner-Weiss, *Resisting the State*, 21.

181. Hale, "Eurasian Polities," 36.

182. Sakwa, "Putin and the Oligarchs."

183. Stoner-Weiss, *Resisting the State*; Golosov, "Proportional Representation."

184. Although the system was reformed in 2013 to allow for direct gubernatorial elections, the new law was never implemented in the North Caucasus.

185. Manning and Parison, *International Public Administration Reform*.

186. Ledeneva, *Can Russia Modernise?*, 69.

187. Smyth, Lowry, and Wilkening, "Engineering Victory," 134.

188. Ledeneva, *Can Russia Modernise?*, 252.

189. Ibid., 25.

190. Smyth, Lowry, and Wilkening, "Engineering Victory," 120.

191. Sakwa, "Dual State," 185.

192. Collins, *Clan Politics*; Rasanayagam, "Informal Economy, Informal State."

193. Gel'man, "Unrule of Law," 1028.

194. Ibid., 1030.

195. Morozov, "Sovereignty and Democracy."

196. Gel'man, "Unrule of Law," 1036.

197. Ambrosio, "Insulating Russia."

198. Collins, *Clan Politics*, 2.

199. Luong, *Institutional Change*, 108.

200. Collins, *Clan Politics*, 175.

201. Ibid., 249.

202. Bunce and Wolchik, *Defeating Authoritarian Leaders*, 170.

203. Luong, *Institutional Change*, 166.

204. Beacháin and Polese, *Colour Revolutions*.

205. Bunce and Wolchik, *Defeating Authoritarian Leaders*; Levitsky and Way, *Competitive Authoritarianism*.

206. Bunce and Wolchik, *Defeating Authoritarian Leaders*.

207. Hale, "Formal Constitutions," 597.

208. See, for example, http://reforma.kg/articles/view/81 (in Russian).

209. See, for example, http://kloop.kg/blog/2013/12/16/hronika-press-konferentsiya-atambaeva-po-itogam-goda/ (in Russian).

Chapter Four

1. The *kartvelebi* consist of nearly twenty geographically divided ethnic subgroups, the largest of which are Kartlians, Imeratians, Migrelians, and Svans.

2. See, for example, Altman, *Reconstruction*.

3. Law, "Corruption in Georgia."

4. O'Hearn, "Consumer Second Economy"; Altman, *Reconstruction*; Shelley, Scott, and Latta, *Organized Crime and Corruption*.

5. Kupatadze, *Organized Crime*.

6. Scott, "Georgia's Anti-Corruption Revolution," 19.

7. Altman, *Georgian Feast*.

8. Confidential interview with an NGO official, September 10, 2013, Tbilisi.

9. Toptygyn, *Neizvestnyi Beriia*.

10. Slider, "Note," 539.

11. As Beissinger describes, "Stalin became a major symbol of identification with the Soviet Union for many Georgians" (*Nationalist Mobilization*, 178).

12. Shelley, introduction, 1.

13. Light, "Police Reforms," 322.

14. Ofer and Vinokur, *Private Sources of Income*; O'Hearn, "Consumer Second Economy"; Mars and Altman, "Cultural Bases."

15. Kukhianidze, "Corruption and Organized Crime," 217.

16. Kupatadze, *Organized Crime*, 19.

17. See Greenslade and Grossman, *Regional Dimensions*, 7. According to O'Hearn, "99% of the money spent by urban Georgians on repairs to furniture and household articles, and 97% of that spent by rural residents, went to the second economy" ("Consumer Second Economy," 225).

18. Parsons, "National Integration," 561.

19. Law, "Corruption in Georgia," 101.

20. Shelley, introduction, 1.

21. According to Slider, Georgians and Jews had the highest per capita rates of student enrollment in institutes of higher education of all the ethnic groups in the USSR ("Note," 536–37).

22. Goskomstat USSR, *Narodnoe Khozyaistvo*, 519; According to Robert A. Lewis and Richard H. Rowland, in 1970, Jews and Georgians enrolled in

higher education at rates far higher than those of all other Soviet nationalities ("East Is West and West Is East," 19). See also Slider, "Note," 536–37.

23. Kramer, "Political Corruption," 214.

24. Parsons, "National Integration," 558.

25. Feldbrugge, "Government and Shadow Economy."

26. Razzakov, *Bandity Semidesiatykh*. In the 1970s, the average monthly salary of a Soviet white collar worker ranged between eighty and one hundred rubles per month.

27. Kupatadze, *Organized Crime*, 20.

28. Parsons, "National Integration," 558.

29. Mars and Altman, "Cultural Bases," 546.

30. Altman, *Reconstruction*, 5–4.

31. Mars and Altman, "Case of a Factory," 103.

32. Altman, *Georgian Feast.*

33. Schatz, *Modern Clan Politics*; Mars and Altman, "Cultural Bases," 550.

34. Mars and Altman, "Cultural Bases," 555.

35. Ibid., 559.

36. Parsons, "National Integration."

37. Shelley, introduction, 1.

38. Mars and Altman, "Cultural Bases," 555, 546.

39. Ibid., 549.

40. Godson et al., "Building Societal Support," 10.

41. The Soviet caste of elite criminals known in Russian as *vory-v-zakone* and in Georgian as *kanonieri qurdi* (thieves-in-law), became deeply entrenched in Georgia during Brezhnev's period. Georgian nationals comprised more than 30 percent of all known *vory-v-zakone* in the USSR. As Slade notes, "Georgia became the biggest producer of thieves-in-law of all the Soviet republics" ("No Country for Made Men," 626).

42. Parsons, "National Integration."

43. Two years following his appointment as first secretary, Shevardnadze made a speech at the Georgian Communist Party's meeting at its Tbilisi headquarters in which he claimed that despite the mass arrests and expulsion, many Georgia party branches continued to distribute patronage via nepotism and favoritism. See *Zarya Vostoka*, February 8, 1974.

44. Shelley, introduction, 3.

45. Law, "Corruption in Georgia," 105.

46. Kupatadze, *Organized Crime*, 21.

47. Mars and Altman, "Cultural Bases," 558.

48. Parsons, "National Integration," 559.

49. Kupatadze, *Organized Crime.*

50. Ibid., 21.

51. Parsons, "National Integration," 555.

52. Sakwa, *Soviet Politics,* 71.

53. Baev, "Civil Wars in Georgia."

54. Nodia, "Dynamics of State-Building," 10.

55. Machavariani, "Overcoming Economic Crime," 37; Belli, Gotsadze, and Shahriari, "Out-of-Pocket and Informal Payments," 110.

56. Schneider, *Size of the Shadow Economies,* 25.

57. Bunce and Wolchik, *Defeating Authoritarian Leaders,* 153.

58. Kupatadze, *Organized Crime.*

59. Ibid., 120.

60. Light, "Police Reforms."

61. Shelley, introduction, 3.

62. See World Values Survey, Wave 3: 1995–99, at: http://www.worldvaluessurvey.org/WVSOnline.jsp

63. Shelley, introduction, 4.

64. Mitchell, "Compromising Democracy," 173.

65. Shelley, "Georgian Organized Crime," 55.

66. Aliyev, "Effects."

67. Transparency International, *Corruption Perceptions Index.*

68. Mitchell, "Compromising Democracy," 176.

69. Engvall, *Against the Grain.*

70. Orkodashvili, "Higher Education Reforms," 360.

71. See Gotsadze, Zoidze, and Vasadze, "Reform Strategies"; Belli, Gotsadze, and Shahriari, "Out-of-Pocket and Informal Payments."

72. Stefes, *Understanding Post-Soviet Transitions,* 95.

73. Shelley, introduction, 5. See also Tudoroiu, "Rose, Orange, and Tulip," 319–20.

74. The residents of the capital city, Tbilisi, had access to electricity for several hours per day, while many rural settlements had no electricity at all.

75. Broers, "After the 'Revolution,'" 335.

76. Kupatadze, *Organized Crime.*

77. Scott, "Georgia's Anti-Corruption Revolution," 18.

78. The 1996 World Values Surveys conducted in Georgia found that more than 96 percent of respondents had been better off financially ten

years earlier. In addition, more 80 percent of survey participants expressed their dissatisfaction with the government and political system. See World Values Survey, Wave 3.

79. Scott, "Georgia's Anti-Corruption Revolution," 22.

80. Mitchell, "Compromising Democracy."

81. Ibid., 174.

82. Bunce and Wolchik, *Defeating Authoritarian Leaders*, 153.

83. Broers, "After the 'Revolution,'" 336; Esadze, "Georgia's Rose Revolution," 112; Muskhelishvili and Jorjoliani, "Georgia's Ongoing Struggle."

84. Gould and Sickner, "Making Market Democracies?," 757.

85. Devdariani, "Georgia," 81.

86. Kupatadze, *Organized Crime*, 22.

87. Broers, "After the 'Revolution,'" 334.

88. Shelley, "Georgian Organized Crime," 53.

89. Cheterian, "Georgia's Rose Revolution," 693.

90. Particularly since the late 1990s, Aslan Abashidze, the leader of a semi-independent region of Adjara in the south-west of Georgia, was one of the key informal veto-brokers supporting Shevardnadze's regime and preventing institutional changes.

91. Bunce and Wolchik, *Defeating Authoritarian Leaders*, 164.

92. See, for example, Fairbanks, "Georgia's Rose Revolution"; Mitchell, "Democracy in Georgia"; Wheatley, *Georgia*.

93. See Transparency International, *Corruption Perceptions Index*.

94. For specific anticorruption policies in Saakashvili's Georgia, see Organisation for Economic Cooperation and Development, *Fighting Corruption*; Kupatadze, "Explaining Georgia's Anti-Corruption Drive."

95. Stefes, *Understanding Post-Soviet Transitions*, 166.

96. See Georgian Opinion Research Business International, http://gorbi.com

98. di Puppo, *Police Reform*, 2.

99. Kupatadze, *Organized Crime*.

100. Engvall, *Against the Grain*, 23.

101. Kupatadze, "Explaining Georgia's Anti-Corruption Drive."

102. See Kupatadze, *Organized Crime*, 126; Slade, "No Country for Made Men."

103. Confidential interview with a government official, August 22, 2013, Tbilisi.

104. Engvall, *Against the Grain*, 30.

105. See, for example, Orkodashvili, "Higher Education Reforms."

106. Ibid.

107. World Bank, *Fighting Corruption*, 75.

108. Ibid., 75–78.

109. World Bank, *Fighting Corruption*, 64.

110. Engvall, *Against the Grain*, 21–23.

111. World Bank, *Fighting Corruption*, 63–74.

112. Confidential interview with a government official, August 16, 2013, Tbilisi.

113. Torosyan and Filer, *Tax Reform.*

114. Confidential interview with a civil society official, September 9, 2013, Tbilisi.

115. United Nations Development Programme, *Georgia Human Development Report.*

116. Confidential interview with a civil service official, September 11, 2013, Tbilisi.

117. Confidential interview with an official of the State Statistics Service, October 2, 2013, Tbilisi.

118. Papava, "Political Economy."

119. World Bank, *Fighting Corruption*, 53.

120. Confidential interview with a government official, September 20, 2013, Tbilisi.

121. Mitchell, "Compromising Democracy"; Wertsch, "Georgia as a Laboratory."

122. Levitsky and Way, *Competitive Authoritarianism*, 227.

123. For example, the 2007 Georgian National Study survey reported that only 27 percent of respondents believed that their life conditions had improved during Saakashvili's presidency. By contrast, 60 percent of survey participants thought that they had a better life in Soviet times. Georgian National Study (GNS) survey,see: http://www.iri.org/resource/iri-releases-survey-georgian-public-opinion

124. More than twenty former government officials were detained after being suspected of corruption and embezzlement. See Socor, "Merabishvili's Arrest."

125. Hammarberg, *Georgia in Transition*; Rukhadze, "Few Successes."

126. Buckley, "Saakashvili Likely to Face Questioning."

127. Fuller, "Is The Georgian Government Living on Borrowed Time?"

128. Confidential interview with a Georgian political analyst, July 15, 2015, Kiev.

129. Shelley, "Georgian Organized Crime"; Kupatadze, *Organized Crime*; Mitchell, "Compromising Democracy"; United Nations Development Programme, *Georgia Human Development Report*; World Bank, *Fighting Corruption*.

130. di Puppo, "Anti-Corruption Interventions," 225; Transparency International, *Corruption Perceptions Index*.

131. Confidential interview with an official of an international watchdog, June 28, 2013, Tbilisi.

132. Confidential interview with an NGO official, September 16, 2013, Tbilisi.

133. Caucasus Research Resource Centers. (Georgia 2008; 2013) "Caucasus Barometer," http://www.crrccenters.org/caucasusbarometer/

134. Fairbanks and Gugushvili, "New Chance," 118; Kupatadze, *Organized Crime*, 28; confidential interviews with representatives of international intergovernmental organizations, July 9–11, 2013, Brussels; "Three IDA Countries among Top 10 Business Reformers," http://go.worldbank.org/TAP-79WUP80

135. Rukhadze, "Looking Back."

136. Shelley, introduction, 7; World Bank, *Fighting Corruption*, 102.

137. Torosyan and Filer, *Tax Reform*.

138. Devdariani, "Georgia."

139. Broers, "After the 'Revolution,'" 345.

140. di Puppo, "Anti-Corruption Interventions," 224; Frederiksen, "Would-Be State."

141. Tudoroiu, "Rose, Orange, and Tulip," 324; Dobbins, "Post–Rose Revolution Reforms," 761.

142. Fairbanks and Gugushvili, "New Chance," 124.

143. Gould and Sickner, "Making Market Democracies?," 760.

144. Esadze, "Georgia's Rose Revolution," 114.

145. Confidential interview with a Georgian political analyst, July 15, 2015, Kiev.

146. See, for example, North, *Institutions*; de Soto, *Other Path*.

147. Shelley, introduction, 1; Parsons, "National Integration."

148. See Transparency International, *Global Corruption Barometer*.

149. Schneider, Buehn, and Montenegro, *Shadow Economies*, 29.

150. For Georgian National Study (GNS) survey see: http://www.iri.org/re-source/iri-releases-survey-georgian-public-opinion

151. Caucasus Research Resource Centers. (Georgia 2013) "Caucasus Barometer." http://www.crrccenters.org/caucasusbarometer/

152. Ibid.

153. Ibid.

154. Shelley, introduction, 8.

155. Aliyev, "Informality."

156. Scott, "Georgia's Anti-Corruption Revolution," 21.

157. For Georgia's National Statistics Office, see http://geostat.ge

158. Confidential interview with an NGO official, August 27, 2013, Tbilisi.

159. Confidential interview with a representative of an international think tank, September 24, 2013, Tbilisi.

160. Caucasus Research Resource Centers. (Georgia 2010; 2012; 2014) "Caucasus Barometer." http://www.crrccenters.org/caucasusbarometer/

161. di Puppo, "Anti-Corruption Interventions."

162. Caucasus Research Resource Centers. (Georgia 2011) "Caucasus Barometer." http://www.crrccenters.org/caucasusbarometer/

163. Granovetter, "Strength of Weak Ties."

164. EBRD, "Life in Transition," 2011.

165. Caucasus Research Resource Centers. (Georgia 2010; 2014) "Caucasus Barometer." http://www.crrccenters.org/caucasusbarometer/

166. Zakharova, "Street Life."

167. Ibid.; Curro, "Birzha."

Chapter Five

1. Georgescu and Călinescu, *Romanians*, 146–47.

2. King, *Moldovans*, 96.

3. Schevchenko, "Otnoshenie Naselenia."

4. King, *Moldovans*, 95.

5. Bater, *Soviet Scene*; Crowther, "Politics of Democratization," 3.

6. Crowther, "Politics of Democratization," 286. March explicitly refers to Soviet Moldova as more a "Central Asian than European" republic of the USSR ("Power and the Opposition," 347).

7. Livezeanu, "Urbanization," 334; Rahr, "Moldavian Party Chief."

8. Kirke, *Regional`nye Problemy*, 65.

9. Caşu, *Politica Naţională*, 95.

10. According to Soviet statistics, 82 percent of Moldova's population was rural in the 1950s, but by the 1980s, that number was just over 60 percent (Kozlov, *Peoples of the Soviet Union*, 64–65). In 1970, the Moldovan SSR had the highest share of kolkhoz among its population (Slider, "Note," 538).

11. Greenslade and Grossman, *Regional Dimensions*, 15.

12. Ibid., 20.

13. Johnson et al., "Unofficial Economy."

14. According to Greenslade and Grossman, in Georgia, 64 percent of meat and 53 percent of milk products were produced by the informal economy, while in Azerbaijan those numbers were 66 percent and 57 percent, respectively (Greenslade and Grossman, *Regional Dimensions*, 46).

15. Diorditsa, *Moldavia*.

16. Ibid.

17. King, *Moldovans*, 103; Crowther, "Politics of Ethno-National Mobilization," 185.

18. Greenslade and Grossman, *Regional Dimensions*, 40.

19. Robert A. Lewis and Rowland, "East Is West and West Is East," 19.

20. Jones and Grupp, "Modernisation and Ethnic Equalisation," 171.

21. King, *Moldovans*, 98.

22. Crowther, "Politics of Democratization," 185–86; King, *Moldovans*, 100–101.

23. Roman, "Multi-Shade Paradox," 72; Carasciuc, *Corruption and Quality of Governance*.

24. See, for example, Roman, "Multi-Shade Paradox."

25. King, *Moldovans*, 100–102; Ledeneva, *Russia's Economy of Favours*.

26. Narodnoe Khoziaistvo SSSR, *Reference Book*; King, *Moldovans*, 116.

27. Willerton, "Patronage Networks," 188.

28. King, *Moldovans*, 98.

29. Ibid., 99.

30. Crowther, "Politics of Ethno-National Mobilization," 186.

31. Jones and Grupp, "Modernisation," 174.

32. See, for example, King, *Moldovans*, 102; Crowther, "Ethnic Politics," 3.

33. Crowther, "Politics of Ethno-National Mobilization," 187.

34. Clark, "Crime and Punishment," 269.

35. Ibid.

36. Crowther, "Politics of Democratization," 287.

37. King, *Moldovans*, 123–27.

38. Crowther, "Ethnic Politics," 148.

39. Crowther and Matonyte, "Parliamentary Elites."

40. Orlova and Ronnas, "Crippling Cost," 374.

41. Poppe, *Expenditure Patterns*, 2; Crăciun, *Migration and Remittances*.

42. Orlova and Ronnas, "Crippling Cost," 373.

43. Crowther, "Ethnic Politics," 148-49.

44. By 1994, 800 firms had been privatized. A new scheme approved in 1995 resulted in the privatization of another 1,450 enterprises (Crowther, "Politics of Democratization," 319).

45. Levitsky and Way, *Competitive Authoritarianism*.

46. Horowitz, *From Ethnic Conflict to Stillborn Reform*, 119.

47. Way, "Weak States and Pluralism," 478; Tudoroiu, "Structural factors vs. regime change."

48. Way, "Weak States and Pluralism," 478.

49. McDonagh, "Is Democracy Promotion Effective."

50. Crowther "Politics of Democratization," 299-300.

51. Way, "Weak States and Pluralism," 455.

52. Ibid., 473, 470.

53. Orlova and Ronnas, "Crippling Cost," 373.

54. Gorton and White, "Politics of Agrarian Collapse," 305.

55. Ibid., 306.

56. Vaculovschi, Vremis, and Craievschi-Toarta, *Republic of Moldova*; Hill, "PROFILE," 132.

57. Lubarova, Petrushin, and Radziwill, *Is Moldova Ready to Grow?*, 43.

58. Johnson et al., "Unofficial Economy," 182-83.

59. Schneider et al., *Shadow Economies*, 63.

60. See Center for Strategic Studies and Reforms, http://www.eldis.org

61. Center for Strategic Studies and Reforms, *Moldova in Transition*, 62.

62. International Labour Organization, *Employment in the Informal Economy*, 15.

63. Obreja and Carașciuc, *Corruption in Moldova*, 26, 32.

64. Ibid., 28.

65. See Transparency International, *Corruption Perceptions Index*.

66. European Bank for Reconstruction and Development, *Transition Report 1999*; Hellman, Jones, and Kaufmann, *Seize the State*.

67. Tudoroiu, "Democracy and State Capture."

68. Hill, "PROFILE," 137.

69. March, "From Moldovanism to Europeanization?," 601.

70. Way, "Weak States and Pluralism," 479.

71. Institutul de Opinii Publice, Barometer of Public Opinion (November 2009), http://www.ipp.md/libview.php?l=en&id=450&idc=156

72. Kuzio, "Back to the USSR."

73. Karatnycky, Motyl, and Piano, Nations in Transit, 446.

74. Freedom House, Nations in Transit.

75. Ibid.

76. Hale, "Did the Internet Break the Political Machine?," 487.

77. European Bank for Research and Development, Life in Transition 2011, 32.

78. Ibid., 10.

79. Ibid, 61.

80. Tudoroiu, "Democracy and State Capture"; Hellman, Jones, and Kaufmann, "Seize the State"; Gray, Hellman, and Ryterman, Anticorruption in Transition 2, 10.

81. Hellman, Jones, and Kaufmann, "Seize the State."

82. Tudoroiu, "Structural Factors," 240.

83. Freedom House, Nations in Transit.

84. See European Union, European External Action Service, http://eeas.europa.eu/moldova/

85. Culiuc, "Corruption in Higher Education."

86. Moldova's corruption score decreased from 3.2 in 2006 to 2.8 in 2009. See Transparency International Corruption Perceptions Index, http://www.transparency.org/research/cpi/overview

87. Tudoroiu, "Democracy and State Capture"; March, "Power and the Opposition."

88. Hale, "Did the Internet Break the Political Machine?"

89. Confidential interview with a former Moldovan government official, June 2, 2015, Berlin.

90. See Transparency International–Moldova, National Integrity System Assessment.

91. European Union, Delegation of the European Union to Moldova.

92. Bordeianu, Cruc, and Osoian, Evaluation of Moldovan Authorities' Attitudes, 28–32.

93. Reuters, "EU Says Moldova Aid"; Transparency International–Moldova, Sociological Study.

94. Ministry of Justice, "Justice Ministry Began Drafting Package of Laws to Combat Corruption in The Justice System," news release, September 6, 2012, http://justice.gov.md/libview.php?l=ro&idc=4&id=1078

95. Transparency International–Moldova, *National Integrity System Assessment*.

96. Teleradio Moldova, "CCCEC Devine CAN," http://trm.md/ro/social/cccec-devine-cna/

97. In 2011, Moldova ranked 112th in Transparency International's *Corruption Perceptions Index*; in 2012, Moldova ranked 94th.

98. Moldova ranked 102nd in 2013 and 103rd in 2014 in Transparency International's *Corruption Perceptions Index*.

99. Radio Chişinău, "700 de Poliţişti."

100. See World Bank Group, Doing Business, http://www.doingbusiness.org/rankings; Calus, "Reforms in Moldova," 4.

101. Lupuşor et al., *MEGA*.

102. See Index Mundi assessment, http://www.indexmundi.com/moldova/economy_profile.html

103. One of the specific measures adopted by the AIE government to tackle informal employment was the introduction of fines for both employers and employees who engaged in the practice of "envelope wages," or salaries paid informally to avoid taxes. See Moldova Azi (azi.md), "Both Employees and Employers Will Be Fined for Informal Pays," June 23, 2011, http://www.azi.md/en/story/19235

104. See European Union, *Delegation of the European Union to Moldova*.

105. See World Bank, http://www.worldbank.org/en/country/moldova/overview

106. Confidential interview with a European Union official working in the EU mission in Moldova, May 28, 2015, Berlin.

107. Socor, "Moldova."

108. According to the 2015 Barometer for Public Opinion survey, only 11 percent of respondents supported the minority government and 55 percent did not. See Institute for Public Policy, *Barometer of Public Opinion*.

109. European Bank for Research and Development, *Life in Transition: A Survey of People's Experiences and Attitudes*; European Bank for Research and Development, *Life in Transition: After the Crisis*.

110. However, relatively low levels of public trust in formal institutions are not unique to Moldova and have been recorded in Moldova's EU

neighbors, particularly Romania and Slovakia. For example, in 2012, trust in the judicial system was even lower in Romania (24 percent) than in Moldova (27 percent), and confidence in government was 12 percent in Romania versus 24 percent in Moldova. See Gallup World View, http:// gallup.com

111. Institute for Public Policy, *Barometer of Public Opinion.*

111. Ibid.

113. International Republican Institute, "Moldova."

114. Ibid.

115. Carasciuc, *Corruption and Quality of Governance.*

116. Ledeneva, *Russia's Economy of Favours*, 178.

117. Carasciuc, *Corruption and Quality of Governance*, 25–26.

118. Roman, "Multi-Shade Paradox."

119. Confidential interview with an NGO official, June 6, 2015, Chișinău.

120. Confidential interview with a public official from the Ministry of Interior, June 8, 2015, Chișinău.

121. Crowther and Matonyte, "Parliamentary Elites," 285–86.

122. Confidential interview with a government official, June 8, 2015, Chișinău.

123. Confidential interview with a civil society representative, June 4, 2015, Chișinău.

124. Confidential interview with a public administrator, June 7, 2015, Chișinău.

125. Abbott, "Cultural Trauma," 229.

126. See Transparency International, *Global Corruption Barometer.*

127. Bejakovic and Meinardus, *Equity vs. Efficiency*, 137; World Health Organization, *European Health for All*, http://www.euro.who.int/en/data-and-evidence/databases/european-health-for-all-database-hfa-db

128. Bejakovic and Meinardus, *Equity vs. Efficiency*, 131.

129. Ibid., 126; Lupușor et al., *MEGA*, 25.

130. Polese, "'If I Receive It.'"

131. Institute of Public Policy, *Barometer of Public Opinion.*

132. As Western sanctions and decreasing oil prices hit the Russian economy hard in early 2015, Moldovan remittances from Russia began to drop, negatively affecting Moldova's struggling economy and further reducing its chance of recovery.

133. Evropeiska Pravda, "Chto Proisxodit."

Chapter Six

1. For the social organization of pre-Soviet Ukraine, see Magocsi, *History of Ukraine*, 422.

2. Kubicek, *History of Ukraine*, 97–100.

3. Subtelny, *Ukraine*, 408.

4. Kubicek, *History of Ukraine*, 100; Khrushchev, *Memoirs*.

5. Subtelny, *Ukraine*, 497.

6. Ibid., 514.

7. Ibid., 505.

8. Kubicek, *History of Ukraine*, 112.

9. Lewytzkyj, *Politics and Society*, 72.

10. Magocsi, *History of Ukraine*, 663–64; Lewytzkyj, *Politics and Society*, 177.

11. Kubicek, *History of Ukraine*, 115.

12. Lewytzkyj, *Politics and Society*, 173.

13. Ibid.

14. Willerton, "Patronage Networks," 181.

15. Magocsi, *History of Ukraine*, 659; Kubicek, *History of Ukraine*, 113.

16. Sergei I. Zhuk, "Religion, 'Westernization,' and Youth," 663.

17. Ibid.

18. Subtelny, *Ukraine*, 531. According to Willerton, in the post-Khrushchev's USSR, "a significant ethnic contingent within the top all-union elite has come from the Ukraine" ("Patronage Networks," 194).

19. Subtelny, *Ukraine*, 511. Shelest and Podhorny were members of a the pro-Ukrainian faction that originated in Ukraine's second-largest city, Kharkiv, which was competing for power and influence with Russian-speaking Dnepropetrovsk Clan" (Willerton, "Patronage Networks," 194).

20. Subtelny, *Ukraine*, 512.

21. Kuzio, *Ukraine: Perestroika to Independence*, 43–44.

22. Willerton, "Patronage Networks," 181.

23. Kuzio, *Ukraine: Perestroika to Independence*, 48.

24. Lewytzkyj, *Politics and Society*, 156.

25. Zimmer and Haran, "Unfriendly Takeover," 543.

26. Willerton, "Patronage Networks," 187; During the 1970s and 1980s, fewer than 80 Ukrainian officials were convicted on charges of political corruption, in comparison to over 140 officials in Azerbaijan and almost 400 in the Russian SSR ("Crime and Punishment," 271).

27. The number of Russians in the Ukrainian SSR increased from seven million in 1960 to ten million by 1980. See Subtelny, *Ukraine*, 514.

28. Subtelny, *Ukraine*, 515.

29. Fritz, *State-Building*, 111.

30. Wolczuk, *Moulding of Ukraine*, 65.

31. Ibid., 61.

32. Kuzio, *Ukraine: Perestroika to Independence*, 188.

33. Wynnyckyj, "Institutions and Entrepreneurs," 29.

34. Fritz, *State-Building*, 118.

35. Zimmer and Haran, "Unfriendly Takeover," 553.

36. Ibid., 557.

37. Way, "Rapacious Individualism," 195.

38. Kudelia and Kuzio, "Nothing Personal."

39. Kuzio, *Ukraine: State and Nation Building*, 36.

40. Fritz, *State-Building*, 113.

41. Kaufmann and Kaliberda, *Integrating the Unofficial Economy*.

42. Thießen, "Informal Economy," 21; Round, Williams, and Rodgers, "Corruption in the Post-Soviet Workplace," 153.

43. Isajiw, *Society in Transition*, xxi; Åslund, *How Ukraine Became a Market Economy*, 91.

44. Puglisi, "Rise of the Ukrainian Oligarchs," 105.

45. Åslund, *How Ukraine Became a Market Economy*, 48.

46. Puglisi, "Rise of the Ukrainian Oligarchs," 105.

47. Kubicek, *History of Ukraine*, 146.

48. Puglisi, "Rise of the Ukrainian Oligarchs," 111.

49. Sergei I. Zhuk, "Religion, 'Westernization,' and Youth," 663.

50. Puglisi, "Rise of the Ukrainian Oligarchs," 111.

51. Kubicek, *History of Ukraine*, 151.

52. Åslund, *How Ukraine Became a Market Economy*, 46.

53. Fritz, *State-Building*, 138.

54. Ibid., 123.

55. Way, "Kuchma's Failed Authoritarianism," 136.

56. Ibid., 134.

57. Kuzio, "Regime Type and Politics."

58. Way, "Rapacious Individualism," 196.

59. D'Anieri, *Understanding Ukrainian Politics*, 61.

60. Way, "Rapacious Individualism," 191.

61. Åslund, *Ukraine*, 8.

62. D'Anieri, *Understanding Ukrainian Politics*, 200.

63. Karatnycky, Motyl, and Piano, *Nations in Transit*.

64. See Transparency International, *Corruption Perceptions Index*.

65. Karatnycky, Motyl, and Piano, *Nations in Transit*, 680.

66. Miller, Koshechkina, and Grødeland, "How Citizens Cope," 614.

67. Åslund, *How Ukraine Became a Market Economy*, 128; Way, "Kuchma's Failed Authoritarianism," 134.

68. Åslund, *How Ukraine Became a Market Economy*, 125.

69. Fritz, *State-Building*, 162.

70. Åslund, *How Ukraine Became a Market Economy*, 133.

71. Ibid., 133.

72. Kubicek, *History of Ukraine*, 159.

73. Åslund, *How Ukraine Became a Market Economy*, 6.

74. Ibid.

75. Kuzio, "Regime Type and Politics," 167.

76. Ibid., 169–170.

77. Katchanovski, "Orange Evolution?"

78. Åslund, *How Ukraine Became a Market Economy*, 205.

79. Ibid., 206.

80. Freedom House, *Nations in Transit: Ukraine (2009)*.

81. Confidential interview with a senior adviser for the Ministry of Education, June 21, 2015, Kiev.

82. Ibid.

83. See Transparency International, *Corruption Perceptions Index*.

84. Grødeland, "Elite Perceptions," 241; Global Corruption Barometer.

85. Gorshenin Institute, "Mental Bases of Choice."

86. European Bank for Research and Development, *Life in Transition 2006*.

87. Gorshenin Institute, "Mental Bases of Choice."

88. Schneider and Enste, *Shadow Economies*.

89. Polese, "'If I Receive It,'" 57.

90. Williams and Round, "Retheorizing the Nature," 374.

91. Round, Williams, and Rodgers, "Everyday Tactics," 183.

92. Polese, "'If I Receive It,'" 48–49; Polese, *Limits of a Post-Soviet State*.

93. Miller, Koshechkina, and Grødeland, "How Citizens Cope," 614.

94. Ledeneva, *Russia's Economy of Favours*; Tymczuk, "Public Duties," 64.

95. Confidential interviews with civil society activists and sociology scholars, July 15–17, 2015, Kiev.

96. Confidential interviews with political analysts from several Ukrainian and international think tanks, July 5–8, 2015, Kiev.

97. Confidential interview with a head of an international NGO, July 19, 2015, Kiev.

98. Confidential interview at the Ukrainian Center for Independent Political Research, July 16, 2015, Kiev.

99. Confidential interview with a top manager in the energy sector, July 21, 2015, Kiev.

100. Åslund, *How Ukraine Became a Market Economy*, 233–35.

101. Malygina, "Ukraine," 14.

102. Kuzio, "Crime, Politics, and Business."

103. Chaisty and Chernykh, "Coalitional Presidentialism," 188.

104. Åslund, *Ukraine*, 82–83; Kuzio, "Crime, Politics, and Business," 196.

105. International Republican Institute. "Public Opinion Survey: Residents of Ukraine, February 17–March 7, 2012."

106. Organisation for Security and Co-Operation in Europe, *Ukraine Parliamentary Elections*.

107. Kovalov, "Electoral Manipulations and Fraud."

108. Kuzio, *Ukraine: State and Nation Building*, 137–38.

109. Gorshenin Institute, "Mental Bases of Choice."

110. Darden, "Blackmail as a Tool."

111. Grødeland, "Elite Perceptions," 259.

112. Global Corruption Barometer 2013, http://www.transparency.org/research/gcb/gcb_2015_16. Similarly, the Gallup World Poll revealed that 80 percent of the Ukrainian public provided material gifts to public officials in 2013, up from 73 percent in 2009 (Ray and Esipova, "Corruption a Major Obstacle).

113. Grødeland, "Elite Perceptions," 237.

114. European Bank for Research and Development, *Life in Transition 2011*.

115. Onoshchenko and Williams, "Paying for Favours," 259.

116. Onoshchenko and Williams, "Evaluating the Role," 259, 260, 264.

117. Stepurko et al., "Informal Payments for Health Care Services: The Case of Lithuania, Poland, and Ukraine."

118. Stepurko et al., "Informal Payments for Health Care Services—Corruption or Gratitude?," 423.

119. Confidential interview with a health care sector official, July 16, 2015, Kiev.

120. Confidential interview with managers of a Ukrainian think tank, July 14, 2015, Kiev.

121. Confidential interview with a policy analyst at a local NGO, July 15, 2015, Kiev.

122. Confidential interview with a senior official of Reanimation Package of Reforms NGO, July 10, 2015, Kiev.

123. National Reform Council, *National Reforms Governance and Monitoring Framework*.

124. Sologoub, "Presentation of Strategy-2020."

125. Ukrainian Crisis Media Center, "Dmytro Shymkiv."

126. National Reform Council, *National Reforms Governance and Monitoring Framework*.

127. Unian, "Second Wave."

128. Alyona Zhuk, "Critics Fear Officials."

129. Popova and Post, "What Is Lustration?"

130. "Dmytro Shymkiv: The Purpose of Decentralization Is to Bring Authorities Closer to People," *Official Website of the President of Ukraine*, June 24, 2015, http://www.president.gov.ua/en/news/dmitro-shimkiv-meta-decentralizaciyi-nabliziti-vladu-do-naro-35550

131. Balmforth and Zinets, "Ukraine Guardsman Killed."

132. Confidential interview with a civil society official at CEDOS NGO, July 12, 2015, Kiev.

133. Obozrevatel, "Proschai 'Reshaly.'"

134. Reuters, "Ukraine Names Georgia's Saakashvili."

135. See Olearchyk and Buckley, "Ukraine Looks"; Varshlomidze, "Georgians Guide."

136. Confidential interview with a senior adviser for reforms in higher education, July 21, 2015, Kiev.

137. See, for example, *Business Insider*, "IMF Chief"; Nurshayeva, "EBRD Praises Ukraine Anti-Corruption Drive"; Unian, "Steinmeier."

138. Index for Monitoring Reforms, "Release 18 (August 31st–September 13th, 2015): One of the Lowest Index Values," http://imorevox.in.ua/?page_id=609

139. Confidential interview with a senior manager of the National Bank of Ukraine, July 22, 2015, Kiev.

140. See Vox Ukraine, "Gde Reformy?," http://imorevox.in.ua/wordpress/wp-content/uploads/2015/05/iMoRe_2015_07_02.pdf

141. See Transparency International–Ukraine, "Anti-Corruption Fight."

142. See Open Society Foundation, "Government's Anti-Corruption Program."

143. Jaroszewicz and Żochowski, "Combating Corruption," 1; Denisova-Schmidt and Huber, "Regional Differences," 27-28.

144. Piasecka and Drik, "Current Challenges." Moreover, many lustration subjects have simply made brief visits to the antiterrorism operation zone and then returned to their positions in Kiev. See Alyona Zhuk, "Critics Fear Officials."

145. Confidential interview with a head of a local NGO, July 7, 2015, Kiev.

146. See "Ukraine Reform Monitor: August 2015," http://carnegieendowment.org/2015/08/19/ukraine-reform-monitor-august-2015/iewe

147. Confidential interview with a civil society official at the Reanimation Package of Reforms NGO, July 10, 2015, Kiev.

148. Ibid.

149. Confidential interview with officials of a major Ukrainian research institute, July 14, 2015, Kiev.

150. Confidential interview with officials of a major Ukrainian research institute, July 14, 2015, Kiev.

151. Socor, "Saakashvili Grapples"; Radio Free Europe/Radio Liberty, "Saakashvili, Yatsenyuk Spar."

152. Confidential interview with energy sector official, July 21, 2015, Kiev.

153. Confidential interviews with several energy sector officials, July 22, 2015, Kiev.

154. Confidential interview with a civil society official at CEDOS NGO, July 12, 2015, Kiev.

155. Confidential interview with an official of the Ministry of Transportation, July 18, 2015, Kiev.

156. Freedom House, *Nations in Transit: Ukraine* (2015).

157. According to a survey conducted by the International Republican Institute on July 16-30, 2015, military conflict in Donbas was the key concern for more than 60 percent of the Ukrainian public, followed by corruption within state institutions (43 percent) and unemployment (30 percent) (International Republican Institute, "Public Opinion Survey: Residents of Ukraine, July 16-30, 2015"). A June 2015 public poll by the Rating Group Ukraine and the U.S. Agency for International Development reported simi-

lar results: 60 percent of respondents identified conflict in Donbas as their key concern. See USAID, "Key Findings June 2015 survey in Ukraine, https://www.ifes.org/sites/default/files/ifes_ukraine_june_2015_survey_key_findings_report_final.pdf

158. Democratic Initiative Foundation, "Reforms in Ukraine: Public Opinion of Citizens," https://ukraine-office.eu/en/17-09-2015-reforms-in-ukraine-public-opinion-of-citizens-dif/

159. A February 2015 poll conducted by the Gorshenin Institute ("Ukraine") showed that more than 70 percent of Ukrainians did not feel that any reforms were taking place, while inly 20 percent of respondents felt the effects of reforms.

160. See Rating Pro, "Opinions of Ukrainians."

161. Confidential interview with a health care sector official, July 16, 2015, Kiev.

162. Democratic Initiative Foundation, "Reforms in Ukraine"; Razumkov Centre, http://razumkov.org.ua/eng/

163. Gorshenin Institute, "Ukraine."

164. Ibid.

165. See International Republican Institute, "Public Opinion Survey: Residents of Ukraine, July 16–30, 2015."

165. International Republic Institute and Rating Pro, "Dynamics of Social and Political Opinions."

166. See International Republican Institute, "Public Opinion Survey: Residents of Ukraine, July 16–30, 2015."

167. Confidential interview with civil society members, July 12–14, 2015, Kiev. These activists defined "Saakashvilization" as the replacement of petty institutional bribery with increased top-level corruption, as had allegedly occurred in Saakashvili's Georgia.

168. Confidential interview with a senior manager of the National Bank of Ukraine, July 22, 2015, Kiev.

169. Confidential interview with an ambassador of a European Union state to Ukraine, July 8, 2015, Kiev.

170. Confidential interview with an economic analyst, July 20, 2015, Kiev.

171. Confidential interview at the Ukrainian Center for Independent Political Research, July 16, 2015, Kiev.

172. Ibid.

173. Confidential interview with a top manager in the energy sector, July 21, 2015, Kiev.

174. Confidential interview with a civil society official at the Reanimation Package of Reforms NGO, July 10, 2015, Kiev.

175. Confidential interview with a member of Verkhovnaia Rada, July 28, 2015, Kiev.

176. Confidential interview with a senior official at the Reanimation Package of Reforms NGO, July 13, 2015, Kiev.

177. Confidential interview with a member of Verkhovnaia Rada (Parliament), July 28, 2015, Kiev.

178. Confidential interview with a communication manager at the Reanimation Package of Reforms NGO, July 13, 2015, Kiev.

179. Confidential interview with an energy sector official, July 21, 2015, Kiev.

180. Ibid.

181. Confidential interview with a senior manager of the National Bank of Ukraine, July 22, 2015, Kiev.

182. Confidential interview with a communication manager at the Reanimation Package of Reforms NGO, July 13, 2015, Kiev.

183. Gorshenin Institute, "Ukraine."

184. See Kiev International Institute of Sociology, http://www.kiis.com.ua/?lang=eng

185. Confidential interview with a civil society official at CEDOS NGO, July 12, 2015, Kiev.

186. Ibid.

187. Confidential interview with two anticorruption officials, July 23, 2015, Kiev.

188. Confidential interview with a representative of civil society, July 20, 2015, Kiev.

189. Confidential interview with an energy sector official, July 21, 2015, Kiev.

190. Confidential interview with a civil society official at CEDOS NGO, July 12, 2015, Kiev.

191. See International Foundation for Electoral Systems (http://www.ifes.org/ukraine) and Rating Pro, "Opinion of Ukrainians."

Conclusion

1. Gel'man, "Unrule of Law"; Ledeneva, *Can Russia Modernise?*; Rose, "Russia as an Hour-Glass Society."

2. Linz, *Totalitarian and Authoritarian Regimes.*

3. Lauth, "Informal Institutions"; Helmke and Levitsky, "Informal Institutions and Comparative Politics."

4. Morris and Polese, *Informal Post-Socialist Economy*; Ledeneva, *Russia's Economy of Favours*; Williams, "Surviving Post-Socialism"; Rose, "Getting by without Government."

Bibliography

Aasland, Aadne, Åse Berit Grødeland, and Heiko Pleines. "Trust and Informal Practice among Elites in East Central Europe, South East Europe, and the West Balkans." *Europe-Asia Studies* 64, no. 1 (2012): 115–43.

Abbott, Pamela. "Cultural Trauma and Social Quality in Post-Soviet Moldova and Belarus." *East European Politics and Societies* 21, no. 2 (2007): 219–58.

Adler, Larissa, and Diana Sheinbaum. "Trust, Social Networks, and the Informal Economy: A Comparative Analysis." *Review of Sociology* 10, no. 1 (2004): 5–26.

Aidukaite, Jolanta. "Welfare Reforms and Socio-Economic Trends in the 10 New EU Member States of Central and Eastern Europe." *Communist and Post-Communist Studies* 44, no. 3 (2011): 211–19.

Alberti, Maria Emanuela, and Serena Sabatini, eds. *Exchange Networks and Local Transformation*. Oxford: Oxbow, 2012.

Alexeev, Michael, and William Pyle. "A Note on Measuring the Unofficial Economy in the Former Soviet Republics." *Economics of Transition* 11, no. 1 (2003): 153–75.

Aliyev, Huseyn. "Civil Society in the South Caucasus: Kinship Networks as Obstacles to Civil Participation." *Southeast European and Black Sea Studies* 14, no. 2 (2014): 263–82.

Aliyev, Huseyn. "The Effects of the Saakashvili Era Reforms on Informal Practices in the Republic of Georgia." *Studies of Transition States and Societies* 6, no. 1 (2014): 21–35.

Aliyev, Huseyn. "Informal Networks as Sources of Human (In)Security in the South Caucasus." *Global Change, Peace, and Security* 27, no. 2 (2015): 191–206.

Aliyev, Huseyn. "Informality within the Post-Soviet NGO Sector: Examining the Use of Informal Networks by NGOs in Azerbaijan and Georgia." *Journal of Civil Society* 11, no. 13 (2015): 317–32.

Aliyev, Huseyn. "Institutional Transformation and Informality in Azerbaijan and Georgia." In *Informal Economies in Post-Socialist Spaces: Practices, Institutions, and Networks,* edited by Jeremy Morris and Abel Polese. Basingstoke: Palgrave Macmillan, 2015.

Aliyev, Huseyn. *Post-Communist Civil Society and the Soviet Legacy: Challenges of Democratisation and Reform in the Caucasus.* Basingstoke: Palgrave Macmillan, 2015.

Aliyev, Huseyn. "Post-Communist Informal Networking: Blat in the South Caucasus." *Demokratizatsiya: The Journal of Post-Soviet Democratization* 21, no. 1 (2013): 89–112.

Aliyev, Huseyn. "Post-Soviet Informality: Towards Theory Building." *International Journal of Sociology and Social Policy* 35, nos. 1–2 (2015): 182–98.

Almond, Gabriel, and Sidney Verba. *The Civic Culture: Political Attitudes and Democracy in Five Nations.* Boston: Little, Brown, 1963.

Altman, Yochanan. *The Georgian Feast: Wine and Food as Embodiment of Networks.* Bordeaux: 6th AWBR International Conference Bordeaux Management School, 2011.

Altman, Yochanan. *A Reconstruction Using Anthropological Methods of the Second Economy of Soviet Georgia.* Enfield: Middlesex Polytechnic, 1983.

Amado, Gelles, and Haroldo Vinagre Brasil. "Organizational Behaviors and Cultural Context: The Brazilian 'Jeitinho.'" *International Studies of Management and Organization* 21, no. 3 (1991): 38–61.

Ambrosio, Thomas. "Insulating Russia from a Colour Revolution: How the Kremlin Resists Regional Democratic Trends." *Democratisation* 14, no. 2 (2007): 232–52.

Ashwin, Sarah. "Endless Patience: Explaining Soviet and Post-Soviet Social Stability." *Communist and Post-Communist Studies* 31, no. 2 (1998): 187–98.

Åslund, Anders. *How Ukraine Became a Market Economy and Democracy.* Washington, DC: Peterson Institute, 2009.

Åslund, Anders. *Ukraine: What Went Wrong and How to Fix It.* Washington, DC: Peterson Institute, 2015.

Babajanian, Babken. "Local Governance in Post-Soviet Armenia: Leadership, Local Development, and Accountability." *Communist and Post-Communist Studies* 41, no. 3 (2008): 375–96.

Babajanian, Babken. "Social Capital and Community Participation in Post-Soviet Armenia: Implications for Policy and Practice." *Europe-Asia Studies* 60, no. 8 (2008): 1299–1319.

Babajanian, Babken. "Social Welfare in Post-Soviet Armenia: From Socialist to Liberal and Informal?" *Post-Soviet Affairs* 24, no. 4 (2008): 383–404.

Baev, Pavel. "Civil Wars in Georgia: Corruption Breeds Violence." In *Potentials of Disorder: Explaining Conflict and Stability in the Caucasus and in the Former Yugoslavia*, edited by Jan Koehler and Christoph Zurcher. Manchester: Manchester University Press, 2003.

Bailey, Deborah C. "Women and Wasta: The Use of Focus Groups for Understanding Social Capital and Middle Eastern Women." *Qualitative Report* 17, no. 33 (2012): 1–18.

Balabanova, Dina, and Martin McKee. "Understanding Informal Payments for Health Care: The Example of Bulgaria." *Health Policy* 62, no. 3 (2002): 243–73.

Balabanova, Dina, Martin McKee, Joceline Pomerleau, Richard Rose, and Christian Haerpfer. "Health Service Utilization in the Former Soviet Union: Evidence from Eight Countries." *Health Services Research* 39, no. 6 (2004): 1927–50.

Balmforth, Richard, and Natalia Zinets. "Ukraine Guardsman Killed in Nationalist Protest outside Parliament." *Reuters*, August 31, 2015.

Barnett, Andy, Bruce Yandle, and George Naufal. "Regulation, Trust, and Cronyism in Middle Eastern Societies: The Simple Economics of 'Wasta.'" *Journal of Socio-Economics* 44, no. C (2013): 41–46.

Bater, James H. *The Soviet Scene: A Geographical Perspective*. London: Arnold, 1989.

Beacháin, Donnacha Ó., and Abel Polese, eds. *The Colour Revolutions in the Former Soviet Republics: Successes and Failures*. London: Routledge, 2010.

Begg, Robert, and John Pickles. "Institutions, Social Networks, and Ethnicity in the Cultures of Transition." In *Theorizing Transition—The Political Economy of Post-Communist Transformation*, edited by John Pickles and Adrian Smith. London: Routledge, 1998.

Beissinger, Mark. *Nationalist Mobilization and the Collapse of the Soviet State*. Cambridge: Cambridge University Press, 2002.

Beissinger, Mark. "Structure and Example in Modular Political Phenomena: The Diffusion of Bulldozer/Rose/Orange/Tulip Revolutions." *Perspectives on Politics* 5, no. 2 (2007): 259–76.

Beissinger, Mark, and Crawford Young, eds. *Beyond State Crisis? Post-Colonial Africa and Post-Soviet Eurasia in Comparative Perspective*. Baltimore: Johns Hopkins University Press, 2002.

Bejakovic, Predrag, and Marc Meinardus, eds. *Equity vs. Efficiency: Possibilities to Lessen the Trade-Off in Social, Employment, and Education Policy in South-East Europe*. Sofia: Ebert Foundation, 2011.

Belli, Paolo, George Gotsadze, and Helen Shahriari. "Out-of-Pocket and Informal Payments in Health Sector: Evidence from Georgia." *Health Policy* 70, no. 1 (2004): 109–23.

Bernhard, Michael, and Ekrem Karakoç. "Civil Society and the Legacies of Dictatorship." *World Politics* 59, no. 4 (2007): 539–67.

Besstremyannaya, Galina. "Out-of-Pocket Health Care Expenditures by Russian Consumers with Different Health Status." *Transition Studies Review* 14, no. 2 (2007): 331–38.

Blunter, Herbert. "Society as Symbolic Interaction." In *Human Behaviour and Social Processes*, edited by Arnold M. Rose. London: Routledge, 1962.

Boeke, Julius H. *Economics and Economic Policy of Dual Societies as Exemplified by Indonesia*. Harlem: Willnik, 1942.

Bordeianu, Mircea, Olesea Cruc, and Ion Osoian. *Evaluation of Moldovan Authorities' Attitudes, Capacities, and Needs in Terms of the EU Integration Process*. Chişinău: Institute for Development and Social Initiatives (IDIS) "Viitorul," 2011.

Böröcz, József. "Informality Rules." *East European Politics and Societies* 14, no. 2 (2000): 348–80.

Börzel, Tanja A., and Yasemin Pamuk. *Europeanization Subverted?: The European Union's Promotion of Good Governance and the Fight against Corruption in the Southern Caucasus*. Berlin: Free University Berlin, 2011.

Börzel, Tanja A., and Yasemin Pamuk. "Pathologies of Europeanisation: Fighting Corruption in the Southern Caucasus." *West European Politics* 35, no. 1 (2012): 79–97.

Brie, Michael, and Erhard Stölting. "Formal Institutions and Informal Institutional Arrangements." In *International Handbook on Informal Governance*, edited by Thomas Christiansen and Christine Neuhold. Cheltenham: Elgar, 2012.

Broers, Laurence. "After the 'Revolution': Civil Society and the Challenges of Consolidating Democracy in Georgia." *Central Asian Survey* 24, no. 3 (2005): 333–50.

Bromley, Ray, and Chris Gerry. *Casual Work and Poverty in Third World Cities*. Chichester: Wiley, 1979.

Buckley, Neil. "Saakashvili Likely to Face Questioning, says Georgia PM." *Financial Times*, October 27, 2013.

Bunce, Valerie. "Comparative Democratization: Big and Bounded General-izations." *Comparative Political Studies* 33, nos. 6–7 (2000): 703–34.

Bunce, Valerie. "Rethinking Recent Democratization: Lessons from the Post-communist Experience." *World Politics* 55, no. 2 (2003): 167–92.

Bunce, Valerie. "Should Transitologists Be Grounded?" *Slavic Review* 54, no. 1 (1995): 111–27.

Bunce, Valerie, Michael McFaul, and Kathryn Stoner-Weiss, eds. *Democracy and Authoritarianism in the Postcommunist World.* Cambridge: Cambridge University Press, 2010.

Bunce, Valerie, and Sharon Wolchik, eds. *Defeating Authoritarian Leaders in Postcommunist Countries.* Cambridge: Cambridge University Press, 2011.

Bunce, Valerie, and Sharon Wolchik. "Favorable Conditions and Electoral Revolutions." *Journal of Democracy* 17, no. 4 (2006): 5–18.

Burnham, Peter, Wyn Grant, Karin Gilland Lutz, and Zig Layton-Henry. *Research Methods in Politics.* Basingstoke: Palgrave Macmillan, 2008.

Burns, Tom R., and Helena Flam. *The Shaping of Social Organization.* London: Sage, 1987.

Business Insider. "IMF Chief Says 'Extremely Encouraged' by Ukraine Reforms." September 6, 2015.

Calus, Kamil. "Reforms in Moldova: Moderate Progress and an Uncertain Outlook for the Future." *OSW/Commentary* 100, no. 23 (2013): 1–7.

Cameron, David R., and Mitchell A. Orenstein. "Post-Soviet Authoritarian-ism: The Influence of Russia in Its 'Near Abroad.'" *Post-Soviet Affairs* 28, no. 1 (2012): 1–44.

Carasciuc, Lilia. *Corruption and Quality of Governance: The Case of Moldova.* Chișinău: Transparency International–Moldova, 2000.

Carothers, Thomas. "The End of the Transition Paradigm." *Journal of Democracy* 13, no. 1 (2002): 5–21.

Castells, Manuel. *The Rise of the Network Society.* Chichester: Wiley, 2011.

Castells, Manuel, and Alejandro Portes. "World Underneath: The Origins, Dynamics, and Effects of the Informal Economy." In *The Informal Economy: Studies in Advanced and Less Developed Countries*, edited by Alejandro Portes, Manuel Castells, and Lauren A. Benton. Baltimore: Johns Hopkins University Press, 1989.

Cașu, Igor. *Politica Națională în Moldova Sovietică, 1944–1989.* Chișinău: Cartdidact, 2000.

Caucasus Research Resource Centers. (Georgia 2010; 2011; 2012; 2013; 2014) "Caucasus Barometer." http://www.crrccenters.org/caucasusbarometer/

Center for Strategic Studies and Reforms. *Moldova in Transition: Economic Survey*. Chișinău: CISR, 1998.

Chaisty, Paul, and Svitlana Chernykh. "Coalitional Presidentialism and Legislative Control in Post-Soviet Ukraine." *Post-Soviet Affairs* 31, no. 3 (2015): 177–200.

Chavance, Bernard. "Formal and Informal Institutional Change: The Experience of Postsocialist Transformation." *European Journal of Comparative Economics* 5, no. 1 (2008): 57–71.

Chavdarova, Tanya. "Institutionalization of Market Order and Reinstitutionalization of *Vruzki* (Connections) in Bulgaria." In *Informality in Eastern Europe: Structures, Political Cultures, and Social Practices*, edited by Christian Giordano and Nicolas Hayoz. Bern: Lang, 2013.

Chen, Chao C., Xiao-Ping Chen, and Shengsheng Huang. "Chinese *Guanxi*: An Integrative Review and New Directions for Future Research." *Management and Organization Review* 9, no. 1 (2013): 167–207.

Cheterian, Vicken. "Georgia's Rose Revolution: Change or Repetition? Tension between State-Building and Modernization Projects." *Nationalities Papers* 36, no. 4 (2008): 689–712.

Chong, Alberto, and Mark Gradstein. "Inequality and Informality." *Journal of Public Economics* 91, no. 1 (2007): 159–79.

Chow, Irene Hau-Siu, and Ignace Ng. "The Characteristics of Chinese Personal Ties (Guanxi): Evidence from Hong Kong." *Organization Studies* 25, no. 7 (2004): 1075–93.

Chowdhury, Savinna. *Everyday Economic Practices: The "Hidden Transcripts" of Egyptian Voices*. London: Routledge, 2007.

Christiansen, Thomas, and Christine Neuhold, eds. *International Handbook on Informal Governance*. Cheltenham: Elgar, 2012.

Clark, William A. "Crime and Punishment in Soviet Officialdom, 1965–90." *Europe-Asia Studies* 45, no. 2 (1993): 259–79.

Closson, Stacy. "Networks of Profit in Georgia's Autonomous Regions: Challenges to Statebuilding." *Journal of Intervention and Statebuilding* 4, no. 2 (2010): 179–204.

Colignon, Richard A., and Chikako Usui. *Amakudari: The Hidden Fabric of Japan's Economy*. Ithaca: Cornell University Press, 2003.

Collins, Kathleen. *Clan Politics and Regime Transition in Central Asia*. Cambridge: Cambridge University Press, 2006.

Collins, Kathleen. "Clans, Pacts, and Politics in Central Asia." *Journal of Democracy* 13, no. 3 (2002): 137–52.

Collins, Kathleen. "Economic and Security Regionalism among Patrimonial Authoritarian Regimes: The Case of Central Asia." *Europe-Asia Studies* 61, no. 2 (2009): 249–81.

Collins, Kathleen. "The Political Role of Clans in Central Asia." *Comparative Politics* 35, no. 2 (2003): 171–90.

Colomer, Josep. *Strategic Transitions: Game Theory and Democratization.* Baltimore: Johns Hopkins University Press, 2000.

Crăciun, Cristina. *Migration and Remittances in the Republic of Moldova: Empirical Evidence at Micro-Level.* Kiev: Kyiv-Mohyla Academy, 2006.

Crawford, Beverly, and Arend Lijphart, eds. *Liberalization and Leninist Legacies: Comparative Perspectives on Democratic Transitions.* Berkeley: University of California Press, 1997.

Crenson, Matthew A. "Social Networks and Political Processes in Urban Neighborhoods." *American Journal of Political Science* 22, no. 3 (1978): 289–95.

Crowther, William. "Ethnic Politics and the Post-Communist Transition in Moldova." *Nationalities Papers* 26, no. 1 (1998): 147–64.

Crowther, William. "The Politics of Democratization in Post-Communist Moldova." In *Democratic Changes and Authoritarian Reactions in Russia, Ukraine, Belarus, and Moldova,* edited by Karen Dawisha and Bruce Parrott. Cambridge: Cambridge University Press, 1997.

Crowther, William. "The Politics of Ethno-National Mobilization: Nationalism and Reform in Soviet Moldavia." *Russian Review* 50, no. 2 (1991): 183–202.

Crowther, William, and Irmina Matonyte. "Parliamentary Elites as a Democratic Thermometer: Estonia, Lithuania, and Moldova Compared." *Communist and Post-Communist Studies* 40, no. 3 (2007): 281–99.

Culiuc, Alexandru. "Corruption in Higher Education in Moldova." *AlmaMater,* April 17, 2007.

Curro, Costanza. "Birzha." In *Global Encyclopedia of Informality,* edited by Alena Ledeneva. Cambridge: Cambridge University Press, forthcoming.

Cutright, Phillips. "National Political Development: Measurement and Analysis." *American Sociological Review* 28, no. 2 (1963): 253–64.

Danet, Brenda. *Pulling Strings: Biculturalism in Israeli Bureaucracy.* Albany: State University of New York Press, 1989.

D'Anieri, Paul J. *Understanding Ukrainian Politics: Power, Politics, and Institutional Design.* Armonk, NY: Sharpe, 2007.

Darden, Keith A. "Blackmail as a Tool of State Domination: Ukraine under Kuchma." *East European Constitutional Review* 10 (2001): 67–71.

Daymon, Christine, and Caroline Hodges. "Researching the Occupational Culture of Public Relations in Mexico." *Public Relations Review* 35, no. 4 (2009): 429–33.

Denisova-Schmidt, Elena, and Martin Huber. "Regional Differences in Perceived Corruption among Ukrainian Firms." *Eurasian Geography and Economics* 55, no. 1 (2014): 10–36.

Democratic Initiative Foundation. Ukraine exit polls. http://2008.dif.org.ua/en/about/info

Dershem, Larry, and David Gzirishvili. "Informal Social Support Networks and Household Vulnerability: Empirical Findings from Georgia." *World Development* 26, no. 10 (1998): 1827–38.

de Soto, Hernando. *The Mystery of Capital: Why Capitalism Triumphs in the West and Fails Everywhere Else.* New York: Basic Books, 2000.

de Soto, Hernando. *The Other Path: The Invisible Revolution in the Third World.* New York: Harper and Row, 1989.

de Sousa, Luis. "'I Don't Bribe, I Just Pull Strings': Assessing the Fluidity of Social Representations of Corruption in Portuguese Society." *Perspectives on European Politics and Society* 9, no. 1 (2008): 8–23.

de Soysa, Indra, and Johannes Jütting. *Informal Institutions and Development—What Do We Know and What Can We Do?* Paris: OECD Development Center, 2006.

Devdariani, Jaba. "Georgia: Rise and Fall of the Façade Democracy." *Demokratizatsiya: The Journal of Post-Soviet Democratization* 12, no. 1 (2004): 79–115.

Diamond, Larry J. "Is the Third Wave Over?" *Journal of Democracy* 7, no. 3 (1996): 20–37.

Diamond, Larry J. "Thinking about Hybrid Regimes." *Journal of Democracy* 13, no. 2 (2002): 21–35.

Dimitrova-Grajzl, Valentina, and Eszter Simon. "Political Trust and Historical Legacy: The Effect of Varieties of Socialism." *East European Politics and Societies* 24, no. 2 (2010): 206–28.

Diorditsa, Alexander. *Moldavia: A Flourishing Orchard.* London: Soviet Booklet, 1960.

Di Palma, Giuseppe. *To Craft Democracies: An Essay on Democratic Transitions.* Berkeley: University of California Press, 1990.

Di Palma, Giuseppe. "Why Democracy Can Work in Eastern Europe." *Journal of Democracy* 2, no. 1 (1991): 21–31.

di Puppo, Lili. "Anti-Corruption Interventions in Georgia." *Global Crime* 11, no. 2 (2010): 220–36.

di Puppo, Lili. *Police Reform in Georgia*. Bergen: Anti-Corruption Resource Centre, 2010.

Dobbins, Michael. "The Post–Rose Revolution Reforms as a Case of Misguided Policy Transfer and Accidental Democratisation?" *Europe-Asia Studies* 66, no. 5 (2014): 759–74.

Dobovšek, Bojan, and Gorazd Meško. "Informal Networks in Slovenia: A Blessing or a Curse?" *Problems of Post-Communism* 55, no. 2 (2008): 25–37.

Dynko, Andrej. "Europe's Last Dictatorship." *New York Times*, July 16, 2012.

Eggertsson, Thrainn. *Imperfect Institutions: Possibilities and Limits of Reform*. Ann Arbor: University of Michigan Press, 2005.

Ekiert, Grzegorz. "Patterns of Postcommunist Transformation in Central and Eastern Europe." In *Capitalism and Democracy in Central and Eastern Europe: Assessing the Legacy of Communist Rule*, edited by Grzegorz Ekiert and Stephen E. Hanson. Cambridge: Cambridge University Press, 2003.

Ekiert, Grzegorz, and Stephen E. Hanson, eds. *Capitalism and Democracy in Central and Eastern Europe: Assessing the Legacy of Communist Rule*. Cambridge: Cambridge University Press, 2003.

Ekiert, Grzegorz, Jan Kubik, and Milada Anna Vachudova. "Democracy in Central and Eastern Europe One Hundred Years On." *East European Politics and Societies* 27, no. 1 (2013): 90–107.

Engvall, Johan. *Against the Grain: How Georgia Fought Corruption and What It Means*. Washington, DC: Johns Hopkins University–SAIS and Central Asia-Caucasus Institute, 2012.

Esadze, Londa. "Georgia's Rose Revolution: People's Anti-Corruption Revolution?" In *Organized Crime and Corruption in Georgia*, edited by Louise Shelley, Erik R. Scott, and Anthony Latta. London: Routledge, 2007.

European Bank for Reconstruction and Development. *Life in Transition: A Survey of People's Experiences and Attitudes*. London: EBRD, 2006.

European Bank for Reconstruction and Development. *Life in Transition: After the Crisis*. London: EBRD, 2011.

European Bank for Reconstruction and Development. *Transition Report 1999: Ten Years of Transition*. London: EBRD, 1999.

European Union. *Delegation of the European Union to Moldova*. http://eeas.europa.eu/archives/delegations/moldova/index_en.htm

Evropeiska Pravda. "Chto Proisxodit v Moldove I Kto Stoit Za Protestami." *europeanintegration.co.ua*, September 8, 2015.

Fairbanks, H. Charles. "Georgia's Rose Revolution." *Journal of Democracy* 15, no. 2 (2004): 110–24.

Fairbanks, H. Charles, and Alexi Gugushvili. "A New Chance for Georgian Democracy." *Journal of Democracy* 24, no. 1 (2013): 116–27.

Feldbrugge, F. J. M. "Government and Shadow Economy in the Soviet Union." *Europe-Asia Studies* 36, no. 4 (1984): 528–43.

Ferreira, Maria Cristina, Ronald Fischer, Juliana Barreiros Porto, Ronaldo Pilati, and Taciano L. Milfont. "Unraveling the Mystery of Brazilian Jeitinho: A Cultural Exploration of Social Norms." *Personality and Social Psychology Bulletin* 38, no. 3 (2012): 331–44.

Fish, M. Steven. "The Hazards of Half-Measures: Perestroika and the Failure of Post-Soviet Democratization." *Demokratizatsiya: The Journal of Post-Soviet Democratization* 13, no. 2 (2005): 241–54.

Fish, M. Steven. "Postcommunist Subversion: Social Science and Democratization in East Europe and Eurasia." *Slavic Review* 58, no. 4 (1999): 794–823.

Fitzpatrick, Sheila. *Everyday Stalinism: Ordinary Life in Extraordinary Times: Soviet Russia in the 1930s*. Oxford: Oxford University Press, 1999.

Folodare, Irving S. "The Effect of Neighborhood on Voting Behaviour." *Political Science Quarterly* 83, no. 4 (1968): 516–29.

Fox, Kate. *Watching the English: The Hidden Rules of English Behaviour*. London: Brealey, 2008.

Franke, Anja, Andrea Gawrich, and Gurban Alakbarov. "Kazakhstan and Azerbaijan as Post-Soviet Rentier States: Resource Incomes and Autocracy as a Double 'Curse' in Post-Soviet Regimes." *Europe-Asia Studies* 61, no. 1 (2009): 109–40.

Frederiksen, Martin D. "The Would-Be State: Reforms, NGOs, and Absent Presents in Postrevolutionary Georgia." *Slavic Review* 73, no. 2 (2014): 307–21.

Freedom House. *Nations in Transit*. https://freedomhouse.org/report-types/nations-transit#.VNmW7y75M1Q

Freedom House. *Nations in Transit: Ukraine*. 2009. https://freedomhouse.org/report/nations-transit/2009/ukraine

Freedom House. *Nations in Transit: Ukraine*. 2015. https://freedomhouse.org/report/nations-transit/2015/ukraine

Freeman, Linton C. "Centrality in Social Networks Conceptual Clarification." *Social Networks* 1, no. 3 (1978): 215–39.

Fritz, Verena. *State-Building: A Comparative Study of Ukraine, Lithuania, Belarus, and Russia*. Budapest: Central European University Press, 2007.

Fuller, Liz. "Is the Georgian Government Living on Borrowed Time?" *Radio Free Europe/Radio Liberty*, March 27, 2015.

Gans-Morse, Jordan. "Searching for Transitologists: Contemporary Theories of Post-Communist Transitions and the Myth of a Dominant Paradigm." *Post-Soviet Affairs* 20, no. 4 (2004): 320–49.

Garfinkel, Harold. *Studies in Ethnomethodology*. Englewood Cliffs, NJ: Prentice-Hall, 1967.

Gaughan, Joseph P., and Louis A. Ferman. "Toward an Understanding of the Informal Economy." *Annals of the American Academy of Political and Social Science* 493, no. 1 (1987): 15–25.

Gel'man, Vladimir. "Post-Soviet Transitions and Democratization: Towards Theory-Building." *Democratization* 10, no. 2 (2003): 87–104.

Gel'man, Vladimir. "The Unrule of Law in the Making: The Politics of Informal Institution Building in Russia." *Europe-Asia Studies* 56, no. 7 (2004): 1021–40.

Georgescu, Vlad, and Matei Călinescu. *Romanians: A History*. Columbus: Ohio State University Press, 1991.

Gërxhani, Klarita. "The Informal Sector in Developed and Less Developed Countries: A Literature Survey." *Public Choice* 120, nos. 3–4 (2004): 267–300.

Gibson, Anne. "Old-Boys Network Locks Women Out: Boss." *New Zealand Herald*, April 5, 2014.

Gibson, James L. "Social Networks, Civil Society, and the Prospects for Consolidating Russia's Democratic Transition." *American Journal of Political Science* 45, no. 1 (2001): 51–68.

Gilbert, Leah, and Payam Mohseni. "Beyond Authoritarianism: The Conceptualization of Hybrid Regimes." *Studies in Comparative International Development* 46, no. 3 (2011): 270–97.

Giordano, Christian. "The Social Organization of Informality: The Rationale Underlying Personalized Relationships and Coalitions." In *Informality in Eastern Europe: Structures, Political Cultures, and Social Practices*, edited by Christian Giordano and Nicolas Hayoz. Bern: Lang, 2013.

Giordano, Christian, and Nicolas Hayoz, eds. *Informality in Eastern Europe: Structures, Political Cultures, and Social Practices*. Bern: Lang, 2013.

Gobel, Christian. "Towards a Consolidated Democracy?: Informal and Formal Institutions in Taiwan's Political Process." Paper presented at the annual meeting of the American Political Science Association, San Francisco, August 30–September 2, 2001.

Godfrey, Paul C. "Toward a Theory of the Informal Economy." *Academy of Management Annals* 5, no. 1 (2011): 231–77.

Godson, Roy, Dennis Jay Kenney, Margaret Litvin, and Gigi Tevzadze. "Building Societal Support for the Rule of Law in Georgia." *Trends in Organized Crime* 8, no. 2 (2004): 5–27.

Goffman, Erving. *Behavior in Public Places*. New York: Free Press, 1963.

Gold, Gary D., and George S. Naufal. "Wasta: The Other Invisible Hand: A Case Study of University Students in the Gulf." *Journal of Arabian Studies* 2, no. 1 (2012): 59–73.

Gold, Thomas, Doug Guthrie, and David Wank, eds. *Social Connections in China: Institutions, Culture, and the Changing Nature of Guanxi*. Cambridge: Cambridge University Press, 2002.

Golosov, Grigorii V. "Proportional Representation and Authoritarianism: Evidence from Russia's Regional Election Law Reform." *Representation* 49, no. 1 (2013): 83–95.

Gorshenin Institute. "Mental Bases of Choice." March 13, 2008. http://gorshenin.eu/programs/annual/362_mental_bases_of_choice.html

Gorshenin Institute. "Ukraine: Stress Test." April 4, 2008. http://gorshenin.eu/programs/researches/926_ukraine_stress_test.html

Gorton, Matthew, and John White. "The Politics of Agrarian Collapse: Decollectivisation in Moldova." *East European Politics and Societies* 17, no. 2 (2003): 305–31.

Goskomstat USSR. *Narodnoe Khozyaistvo SSSR za 70 Let*. Moscow: Goskomstat, 1987.

Gotsadze, George, Akaki Zoidze, and Otar Vasadze. "Reform Strategies in Georgia and Their Impact on Health Care Provision in Rural Areas: Evidence from a Household Survey." *Social Science and Medicine* 60, no. 4 (2005): 809–21.

Gould, John A., and Carl Sickner. "Making Market Democracies?: The Contingent Loyalties of Post-Privatization Elites in Azerbaijan, Georgia, and Serbia." *Review of International Political Economy* 15, no. 5 (2008): 740–69.

Graeber, David. *Debt: The First 5,000 Years*. Brooklyn, NY: Melville, 2011.

Granovetter, Mark S. "The Strength of Weak Ties." *American Journal of Sociology* 78, no. 6 (1973): 1360–80.

Gray, Cheryl, Joel Hellman, and Randi Ryterman. *Anticorruption in Transition 2: Corruption in Enterprise-State Interactions in Europe and Central Asia, 1999–2002*. Washington, DC: World Bank, 2004.

Greenslade, Gertrude S., and Gregory Grossman. *Regional Dimensions of the Legal Private Economy in the USSR*. Berkeley, CA: National Council for Soviet and East European Research, 1986.

Grødeland, Åse Berit. "Elite Perceptions of Anti-Corruption Efforts in Ukraine." *Global Crime* 11, no. 2 (2010): 237–60.

Grødeland, Åse Berit. "'Red Mobs,' 'Yuppies,' 'Lamb Heads,' and Others: Contacts, Informal Networks and Politics in the Czech Republic, Slovenia, Bulgaria, and Romania." *Europe-Asia Studies* 59, no. 2 (2007): 217–52.

Grzymala-Busse, Anna. "The Best Laid Plans: The Impact of Informal Rules on Formal Institutions in Transitional Regimes." *Studies in Comparative International Development* 45, no. 3 (2010): 311–33.

Grzymala-Busse, Anna. *Rebuilding Leviathan: Party Competition and State Exploitation in Post-Communist Democracies*. Cambridge: Cambridge University Press, 2007.

Grzymala-Busse, Anna, and Pauline Jones Luong. "Reconceptualizing the State: Lessons from Post-Communism." *Politics and Society* 30, no. 4 (2002): 529–54.

Habdank-Kołaczkowska, Sylvana. *Eurasia's Rupture with Democracy: Nations in Transit 2014*. Washington, DC: Freedom House, 2014.

Habicht, Jarno, Raul-Allan Kiivet, Triin Habicht, and Anton E. Kunst. "Social Inequalities in the Use of Health Care Services after 8 Years of Health Care Reforms—A Comparative Study of the Baltic Countries." *International Journal of Public Health* 54, no. 4 (2009): 250–59.

Hale, Henry E. "Did the Internet Break the Political Machine?: Moldova's 2009 'Twitter Revolution That Wasn't.'" *Demokratizatsiya: The Journal of Post-Soviet Democratization* 21, no. 4 (2013): 481–506.

Hale, Henry E. "Eurasian Polities as Hybrid Regimes: The Case of Putin's Russia." *Journal of Eurasian Studies* 1, no. 1 (2010): 33–41.

Hale, Henry E. "Formal Constitutions in Informal Politics: Institutions and Democratization in Post-Soviet Eurasia." *World Politics* 63, no. 4 (2011): 581–617.

Hale, Henry E. *Patronal Politics: Eurasian Regime Dynamics in Comparative Perspective*. Cambridge: Cambridge University Press, 2014.

Hale, Henry E. "Regime Cycles: Democracy, Autocracy, and Revolution in Post-Soviet Eurasia." *World Politics* 58, no. 1 (2005): 133–65.

Haller, Dieter, and Cris Shore, eds. *Corruption: Anthropological Perspectives.* London: Pluto, 2005.

Hammarberg, Thomas. *Georgia in Transition: Report on the Human Rights Dimension: Background, Steps Taken, and Remaining Challenges.* Tbilisi: EU Special Adviser on Constitutional and Legal Reform and Human Rights in Georgia, 2013.

Harris, John R., and Michael P. Todaro. "Migration, Unemployment, and Development: A Two-Sector Analysis." *American Economic Review* 60, no. 1 (1970): 126–42.

Hart, Keith. "Informal Income Opportunities in Urban Employment in Ghana." *Journal of Modern African Studies* 11, no. 1 (1973): 61–89.

Hartlyn, Jonathan. *The Struggle for Democratic Politics in the Dominican Republic.* Chapel Hill: University of North Carolina Press, 1998.

Hayoz, Nicolas. "Observations on the Changing Meanings of Informality." In *Informality in Eastern Europe: Structures, Political Cultures, and Social Practices,* edited by Christian Giordano and Nicolas Hayoz. Bern: Lang, 2013.

Heidenheimer, Arnold J. "Perspectives on the Perception of Corruption." In *Political Corruption: Concepts and Contexts,* edited by Arnold J. Heidenheimer and Michael Johnston. New Brunswick, NJ: Transaction, 2005.

Heinzen, James. "The Art of the Bribe: Corruption and Everyday Practice in the Late Stalinist USSR." *Slavic Review* 66, no. 3 (2007): 389–412.

Hellman, Joel S., Geraint Jones, and Daniel Kaufmann. *Seize the State, Seize the Day: State Capture, Corruption, and Influence in Transition.* Washington, DC: World Bank, 2000.

Helmke, Gretchen, and Steven Levitsky. "Informal Institutions and Comparative Politics: A Research Agenda." *Perspectives on Politics* 2, no. 4 (2004): 725–40.

Helmke, Gretchen, and Steven Levitsky, eds. *Informal Institutions and Democracy: Lessons from Latin America.* Baltimore: Johns Hopkins University Press, 2006.

Higley, John, and Michael Burton. "The Elite Variable in Democratic Transitions and Breakdowns." *American Sociological Review* 54, no. 1 (1989): 17–32.

Hill, Ronald. "PROFILE—Moldova Votes Backwards: The 2001 Parliamentary Election." *Journal of Communist Studies and Transition Politics* 17, no. 4 (2001): 130–39.

Homans, George C. *Sentiments and Activities.* New York: Free Press, 1962.

Homans, George C. *Social Behavior: Its Elementary Forms*. Rev. ed. New York: Harcourt Brace Jovanovich, 1974.

Horowitz, Shale. *From Ethnic Conflict to Stillborn Reform: The Former Soviet Union and Yugoslavia*. College Station: Texas A&M University Press, 2005.

Howard, Marc Morjé. *The Weakness of Civil Society in Post-Communist Europe*. Cambridge: Cambridge University Press, 2003.

Hsiung, Bingyuan. "*Guanxi*: Personal Connections in Chinese Society." *Journal of Bioeconomics* 15, no. 1 (2013): 17–40.

Huntington, Samuel P. "Democracy for the Long Haul." *Journal of Democracy* 7, no. 2 (1996): 3–13.

Huntington, Samuel P. "Democracy's Third Wave." *Journal of Democracy* 2, no. 2 (1991): 12–34.

Huntington, Samuel P. *The Third Wave: Democratization in the Late Twentieth Century*. Norman: University of Oklahoma Press, 1993.

Hutchings, Kate, and Georgina Murray. "Australian Expatriates' Experiences in Working behind the Bamboo Curtain: An Examination of Guanxi in Post-Communist China." *Asian Business and Management* 1, no. 3 (2002): 373–93.

Hutchings, Kate, and David Weir. "Guanxi and Wasta: A Comparison." *Thunderbird International Business Review* 48, no. 1 (2006): 141–56.

Hwang, Dennis B., Patricia L. Golemon, Yan Chen, Teng-Shih Wang, and Wen-Shai Hung. "*Guanxi* and Business Ethics in Confucian Society Today: An Empirical Case Study in Taiwan." *Journal of Business Ethics* 89, no. 2 (2009): 235–50.

Inglehart, Ronald, and Christian Welzel. "How Development Leads to Democracy: What We Know about Modernization." *Foreign Affairs* 88, no. 2 (2009): 33–48.

Institute of Public Policy. *Barometer of Public Opinion*. http://ipp.md

International Foundation for Electoral Systems (IFES). "Ukraine." http://www.ifes.org/ukraine

International Labour Organization. *Employment in the Informal Economy in the Republic of Moldova*. Geneva: ILO, 2004.

International Labour Organization. *Incomes, Employment, and Equality in Kenya*. Geneva: ILO, 1972.

International Labour Organization. *Measuring Informality: Statistics on the Informal Sector and Informal Employment*. New York: ILO, 2012.

International Republican Institute. "Georgian National Study." http://www.iri.org/country/georgia

International Republican Institute. "Moldova." http://www.iri.org/country/
    moldova

International Republican Institute. "Public Opinion Survey: Residents of
    Ukraine, February 17–March 7, 2012." April 12, 2012. http://www.iri.org/
    sites/default/files/2012%20April%2012%20Survey%20of%20Ukrai-
    nian%20Public%20Opinion%2C%20February%2017-March%207%2C%20
    2012.pdf

International Republican Institute. "Public Opinion Survey: Residents of
    Ukraine, July 16–30, 2015." August 24, 2015. http://www.iri.org/sites/de-
    fault/files/wysiwyg/2015-08-24_survey_of_residents_of_ukraine_july_16-
    30_2015.pdf

International Republican Institute and Rating Pro, "Dinamika
    Obschestvenno-Politicheskikh Vzgliadov v Ukraine" [Dynamics of Social
    and Political Opinions in Ukraine], July 10–30, 2015. http://ratinggroup.
    ua/ru/research/ukraine/dinamika_obschestvenno-politicheskih_
    vzglyadov_v_ukraine.html

Isaacs, Rico. "Nur Otan, Informal Networks, and the Countering of Elite In-
    stability in Kazakhstan: Bringing the 'Formal' Back In." *Europe-Asia Stud-
    ies* 65, no. 6 (2013): 1055–79.

Isajiw, Wsevolod W., ed. *Society in Transition: Social Change in Ukraine in West-
    ern Perspectives*. Toronto: Canadian Scholars, 2003.

Ishkanian, Armine. *Democracy Building and Civil Society in Post-Soviet Arme-
    nia*. London: Routledge, 2008.

Izraeli, Dove. "Business Ethics in the Middle East." *Journal of Business Ethics*
    16, no. 14 (1997): 1555–60.

Jaroszewicz, Marta, and Piotr Żochowski. "Combating Corruption in
    Ukraine—The Beginning of a Long March." *OSW Commentary* 107 (2015):
    1–10.

Johnson, Simon, Daniel Kaufmann, Andrei Shleifer, Marshall I. Goldman,
    and Martin L. Weitzman. "The Unofficial Economy in Transition." *Brook-
    ings Papers on Economic Activity* (1997): 159–239.

Jones, Ellen, and Fred W. Grupp. "Modernisation and Ethnic Equalisation in
    the USSR." *Europe-Asia Studies* 36, no. 2 (1984): 159–84.

Jović, Dejan. "Problems of Early Post-Communist Transition Theory: From
    Transition from to Transition To." *Politička Misao* 47, no. 5 (2011): 44–68.

Jowitt, Kenneth. *New World Disorder: The Leninist Extinction*. Berkeley: Uni-
    versity of California Press, 1992.

Karakoç, Ekrem. "Economic Inequality and Its Asymmetric Effect on Civic

Engagement: Evidence from Post-Communist Countries." *European Political Science Review* 5, no. 2 (2013): 197–223.

Karanikolos, Marina, Philipa Mladovsky, Jonathan Cylus, Sarah Thomson, Sanjay Basu, David Stuckler, Johan P. Mackenbach, and Martin McKee. "Financial Crisis, Austerity, and Health in Europe." *The Lancet* 381, no. 9874 (2013): 1323–31.

Karatnycky, Adrian, Alexander J. Motyl, and Aili Piano, eds. *Nations in Transit, 1999–2000: Civil Society, Democracy, and Markets in East Central Europe and the Newly Independent States*. New Brunswick, NJ: Transaction, 2001.

Karl, Terry L. "Dilemmas of Democratization in Latin America." *Comparative Politics* 23, no. 1 (1990): 1–21.

Karl, Terry L., and Philippe C. Schmitter. "From an Iron Curtain to a Paper Curtain: Grounding Transitologists or Students of Postcommunism?" *Slavic Review* 54, no. 4 (1995): 965–78.

Karl, Terry L., and Philippe C. Schmitter. "Modes of Transition in Latin America, Southern, and Eastern Europe." *International Social Science Journal* 128, no. 2 (1991): 267–82.

Katchanovski, Ivan. "The Orange Evolution?: The 'Orange Revolution' and Political Changes in Ukraine." *Post-Soviet Affairs* 24, no. 4 (2008): 351–82.

Kaufmann, Daniel, and Aleksander Kaliberda. *Integrating the Unofficial Economy into the Dynamics of Post-Socialist Economies: A Framework of Analysis and Evidence*. Washington, DC: World Bank, 1996.

Keenan, Edward L. "Muscovite Political Folkways." *Russian Review* 45, no. 2 (1986): 115–81.

Khrushchev, Nikita. *Memoirs of Nikita Khrushchev*. Edited by Sergei Khrushchev. Translated by George Shriver. Vol. 3. University Park: Pennsylvania State University Press, 2007.

Kim, Byung-Yeon, and Yu Mi Koh. "The Informal Economy and Bribery in North Korea." *Asian Economic Papers* 10, no. 3 (2011): 104–17.

King, Charles. *The Moldovans: Romania, Russia, and the Politics of Culture*. Stanford, CA: Hoover Institution Press, 2000.

Kirke, S. *Regional`nye Problemy Protsessa Sozdaniia Material`no-Tekhnicheskoi Bazi Kommunizma v SSSR*. Leningrad: Leningrad Financial-Economic Institute of N. A. Voznesensky, 1978.

Kitschelt, Herbert. "Accounting for Postcommunist Regime Diversity: What Counts as a Good Cause?" In *Capitalism and Democracy in Central and Eastern Europe*, edited by Grzegorz Ekiert and Stephen E. Hanson. Cambridge: Cambridge University Press, 2003.

Kitschelt, Herbert. "Formation of Party Cleavages in Post-Communist Democracies: Theoretical Propositions." *Party Politics* 1, no. 4 (1995): 447–72.

Knight, Jack. *Institutions and Social Conflict.* Cambridge: Cambridge University Press, 1992.

Knudsen, Ida Harboe. "The Story of Šarūnas: An *Invisible Citizen* of Lithuania." In *The Informal Post-Socialist Economy: Embedded Practices and Livelihoods,* edited by Jeremy Morris and Abel Polese. London: Routledge, 2014.

Kononenko, Vadim, and Arkady Moshes, eds. *Russia as a Network State: What Works in Russia When State Institutions Do Not?* Basingstoke: Palgrave Macmillan, 2011.

Kopecký, Petr, and Maria Spirova. "'Jobs for the Boys'?: Patterns of Party Patronage in Post-Communist Europe." *West European Politics* 34, no. 5 (2011): 897–921.

Kopstein, Jeffrey S., and David A. Reilly. "Geographic Diffusion and the Transformation of the Postcommunist World." *World Politics* 53, no. 1 (2000): 1–37.

Koroteyeva, Victoria, and Ekaterina Makarova. "Money and Social Connections in the Soviet and Post-Soviet Uzbek City." *Central Asian Survey* 17, no. 4 (1998): 579–96.

Kotkin, Stephen, and Andras Sajo, eds. *Political Corruption in Transition: A Skeptic's Handbook.* Budapest: Central European University Press, 2002.

Kovalov, Maksym. "Electoral Manipulations and Fraud in Parliamentary Elections: The Case of Ukraine." *East European Politics and Societies* 28, no. 4 (2014): 781–807.

Kozlov, Viktor. *The Peoples of the Soviet Union.* Bloomington: Indiana University Press, 1988.

Kramer, John M. "Political Corruption in the USSR." *Western Political Quarterly* 30, no. 2 (1977): 213–24.

Krastev, Ivan, and Stephen Holmes. "An Autopsy of Managed Democracy." *Journal of Democracy* 23, no. 3 (2012): 33–45.

Kubicek, Paul. *The History of Ukraine.* Westport, CT: Greenwood, 2008.

Kudelia, Serhiy, and Taras Kuzio. "Nothing Personal: Explaining the Rise and Decline of Political Machines in Ukraine." *Post-Soviet Affairs* 31, no. 3 (2015): 250–78.

Kukhianidze, Alexandre. "Corruption and Organized Crime in Georgia before and after the 'Rose Revolution.'" *Central Asian Survey* 28, no. 2 (2009): 215–34.

Kupatadze, Alexander. "Explaining Georgia's Anti-Corruption Drive." *European Security* 21, no. 1 (2012): 16–36.

Kupatadze, Alexander. *Organized Crime, Political Transitions, and State Formation in Post-Soviet Eurasia.* Basingstoke: Palgrave Macmillan, 2012.

Kuzio, Taras. "Back to the USSR; Russia Helps Moldova Follow Belarus' Lead." *Jamestown Foundation Prism* 8, no. 3 (2002): 1–2.

Kuzio, Taras. "Crime, Politics, and Business in 1990s Ukraine." *Communist and Post-Communist Studies* 47, no. 2 (2014): 195–210.

Kuzio, Taras. "Regime Type and Politics in Ukraine under Kuchma." *Communist and Post-Communist Studies* 38, no. 2 (2005): 167–90.

Kuzio, Taras. *Ukraine: Perestroika to Independence.* Basingstoke: Palgrave Macmillan, 2000.

Kuzio, Taras. *Ukraine: State and Nation Building.* London: Routledge, 2002.

Langston, Joy. "The Birth and Transformation of the Dedazo in Mexico." In *Informal Institutions and Democracy: Lessons from Latin America*, edited by Gretchen Helmke and Steven Levitsky. Cambridge: Cambridge University Press, 2006.

Laumann, Edward, and Franz U. Pappi. *Networks of Collective Action.* New York: Academic Press, 1976.

Lauth, Hans-Joachim. "Informal Institutions and Democracy." *Democratization* 7, no. 4 (2000): 21–50.

Law, David. "Corruption in Georgia." *Critique: Journal of Socialist Theory* 3, no. 1 (1974): 99–107.

Ledeneva, Alena. "*Blat* and *Guanxi*: Informal Practices in Russia and China." *Comparative Studies in Society and History* 50, no. 1 (2008): 118–44.

Ledeneva, Alena. *Can Russia Modernise?: Sistema, Power Networks, and Informal Governance.* Cambridge: Cambridge University Press, 2013.

Ledeneva, Alena. "Informality and Informal Politics." In *Routledge Handbook of Russian Politics and Society*, edited by Graeme Gill and James Young. London: Routledge, 2012.

Ledeneva, Alena. "Practices of Exchange and Networking in Russia." *Soziale Welt* 48, no. 2 (1997): 151–70.

Ledeneva, Alena. *Russia's Economy of Favours: Blat, Networking, and Informal Exchange.* Cambridge: Cambridge University Press, 1998.

Lee, Seungjoo, and Sang-Young Rhyu. "The Political Dynamics of Informal

Networks in South Korea: The Case of Parachute Appointment." *Pacific Review* 21, no. 1 (2008): 45–66.

Lennhag, Mi. *Informal Economy as Rational Habit and State Criticism: An Interview Study on Path Dependence in and Perceptions of Ukrainian and Belarusian Petty Corruption.* Prague: Institute of Sociology of Czech Academy of Sciences, 2010.

Letki, Natalia, and Inta Mieriņa. "Getting Support in Polarized Societies: Income, Social Networks, and Socioeconomic Context." *Social Science Research* 49, no. 1 (2015): 217–33.

Levitsky, Steven, and Lucan A. Way. *Competitive Authoritarianism: Hybrid Regimes after the Cold War.* Cambridge: Cambridge University Press, 2010.

Levitsky, Steven, and Lucan A. Way. "The Rise of Competitive Authoritarianism." *Journal of Democracy* 13, no. 2 (2002): 51–65.

Lewis, David. *Convention.* Cambridge: Harvard University Press, 1969.

Lewis, Robert A., and Richard H. Rowland. "East Is West and West Is East . . . : Population Redistribution in the USSR and Its Impact on Society." *International Migration Review* 11, no. 1 (1977): 3–29.

Lewis, W. Arthur. "Economic Development with Unlimited Supplies of Labour." *Manchester School* 22, no. 2 (1954): 139–91.

Lewytzkyj, Borys. *Politics and Society in Soviet Ukraine, 1953–1980.* Edmonton: Canadian Institute of Ukrainian Studies, University of Alberta, 1984.

Liaropoulos, Lycourgos, Olga Siskou, Daphne Kaitelidou, Mamas Theodorou, and Theofanis Katostaras. "Informal Payments in Public Hospitals in Greece." *Health Policy* 87, no. 1 (2008): 72–81.

Light, Matthew. "Police Reforms in the Republic of Georgia: The Convergence of Domestic and Foreign Policy in an Anti-Corruption Drive." *Policing and Society* 24, no. 3 (2014): 318–45.

Lijphart, Arend. *Patterns of Democracy: Government Forms and Performance in Thirty-Six Countries.* New Haven: Yale University Press, 2012.

Lindberg, Steffan I. "It's Our Time to Chop: Do Elections in Africa Feed Net-Patrimonialism Rather Than Counteract It?" *Democratization* 10, no. 2 (2003): 121–40.

Linz, Juan J. *Totalitarian and Authoritarian Regimes.* Boulder, CO: Rienner, 2000.

Linz, Juan J. "Transitions to Democracy." *Washington Quarterly* 13, no. 3 (1990): 143–64.

Linz, Juan J., and Alfred Stepan, eds. *The Breakdown of Democratic Regimes.* Baltimore: Johns Hopkins University Press, 1978.

Linz, Juan J., and Arturo Valenzuela, eds. *The Failure of Presidential Democracy*. Vol. 1, *Comparative Perspectives*. Baltimore: Johns Hopkins University Press, 1994.

Lipset, Seymour Martin. "The Social Requisites of Democracy Revisited: 1993 Presidential Address." *American Sociological Review* 59, no. 1 (1994): 1–22.

Lipset, Seymour Martin. "Some Social Requisites of Democracy: Economic Development and Political Legitimacy." *American Political Science Review* 53, no. 1 (1959): 69–105.

Livezeanu, Irina. "Urbanization in a Low Key and Linguistic Change in Soviet Moldavia. Part 1." *Soviet Studies* 33, no. 3 (1981): 327–51.

Loayza, Norman. "The Economics of the Informal Sector: A Simple Model and Some Empirical Evidence from Latin America." *Carnegie-Rochester Conference Series on Public Policy* 45 (1996): 129–62.

Loayza, Norman, Ana Maria Oviedo, and Luis Servén. *The Impact of Regulation on Growth and Informality: Cross-Country Evidence*. Washington, DC: World Bank, 2005.

Lomnitz, Larissa A. "Informal Exchange Networks in Formal Systems: A Theoretical Model." *American Anthropologist* 90, no. 1 (1988): 42–55.

Lonkila, Markku. "The Social Meaning of Work: Aspects of the Teaching Profession in Post-Soviet Russia." *Europe-Asia Studies* 50, no.4 (1998): 699–712.

Lubarova, Larisa, Oleg Petrushin, and Artur Radziwill. *Is Moldova Ready to Grow?: Assessment of Post-Crisis Policies (1999–2000)*. Warsaw: CASE— Center for Social and Economic Research, 2000.

Lukin, A. V. "The Transitional Period in Russia: Democratization and Liberal Reforms." *Russian Politics and Law* 38, no. 1 (2000): 6–32.

Luong, Pauline Jones. *Institutional Change and Political Continuity in Post-Soviet Central Asia: Power, Perceptions, and Pacts*. Cambridge: Cambridge University Press, 2002.

Lupușor, Adrian, Alexandru Fală, Denis Cenușă, and Victoria Vasilescu. *MEGA: Moldova Economic Growth Analysis*. Chișinău: Expert-Grup, 2013.

Machavariani, Shalva. "Overcoming Economic Crime in Georgia through Public Service Reform." In *Organized Crime and Corruption in Georgia*, edited by Louise Shelley, Erik R. Scott, and Anthony Latta. London: Routledge, 2007.

Magner, Michael. "Civil Society in Poland after 1989: A Legacy of Socialism?" *Canadian Slavonic Papers* 47, nos. 1–2 (2005): 49–69.

Magocsi, Paul Robert. *A History of Ukraine: The Land and Its Peoples*. Toronto: University of Toronto Press, 1996.

Malinowski, Bronislaw. *Argonauts of the Western Pacific: An Account of Native Enterprise and Adventure in the Archipelagos of Melanesian New Guinea*. London: Routledge, 2002.

Malkin, Irad. "Networks and the Emergence of Greek Identity." *Mediterranean Historical Review* 18, no. 2 (2003): 56–74.

Maloney, William F. "Informality Revisited." *World Development* 32, no. 7 (2004): 1159–78.

Malygina, Katerina. "Ukraine as a Neo-Patrimonial State: Understanding Political Change in Ukraine in 2005–2010." *South-East Europe Review for Labour and Social Affairs* 13, no. 1 (2010): 7–27.

Manning, Nick, and Neil Parison. *International Public Administration Reform: Implications for the Russian Federation*. Washington, DC: World Bank, 2004.

March, Luke. "From Moldovanism to Europeanization?: Moldova's Communists and Nation Building." *Nationalities Papers* 35, no. 4 (2007): 601–26.

March, Luke. "Power and the Opposition in the Former Soviet Union. The Communist Parties of Moldova and Russia." *Party Politics* 12, no. 3 (2006): 341–65.

Marples, David R. "Outpost of Tyranny?: The Failure of Democratization in Belarus." *Democratization* 16, no. 4 (2009): 756–76.

Mars, Gerald, and Yochanan Altman. "A Case of a Factory in Uzbekistan: Its Second Economy Activity and Comparison with a Similar Case in Soviet Georgia." *Central Asian Survey* 11, no. 2 (1992): 101–11.

Mars, Gerald, and Yochanan Altman. "The Cultural Bases of Soviet Georgia's Second Economy." *Europe⬚Asia Studies* 35, no. 4 (1983): 546–60.

Marsh, Christopher. "Social Capital and Democracy in Russia." *Communist and Post-Communist Studies* 33, no. 2 (2000): 183–99.

McDonagh, Ecaterina. "Is Democracy Promotion Effective in Moldova?: The Impact of European Institutions on Development of Civil and Political Rights in Moldova." *Democratization* 15, no. 1 (2008): 142–61.

McFaul, Michael. "The Fourth Wave of Democracy and Dictatorship: Noncooperative Transitions in the Postcommunist World." *World Politics* 54, no. 2 (2002): 212–44.

McFaul, Michael. "The Missing Variable: The 'International System' as the Link between Third and Fourth Wave Models of Democratization." In *Democracy and Authoritarianism in the Postcommunist World*, edited by Valerie Bunce, Michael McFaul, and Kathryn Stoner-Weiss. Cambridge: Cambridge University Press, 2010.

Mead, George Herbert. *Mind, Self, and Society: From the Standpoint of a Social Behaviorist*. Chicago: University of Chicago Press, 2009.

Michailova, Snejina, and Verner Worm. "Personal Networking in Russia and China: Blat and Guanxi." *European Management Journal* 21, no. 4 (2003): 509–19.

Mieriņa, Inta, and Edmunds Cers. "Is Communism to Blame for Political Disenchantment in Post-Communist Countries?: Cohort Analysis of Adults' Political Attitudes." *Europe-Asia Studies* 66, no. 7 (2014): 1031–61.

Milanovic, Branko. *Income, Inequality, and Poverty during the Transition from Planned to Market Economy*. Washington, DC: World Bank, 1998.

Miller, William L., Tatyana Koshechkina, and Åse Berit Grødeland. "How Citizens Cope with Postcommunist Officials: Evidence from Focus Group Discussions in Ukraine and the Czech Republic." *Political Studies* 45, no. 3 (1997): 597–625.

Mishler, William, and Richard Rose. "Trust, Distrust, and Skepticism: Popular Evaluations of Civil and Political Institutions in Post-Communist Societies." *Journal of Politics* 59, no. 2 (1997): 418–51.

Misztal, Barbara. *Informality: Social Theory and Contemporary Practice*. London: Routledge, 2000.

Mitchell, Lincoln A. "Compromising Democracy: State Building in Saakashvili's Georgia." *Central Asian Survey* 28, no. 2 (2009): 171–83.

Mitchell, Lincoln A. "Democracy in Georgia since the Rose Revolution." *Orbis* 50, no. 4 (2006): 669–76.

Mitchell, Lincoln A. *Uncertain Democracy: U.S. Foreign Policy and Georgia's Rose Revolution*. Philadelphia: University of Pennsylvania Press, 2009.

Mohamed, Ahmed A., and Mohamad S. Mohamad. "The Effect of *Wasta* on Perceived Competence and Morality in Egypt." *Cross Cultural Management: An International Journal* 18, no. 4 (2011): 412–25.

Morawska, Ewa. "The Malleable Homo Sovieticus: Transnational Entrepreneurs in Post-Communist East Central Europe." *Communist and Post-Communist Studies* 32, no. 4 (1999): 359–78.

Morozov, Viatcheslav. "Sovereignty and Democracy in Contemporary Russia: A Modern Subject Faces the Post-Modern World." *Journal of International Relations and Development* 11, no. 2 (2008): 152–80.

Morris, Jeremy. "Socially Embedded Workers at the Nexus of Diverse Work in Russia: An Ethnography of Blue-Collar Informalization." *International Journal of Sociology and Social Policy* 31, nos. 11–12 (2011): 619–31.

Morris, Jeremy. "Unruly Entrepreneurs: Russian Worker Responses to Insecure Formal Employment." *Global Labour Journal* 3, no. 2 (2012): 217–36.

Morris, Jeremy, and Abel Polese. "Informal Health and Education Sector Payments in Russian and Ukrainian Cities: Structuring Welfare from Below." *European Urban and Regional Studies* (March 26, 2014). http://eur.sagepub.com/content/early/2014/03/30/0969776414522081.abstract

Morris, Jeremy, and Abel Polese, eds. *The Informal Post-Socialist Economy: Embedded Practices and Livelihoods*. London: Routledge, 2014.

Morton, Henry W. "Who Gets What, When, and How?: Housing in the Soviet Union." *Europe-Asia Studies* 32, no. 2 (1980): 235–59.

Muskhelishvili, Marina, and Gia Jorjoliani. "Georgia's Ongoing Struggle for a Better Future Continued: Democracy Promotion through Civil Society Development." *Democratization* 16, no. 4 (2009): 682–708.

Napal, Geetanee. "Is Bribery a Culturally Acceptable Practice in Mauritius?" *Business Ethics: A European Review* 14, no. 3 (2005): 231–49.

Narodnoe Khoziaistvo SSSR. *Reference Book: Education, Welfare, Labour*. Moscow: Central Statistical Office at the Council of Ministers of the Soviet Union, 1970.

National Reform Council. *National Reforms Governance and Monitoring Framework*. April 7, 2015. http://www.reforms.in.ua/sites/default/files/pdf/nr-40-24-04_final3.pdf

Nodia, Ghia. "Dynamics of State-Building in Georgia." *Demokratizatsiya* 6, no. 1 (1998): 6–13.

North, Douglass C. *Institutions, Institutional Change, and Economic Performance*. Cambridge: Cambridge University Press, 1990.

Nurshayeva, Raushan. "EBRD Praises Ukraine Anti-Corruption Drive, Urges More Reform." *Reuters*, June 4, 2015.

Obozrevatel. "Proschai 'Reshaly': Avtomobil` na Uchet Mojno Budet Postavit` po Internetu." *Obozrevatel.ua*, August 3, 2015.

Obreja, Efim, and Lilia Caraşciuc. *Corruption in Moldova: Facts, Analysis, Proposals*. Chişinău: Transparency International, 2002.

O'Donnell, Guillermo A. "Delegative Democracy." *Journal of Democracy* 5, no. 1 (1994): 55–69.

O'Donnell, Guillermo A. "Illusions about Consolidation." *Journal of Democracy* 7, no. 2 (1996): 34–51.

O'Donnell, Guillermo A. "On Informal Institutions, Once Again." In *Informal Institutions and Democracy: Lessons from Latin America*, edited by Gretchen Helmke and Steven Levitsky. Baltimore: Johns Hopkins University Press, 2006.

O'Donnell, Guillermo A., and Philippe C. Schmitter. *Transitions from Author-itarian Rule: Tentative Conclusions about Uncertain Democracies.* Baltimore: Johns Hopkins University Press, 1986.

O'Donnell, Guillermo A., Philippe C. Schmitter, and Laurence Whitehead, eds. *Transitions from Authoritarian Rule: Southern Europe.* Baltimore: Johns Hopkins University Press, 1986.

Ofer, Gur, and Aaron Vinokur. *The Private Sources of Income of the Soviet Urban Household.* Washington, DC: Kennan Institute for Advanced Russian Studies, 1980.

O'Hearn, Dennis. "The Consumer Second Economy: Size and Effects." *Europe–Asia Studies* 32, no. 2 (1980): 218–34.

Okara, Andrei. "Sovereign Democracy: A New Russian Idea or a PR Project?" *Russia in Global Affairs* 5, no. 3 (2007): 8–20.

Olearchyk, Roman, and Neil Buckley. "Ukraine Looks to Foreign-Born Ministers to Kick-Start Reform." *Financial Times*, April 15, 2015.

Onoshchenko, Olga, and Colin C. Williams. "Evaluating the Role of *Blat* in Finding Graduate Employment in Post-Soviet Ukraine: The 'Dark Side' of Job Recruitment?" *Employee Relations* 36, no. 3 (2014): 254–65.

Onoshchenko, Olga, and Colin C. Williams. "Paying for Favours: Evaluating the Role of *Blat* in Post-Soviet Ukraine." *Journal of Contemporary Central and Eastern Europe* 21, nos. 2–3 (2013): 259–77.

Open Society Foundation. "The Government's Anti-Corruption Program Does Not Measure Ukraine's Progress in the Fight against Corruption." April 27, 2015. http://osf.org.ua/en/anticorruption-policy/view/519

Organisation for Economic Cooperation and Development. *Fighting Corruption in Transition Economies: Georgia.* Paris: OECD, 2005.

Organisation for Security and Co-Operation in Europe. *OSCE/ODIHR Final Report on Armenia's Presidential Election Recommends Measures to Increase Integrity of Electoral Process.* May 8, 2013. http://www.osce.org/odihr/elections/101313

Organisation for Security and Co-Operation in Europe. *Ukraine Parliamentary Elections, 28 October 2012: Final Report.* January 3, 2013. http://www.osce.org/odihr/98578

Orkodashvili, Mariam. "Higher Education Reforms in the Fight against Corruption in Georgia." *Demokratizatsiya: The Journal of Post-Soviet Democratization* 18, no. 4 (2010): 357–74.

Orlova, Nina, and Per Ronnas. "The Crippling Cost of an Incomplete Transformation: The Case of Moldova." *Post-Communist Economies* 11, no. 3 (1999): 373–97.

Ostrom, Elinor. *Understanding Institutional Diversity*. Princeton: Princeton University Press, 2009.

Ottaway, Marina. *Democracy Challenged: The Rise of Semi-Authoritarianism*. Washington, DC: Carnegie Endowment for International Peace, 2013.

Oviedo, Ana Maria, Mark Roland Thomas, and Kamer Karakurum-Özdemir. *Economic Informality: Causes, Costs, and Policies: A Literature Survey*. Washington, DC: World Bank, 2009.

Papava, Vladimer. "The Political Economy of Georgia's Rose Revolution." *Orbis* 50, no. 4 (2006): 657–67.

Parry, Jonathan, and Maurice Bloch, eds. *Money and the Morality of Exchange*. Cambridge: Cambridge University Press, 1989.

Parsons, J. W. R. "National Integration in Soviet Georgia." *Europe-Asia Studies* 34, no. 4 (1982): 547–69.

Passy, Florence, and Marco Giugni. "Social Networks and Individual Perceptions: Explaining Differential Participation in Social Movements." *Sociological Forum* 16, no. 1 (2001): 123–53.

Patico, Jennifer. "Chocolate and Cognac: Gifts and the Recognition of Social Worlds in Post-Soviet Russia." *Ethnos: Journal of Anthropology* 67, no. 3 (2002): 345–68.

Pejovich, Svetozar. "The Effects of the Interaction of Formal and Informal Institutions on Social Stability and Economic Development." *Journal of Markets and Morality* 2, no. 2 (2012): 164–81.

Piasecka, Agnieszka, and Oleksandra Drik. "Current Challenges of Lustration in Ukraine." *Opendialogfoundation.eu*, June 8, 2015.

Pierson, Paul. "The Limits of Design: Explaining Institutional Origins and Change." *Governance: An International Journal of Policy and Administration* 13, no. 4 (2000): 475–99.

Polese, Abel. "'If I Receive It, It Is a Gift; If I Demand It, Then It Is a Bribe': On the Local Meaning of Economic Transactions in Post-Soviet Ukraine." *Anthropology in Action* 15, no. 3 (2008): 47–60.

Polese, Abel. "Informal Payments in Ukrainian Hospitals: On the Boundary between Informal Payments, Gifts, and Bribes." *Anthropological Forum: A Journal of Social Anthropology and Comparative Sociology* 24, no. 4 (2014): 381–95.

Polese, Abel. *Limits of a Post-Soviet State: How Informality Replaces, Renegotiates, and Reshapes Governance in Contemporary Ukraine*. Stuttgart: Ibidem-Verlag, 2016.

Pop-Eleches, Grigore. "Historical Legacies and Post-Communist Regime Change." *Journal of Politics* 69, no. 4 (2007): 908–26.

Pop-Eleches, Grigore, and Joshua A. Tucker. "Associated with the Past?: Communist Legacies and Civic Participation in Post-Communist Countries." *East European Politics and Societies* 27, no. 1 (2013): 45–68.

Popova, Maria, and Vincent Post. "What Is Lustration and Is It a Good Idea for Ukraine to Adopt It?" *Washington Post*, April 9, 2014.

Poppe, Robert. *Expenditure Patterns of Migrant Households: Evidence from Moldova.* Hanover: Proceedings of the German Development Economics Conference, 2010.

Portes, Alejandro, Manuel Castells, and Lauren A. Benton, eds. *The Informal Economy: Studies in Advanced and Less Developed Countries.* Baltimore: Johns Hopkins University Press, 1989.

Przeworski, Adam. *Democracy and the Market: Political and Economic Reforms in Eastern Europe and Latin America.* Cambridge: Cambridge University Press, 1991.

Przeworski, Adam, Michael Alvarez, José Antonio Cheibub, and Fernando Limongi. "What Makes Democracies Endure?" *Journal of Democracy* 7, no. 1 (1996): 39–55.

Przeworski, Adam, and Fernando Limongi. "Modernization: Theories and Facts." *World Politics* 49, no. 2 (1997): 155–83.

Puglisi, Rosaria. "The Rise of the Ukrainian Oligarchs." *Democratization* 10, no. 3 (2003): 99–123.

Putnam, Robert. *Making Democracy Work: Civic Traditions in Modern Italy.* Princeton: Princeton University Press, 1993.

Qian, Wang, Mohammed Abdur Razzaque, and Kau Ah Keng. "Chinese Cultural Values and Gift-Giving Behaviour." *Journal of Consumer Marketing* 24, no. 4 (2007): 214–28.

Radio Chişinău. "700 de Poliţişti Şi-Au Dat Demisia în Ultimele Trei Luni [700 Policemen Resigned over Last 3 Months]." November 13, 2012. http://radiochisinau.md/700_de_politisti_si_au_dat_demisia_in_ultimele_trei_luni-5787

Radio Free Europe/Radio Liberty. "Saakashvili, Yatsenyuk Spar over Ukrainian Reforms." *Radio Free Europe/Radio Liberty*, September 10, 2015.

Rahr, Alexander. "Moldavian Party Chief Reprimanded." *Radio Free Europe/ Radio Liberty*, November 3, 1986.

Raiser, Martin, Christian Haerpfer, Thomas Nowotny, and Claire Wallace. "Social Capital in Transition: A First Look at the Evidence." *Czech Sociological Review* 38, no. 6 (2002): 693–720.

Rasanayagam, Johan. "Informal Economy, Informal State: The Case of Uzbekistan." *International Journal of Sociology and Social Policy* 31, nos. 11–12 (2011): 681–96.

Rating Pro. "Opinions of Ukrainians Regarding Medicine Industry." July 3, 2015. http://ratinggroup.ua/en/research/ukraine/ocenka_sostoyaniya_i_vospriyatiya_reform_v_medicine.html

Ray, Julie, and Neli Esipova. "Corruption a Major Obstacle for Ukraine's Next President." *Gallup World Poll*, May 23, 2014.

Razumkov Centre. "Public Opinion Polls." http://razumkov.org.ua/eng/soc-polls.php

Razzakov, Fyodor. *Bandity Semidesiatykh, 1970–1979*. Moscow: EKSMO, 2008.

Redding, S. Gordon. *The Spirit of Chinese Capitalism*. New York: de Gruyter, 1990.

Rehn, Alf, and Saara Taalas. "'Znakomstva I Svyazi' (Acquaintances and Connections)—*Blat*, the Soviet Union, and Mundane Entrepreneurship." *Entrepreneurship and Regional Development* 16, no. 3 (2004): 235–50.

Reuters. "EU Says Moldova Aid Depends on Judicial Reform." *Reuters*, February 22, 2011.

Reuters. "Ukraine Names Georgia's Saakashvili as Governor of Black Sea Hotspot." *Reuters*, May 31, 2015.

Roberts, Sean R. "Doing the Democracy Dance in Kazakhstan: Democracy Development as Cultural Encounter." *Slavic Review* 71, no. 2 (2012): 308–30.

Robertson, Graeme B. *The Politics of Protest in Hybrid Regimes: Managing Dissent in Post-Communist Russia*. Cambridge: Cambridge University Press, 2010.

Rodgers, Peter, and Colin C. Williams. "The Informal Economy in the Former Soviet Union and in Central and Eastern Europe." *International Journal of Sociology* 39, no. 2 (2009): 3–11.

Roman, Alexandru. "The Multi-Shade Paradox of Public Corruption: The Moldovan Case of Dirty Hands and Collective Action." *Crime, Law, and Social Change* 62, no. 1 (2014): 65–80.

Rose, Richard. "Getting by without Government: Everyday Life in Russia." *Daedalus* 123, no. 3 (1994): 41–62.

Rose, Richard. "Getting Things Done in Anti-Modern Society: Social Capital Networks in Russia." In *Social Capital: A Multifaceted Perspective*, edited by Partha Dasgupta and Ismayil Serageldin. Washington, DC: IBRD, 2000.

Rose, Richard. "Postcommunism and the Problem of Trust." *Journal of Democracy* 5, no. 3 (1994): 18–30.

Rose, Richard. "Russia as an Hour-Glass Society: A Constitution without Citizens." *East European Constitutional Review* 4, no. 54 (1995): 34–42.

Rose, Richard. *Understanding Post-Communist Transformation: A Bottom Up Approach*. London: Routledge, 2009.

Rose, Richard. "Uses of Social Capital in Russia: Modern, Premodern, and Anti-Modern." *Post-Soviet Affairs* 16, no. 1 (2000): 33–57.

Rose, Richard, and Doh Chull Shin. "Democratization Backwards: The Problem of Third-Wave Democracies." *British Journal of Political Science* 31, no. 2 (2001): 331–54.

Ross, Cameron. *Federalism and Democratization in Post-Communist Russia*. Manchester: Manchester University Press, 2002.

Round, John, and Peter Rodgers. "The Problems of Corruption in Post-Soviet Ukraine's Higher Education Sector." *International Journal of Sociology* 39, no. 2 (2009): 80–95.

Round, John, and Colin C. Williams. "Coping with the Social Costs of 'Transition': Everyday Life in Post-Soviet Russia and Ukraine." *European Urban and Regional Studies* 17, no. 2 (2010): 183–96.

Round, John, Colin C. Williams, and Peter Rodgers. "Corruption in the Post-Soviet Workplace: The Experiences of Recent Graduates in Contemporary Ukraine." *Work, Employment, and Society* 22, no. 1 (2008): 149–66.

Round, John, Colin C. Williams, and Peter Rodgers. "Everyday Tactics and Spaces of Power: The Role of Informal Economies in Post-Soviet Ukraine." *Social and Cultural Geography* 9, no. 2 (2008): 171–85.

Rukhadze, Vasili. "Few Successes and Many Disappointments—A Net Assessment of Developments in Georgia since the Start of 2014." *Eurasia Daily Monitor* 11, no. 181 (2014).

Rukhadze, Vasili. "Looking Back: Georgia's Troubled Year 2013 Indicates More Trouble in 2014." *Eurasia Daily Monitor* 11, no. 5 (January 11, 2014). https://jamestown.org/program/looking-back-georgias-troubled-year-2013-indicates-more-trouble-in-2014/

Rupnik, Jacques, and Jan Zielonka. "Introduction: The State of Democracy 20 Years On: Domestic and External Factors." *East European Politics and Societies* 27, no. 1 (2013): 3–25.

Rustow, Dankwart A. "Transitions to Democracy: Toward a Dynamic Model." *Comparative Politics* 2, no. 3 (1970): 337–63.

Ruziev, Kobil, and Peter Midmore. "Informal Credit Institutions in Transition Countries: A Study of Urban Money Lenders in Post-Communist Uzbekistan." *Post-Communist Economies* 26, no. 3 (2014): 415–35.

Saavedra, Jaime, and Alberto Chong. "Structural Reform, Institutions, and

Earnings: Evidence from the Formal and Informal Sectors in Urban Peru." *Journal of Development Studies* 35, no. 4 (1999): 95–116.

Safiyev, Rail. "Azerbaijan: A Dictatorship Built on a Capitalist Economy." *Caucasus Analytical Digest* 50 (2013): 7–11.

Sakwa, Richard. "The Dual State in Russia." *Post-Soviet Affairs* 26, no. 3 (2010): 185–206.

Sakwa, Richard. "Putin and the Oligarchs." *New Political Economy* 13, no. 2 (2008): 185–91.

Sakwa, Richard. *Soviet Politics in Perspective.* 2nd ed. London: Routledge, 1988.

Sampson, Steven L. "The Second Economy of the Soviet Union and Eastern Europe." *Annals of the American Academy of Political and Social Science* 493, no. 1 (1987): 120–36.

Schatz, Edward. *Modern Clan Politics: The Power of "Blood" in Kazakhstan and Beyond.* Seattle: University of Washington Press, 2013.

Schevchenko, Rouslan. "Otnoshenie Naselenia k Sovetskomu Rezhimu v Moldove (1944–1947 gg.)." Наукові Записки з Української Історії 94, no. 32 (2012): 171–76.

Schmitter, Philippe C., and Terry L. Karl. "The Conceptual Travels of Transitologists and Consolidologists: How Far to the East Should They Attempt to Go?" *Slavic Review* 53, no. 1 (1994): 173–85.

Scheuch, Erwin K., and Ute Scheuch. *Cliquen, Klüngel, und Karrieren.* Berlin: LIT, 2013.

Schmitz, Hans. "Domestic and Transnational Perspectives on Democratization." *International Studies Review* 6, no. 3 (2004): 403–26.

Schneider, Friedrich. *The Shadow Economy and Work in the Shadow: What Do We (Not) Know?* Bonn: Institute for the Study of Labor, 2012.

Schneider, Friedrich. *The Size of the Shadow Economies of 145 Countries All over the World: First Results over the Period 1999 to 2003.* Bonn: Institute for the Study of Labor, 2004.

Schneider, Friedrich, Andreas Buehn, and Claudio E. Montenegro. *Shadow Economies All over the World: New Estimates for 162 Countries from 1999 to 2007.* Washington, DC: World Bank, 2010.

Schneider, Friedrich, and Dominik H. Enste. "Shadow Economies: Size, Causes, and Consequences." *Journal of Economic Literature* 38, no. 1 (2000): 77–114.

Schneider, Friedrich, and Dominik H. Enste. *Shadow Economies around the World: Size, Causes, and Consequences.* New York: International Monetary Fund, 2000.

Scott, Erik R. "Georgia's Anti-Corruption Revolution." In *Organized Crime and Corruption*, edited by Louise Shelley, Erik R. Scott, and Anthony Latta. London: Routledge, 2007.

Segal, Philip. "Dealing with the Devil: The Hell of Corruption." *IFC Impact* 3, no. 2 (1999). http://documents.worldbank.org/curated/en/32713146803595 2343/pdf/multi0page.pdf

Sheingold, Carl A. "Social Networks and Voting: The Resurrection of a Research Agenda." *American Sociological Review* 38, no. 6 (1975): 712–20.

Shelley, Louise. "Georgian Organized Crime." In *Organized Crime and Corruption in Georgia*, edited by Louise Shelley, Erik R. Scott, and Anthony Latta. London: Routledge, 2007.

Shelley, Louise. Introduction to *Organized Crime and Corruption in Georgia*, edited by Louise Shelley, Erik R. Scott, and Anthony Latta. London: Routledge, 2007.

Shelley, Louise, Erik R. Scott, and Anthony Latta, eds. *Organized Crime and Corruption in Georgia*. London: Routledge, 2007.

Siegel, David A. "Social Networks and Collective Action." *American Journal of Political Science* 53, no. 1 (2009): 122–38.

Sik, Endre. "Network Capital in Capitalist, Communist, and Post-Communist Societies." *International Contributions to Labour Studies* 4 (1994): 73–93.

Sindzingre, Alice. "The Relevance of the Concepts of Formality and Informality: A Theoretical Appraisal." In *Linking the Formal and Informal Economy: Concepts and Policies*, edited by Basudeb Guha-Khasnobis, Ravi Kanbur, and Elinor Ostrom. Oxford: Oxford University Press, 2006.

Sinha, Anushree, and Ravi Kanbur. "Introduction: Informality—Concepts, Facts, and Models." *Margin: The Journal of Applied Economic Research* 6, no. 2 (2012): 91–102.

Slade, Gavin. "No Country for Made Men: The Decline of the Mafia in Post–Soviet Georgia." *Law and Society Review* 46, no. 3 (2012): 623–49.

Slater, Dan. "Institutional Complexity and Autocratic Agency in Indonesia." In *Explaining Institutional Change: Ambiguity, Agency, and Power*, edited by James Mahoney and Kathleen Thelen. Cambridge: Cambridge University Press, 2010.

Slider, Darrell. "A Note on the Class Structure of Soviet Nationalities." *Soviet Studies* 37, no. 4 (1985): 535–40.

Smith, Adrian. "Culture/Economy and Spaces of Economic Practice: Positioning Households in Post–Communism." *Transactions of the Institute of British Geographers* 27, no. 2 (2002): 232–50.

Smith, Adrian, and Alison Stenning. "Beyond Household Economies: Articulations and Spaces of Economic Practice in Postsocialism." *Progress in Human Geography* 30, no. 2 (2006): 190–213.

Smith, Peter B., Claudio Torres, Chan-Hoong Leong, Pawan Budhwar, Mustafa Achoui, and Nadezhda Lebedeva. "Are Indigenous Approaches to Achieving Influence in Business Organizations Distinctive?: A Comparative Study of Guanxi, Wasta, Jeitinho, Svyazi, and Pulling Strings." *International Journal of Human Resource Management* 23, no. 2 (2012): 333–48.

Smyth, Regina, Anna Lowry, and Brandon Wilkening. "Engineering Victory: Institutional Reform, Informal Institutions, and the Formation of a Hegemonic Party Regime in the Russian Federation." *Post-Soviet Affairs* 23, no. 2 (2007): 118–37.

Sneath, David. "Transacting and Enacting: Corruption, Obligation and the Use of Monies in Mongolia." *Ethnos: Journal of Anthropology* 71, no. 1 (2006): 89–112.

Socor, Vladimir. "Merabishvili's Arrest and the Erosion of Rule of Law in Georgia." *Eurasia Daily Monitor* 10, no. 99 (May 24, 2013). https://jamestown.org/program/merabishvilis-arrest-and-the-erosion-of-rule-of-law-in-georgia/

Socor, Vladimir. "Moldova: European Choice with Communist Support?" *Eurasia Daily Monitor* 12, no. 41 (March 5, 2015). http://www.refworld.org/docid/54fd9a6c4.html

Socor, Vladimir. "Saakashvili Grapples with Daunting Odds in Ukraine's Odesa." *Eurasia Daily Monitor* 12, no. 116 (June 22, 2015). https://jamestown.org/program/saakashvili-grapples-with-daunting-odds-in-ukraines-odesa/

Sologoub, Ilona. "Presentation of Strategy-2020 for Ukraine: Impressions and Reflections." *Vox Ukraine*, October 9, 2014.

Stefes, Christoph H. *Understanding Post-Soviet Transitions: Corruption, Collusion, and Clientelism.* Basingstoke: Palgrave Macmillan, 2006.

Stepurko, Tetiana, Milena Pavlova, Irena Gryga, and Wim Groot. "Informal Payments for Health Care Services—Corruption or Gratitude?: A Study on Public Attitudes, Perceptions, and Opinions in Six Central and Eastern European Countries." *Communist and Post-Communist Studies* 46, no. 4 (2013): 419–31.

Stepurko, Tetiana, Milena Pavlova, Irena Gryga, Liubove Murauskiene, and Wim Groot. "Informal Payments for Health Care Services: The Case of

Lithuania, Poland, and Ukraine." *Journal of Eurasian Studies* 6, no. 1 (2015): 46–58.

Stoner-Weiss, Kathryn. *Resisting the State: Reform and Retrenchment in Post-Soviet Russia*. Cambridge: Cambridge University Press, 2006.

Streeck, Wolfgang, and Kathleen Thelen. *Beyond Continuity: Institutional Change in Advanced Political Economies*. Oxford: Oxford University Press, 2005.

Subtelny, Orest. *Ukraine: A History*. Toronto: University of Toronto Press, 2009.

Thelen, Tatjana. "Shortage, Fuzzy Property, and Other Dead Ends in the Anthropological Analysis of (Post) Socialism." *Critique of Anthropology* 31, no. 1 (2011): 43–61.

Thießen, Ulrich. "The Informal Economy in Eastern Europe: The Example of the Ukraine." *Economic Bulletin* 34, no. 6 (1997): 19–24.

Thye, Shane R., Michael J. Lovaglia, and Barry Markovsky. "Responses to Social Exchange and Social Exclusion in Networks." *Social Forces* 75, no. 3 (1997): 1031–47.

Tlaiss, Hayfaa, and Saleema Kauser. "The Importance of *Wasta* in the Career Success of Middle Eastern Managers." *Journal of European Industrial Training* 35, no. 5 (2011): 467–86.

Toptygyn, Aleksey. *Neizvestnyi Beriia*. Moscow: OLMA, 2002.

Torosyan, Karine, and Randall Filer. *Tax Reform in Georgia and the Size of the Shadow Economy*. Bonn: Institute for the Study of Labor, 2012.

Transparency International. *Corruptions Perception Index*. http://www.transparency.org/research/cpi/

Transparency International. *Global Corruption Barometer*. http://www.transparency.org/research/gcb/

Transparency International–Moldova. *National Integrity System Assessment: Moldova 2014*. Chişinău: TI Moldova, 2014.

Transparency International–Moldova. *Sociological Study: Corruption in Republic of Moldova: Perceptions vs. Personal Experiences of Households and Business People*. Chişinău: TI Moldova and the Embassy of the United States of America, 2012.

Transparency International–Ukraine. "Anti-Corruption Fight in Ukraine Is Inhibited by the Influence of Government over Anti-Corruption Institutions and Oligarchs over Political Parties." August 6, 2014. http://ti-ukraine.org/en/news/5441.html

Tudoroiu, Theodor. "Democracy and State Capture in Moldova." *Democratization* 22, no. 4 (2015): 655–78.

Tudoroiu, Theodor. "Rose, Orange, and Tulip: The Failed Post-Soviet Revolutions." *Communist and Post-Communist Studies* 40, no. 3 (2007): 315–42.

Tudoroiu, Theodor. "Structural Factors vs. Regime Change: Moldova's Difficult Quest for Democracy." *Democratization* 18, no. 1 (2011): 236–64.

Tymczuk, Alexander. "Public Duties and Private Obligations: Networking and Personalisation of Relations in Ukraine." *Anthropology of East Europe Review* 24, no. 2 (2006): 62–70.

Uhlin, Anders. *Post-Soviet Civil Society: Democratization in Russia and the Baltic States*. London: Routledge, 2006.

Ukrainian Crisis Media Center. "Dmytro Shymkiv: National Council for Reforms Is a Platform for Consensus for All Branches of Power." August 26, 2014. *http://uacrisis.org/8336-dmitro-shimkiv*

Unian. "Second Wave of Lustration Is to Start in Ukraine." *Unian.info*, January 1, 2015.

Unian. "Steinmeier: Germany Praises Pace of Reforms in Ukraine." *Unian.info*, May 29, 2015.

United Nations Development Programme. *Georgia Human Development Report 2008: The Reforms and Beyond*. Tbilisi: UNDP, 2008.

Urinboyev, Rustamjon. "Law, Social Norms, and Welfare as Means of Public Administration: Case Study of Mahalla Institutions in Uzbekistan." *NISPAcee Journal of Public Administration and Policy* 4, no. 1 (2011): 33–57.

United States Agency for International Development, "Key Findings June 2015 survey in Ukraine." Kiev, 2015.

Uslaner, Eric M. *The Moral Foundations of Trust*. Cambridge: Cambridge University Press, 2002.

Vaculovschi, Dorin, Maria Vremis, and Viorica Craievschi-Toarta. *Republic of Moldova from Social Exclusion towards Inclusive Human Development: National Human Development Report*. Chișinău: "Nova-Imprim" SRL, 2011.

Varshlomidze, Tamila. "Georgians Guide Ukraine's Reform Path away from Russia." *Al-Jazeera*, June 6, 2015.

Vasmer, Maks. *Etymologicheskii Slovar' Russkogo Yazika*. Moscow: Progress, 1964.

Vian, Taryn, and Lydia J. Burak. "Beliefs about Informal Payments in Albania." *Health Policy and Planning* 21, no. 5 (2006): 392–401.

Vinten, Gerald. "Participant Observation: A Model for Organizational Investigation?" *Journal of Managerial Psychology* 9, no. 2 (1994): 30–38.

Wanner, Catherine. "Money, Morality, and New Forms of Exchange in Post-socialist Ukraine." *ethnos* 70, no. 4 (2005): 515–37.

Way, Lucan A. "Authoritarian State Building and the Sources of Regime Competitiveness in the Fourth Wave: The Cases of Belarus, Moldova, Russia, and Ukraine." *World Politics* 57, no. 2 (2005): 231–61.

Way, Lucan A. "The Dilemmas of Reform in Weak States: The Case of Post-Soviet Fiscal Decentralization." *Politics and Society* 30, no. 4 (2002): 579–98.

Way, Lucan A. "Kuchma's Failed Authoritarianism." *Journal of Democracy* 16, no. 2 (2005): 131–45.

Way, Lucan A. "Rapacious Individualism and Political Competition in Ukraine, 1992–2004." *Communist and Post-Communist Studies* 38, no. 2 (2005): 191–205.

Way, Lucan A. "Weak States and Pluralism: The Case of Moldova." *East European Politics and Societies* 17, no. 3 (2003): 454–82.

Way, Lucan A., and Steven Levitsky. "Linkage, Leverage, and the Post-Communist Divide." *East European Politics and Societies* 21, no. 1 (2007): 48–66.

Weatherford, Stephen M. "Interpersonal Networks and Political Behavior." *American Journal of Political Science* 26, no. 1 (1982): 117–43.

Wedel, Janine R. "Clans, Cliques, and Captured States: Rethinking 'Transition' in Central and Eastern Europe and the Former Soviet Union." *Journal of International Development* 15, no. 4 (2003): 427–40.

Werner, Cynthia. "Gifts, Bribes, and Development in Post-Soviet Kazakhstan." *Human Organization* 59, no. 1 (2002): 11–22.

Wertsch, James V. "Georgia as a Laboratory for Democracy." *Demokratizatsiya* 13, no. 4 (2005): 519–35.

Wheatley, Jonathan. *Georgia from National Awakening to Rose Revolution.* Aldershot: Ashgate, 2005.

White, Harrison, Scott Boorman, and Ronald Brieger. "Social Structure from Multiple Networks: Block Models of Roles and Position." *American Journal of Sociology* 81, no. 4 (1976): 730–80.

White, Stephen. "Is There a Pattern?" *Journal of Communist Studies and Transition Politics* 25, nos. 2–3 (2009): 396–412.

Willerton, John P., Jr. "Patronage Networks and Coalition Building in the Brezhnev Era." *Europe–Asia Studies* 39, no. 2 (1987): 175–204.

Williams, Colin C. "Beyond the Formal/Informal Jobs Divide: Evaluating the Prevalence of Hybrid 'Under-Declared' Employment in South-Eastern

Europe." *International Journal of Human Resource Management* 21, no. 14 (2010): 2529–46.

Williams, Colin C. "Surviving Post-Socialism: Coping Practices in East-Central Europe." *International Journal of Sociology and Social Policy* 25, no. 9 (2005): 65–77.

Williams, Colin C., and Mark A. Lansky. "Informal Employment in Developed and Developing Economies: Perspectives and Policy Responses." *International Labour Review* 152, nos. 3–4 (2013): 355–80.

Williams, Colin C., and Jo Padmore. "'Envelope Wages' in the European Union." *International Labour Review* 152, nos. 3–4 (2013): 411–30.

Williams, Colin C., and John Round. "Retheorizing the Nature of Informal Employment: Some Lessons from Ukraine." *International Sociology* 23, no. 3 (2008): 367–88.

Williams, Colin C., John Round, and Peter Rodgers. *The Role of Informal Economies in the Post-Soviet World: The End of Transition.* London: Routledge, 2013.

Williamson, John. "A Short History of the Washington Consensus." *Law and Business Review of the Americas* 15, no. 1 (2009): 7–23.

Wolczuk, Kataryna. *The Moulding of Ukraine: The Constitutional Politics of State Formation.* Budapest: Central European University Press, 2001.

World Bank. *Fighting Corruption in Public Services: Chronicling Georgia's Reforms.* Washington, DC: World Bank, 2012.

World Values Survey, "Wave 3: 1995–99," http://www.worldvaluessurvey.org/WVSOnline.jsp

Wynnyckyj, Mychailo. "Institutions and Entrepreneurs: Cultural Evolution in the 'De Novo' Market Sphere in Post-Soviet Ukraine." Ph.D. diss., University of Cambridge, 2003.

Yalcin-Heckmann, Lale. "Informal Economy Writ Large and Small: From Azerbaijani Herb Traders to Moscow Shop Owners." In *The Informal Post-Socialist Economy*, edited by Jeremy Morris and Abel Polese. London: Routledge, 2013.

Yang, Mayfair. *Gifts, Favors, and Banquets: The Art of Social Relationships in China.* Ithaca: Cornell University Press, 1994.

Yeung, Irene, and Rosalie L. Tung. "Achieving Business Success in Confucian Societies: The Importance of *Guanxi* (Connections)." *Organizational Dynamics* 25, no. 2 (1996): 54–65.

Zakaria, Fareed. "The Rise of Illiberal Democracy." *Foreign Affairs* 76, no. 6 (1997): 22–43.

Zakharova, Evgenia. "Street Life in Tbilisi as a Factor of Male Socialisation." *Laboratorium: Russian Review of Social Research* 2, no. 1 (2010): 182–204.

Zdravomyslova, Elena, and Viktor Voronkov. "The Informal Public in Soviet Society: Double Morality at Work." *Social Research: An International Quarterly* 69, no. 1 (2002): 49–69.

Zhang, Baohui. "Corporatism, Totalitarianism, and Transitions to Democracy." *Comparative Political Studies* 27, no. 1 (1994): 108–36.

Zhuk, Alyona. "Critics Fear Officials Trying to Sabotage Lustration Drive." *Kyiv Post*, April 23, 2015.

Zhuk, Sergei I. "Religion, 'Westernization,' and Youth in the 'Closed City' of Soviet Ukraine, 1964–84." *Russian Review* 67, no. 4 (2008): 661–79.

Zimmer, Kerstin, and Olexiy Haran. "Unfriendly Takeover: Successor Parties in Ukraine." *Communist and Post-Communist Studies* 41, no. 4 (2008): 541–61.

Index